Preface

One aircraft caused more fear, confusion and angst than any other during the Second World War – the Messerschmitt Me 163. And it wasn't just the Me 163's rocket engine which caused such consternation, nor its heavy cannon armament nor even its incredible turn of speed: more than anything it was its shape.

In a world where every aircraft had at least one propeller, straight wings, a long fuselage and a tailplane, Messerschmitt's little interceptor was a radical departure from convention – possessing none of these features. Many Allied aircrew who saw it thought it resembled a bat; others didn't know what to think. It appeared out of nowhere, struck and then dived away at incredible speed. For some, it was truly terrifying.

When I first encountered the Me 163, it had entirely the opposite effect. I was leafing through a copy of William Green's Famous Fighters of the Second World War and there it was, stuck right at the end, a stumpy sad-looking little thing that seemed as though it would barely be able to fly. Compared to the aircraft I had just read about – the beautiful Spitfire, the brutish Thunderbolt and the shark-like Me 262, it was a dismal afterthought.

Some years later, in 1991, George Lucas's Lucasfilm Games brought out a videogame called Secret Weapons of the Luftwaffe for the PC, with cover art depicting two strange-looking jets attacking a formation of B-17s. These unusual fighters had no fuselage or tail to speak of – they were literally all-wing. I wondered again whether something like that could really be made to fly. The booklet accompanying the game, however, made it quite clear that the Germans really had tried to build this aircraft, the Gotha Go 229.

Evidently it had been made to a specification set out by Hermann Göring "that all new aircraft should carry 1000kg of bombs, fly at 1000km/h and have a penetration depth of 1000km". Furthermore, the aircraft's designers, the Horten brothers, made this "flying wing" out of wood because "it was lightweight and metal was in short supply. The Hortens also believed that a wooden wing hit by a cannon shell would sustain less damage than a metal one. The wood construction, covered with a special radar-absorbing paint, made this 'flying wing' virtually undetectable by radar".

This was unbelievable – a futuristic Nazi stealth fighter! Why had I never heard of it before? I re-checked but none of the books I had could offer any further clues.

Then in 1998 I was directed by a friend to a website called Luft46.com where I was amazed to find a vast and bewildering range of 'secret projects' apparently designed by German aircraft companies during the war, though the king of all projects, the Gotha Go 229, was mysteriously absent. What did appear, however, was a huge range of designs clearly related to the Me 163 – some longer, some larger, some even sporting tailplanes.

Books began to become available which fleshed out the story of many of these 'projects', usually translated from German originals, but these were often inconsistent and filled with inexplicable anomalies. One common thread which seemed to run throughout, though, was an admiration for the Horten brothers and their Ho 229 (calling it the Go 229 was apparently a common mistake). It was clear that many of the writers whose work I was now reading were actually fans of these enigmatic designers. Somehow this seemed to colour their writing and I began to wonder just how much of the Horten legend was grounded in hard fact.

In 2015 I wrote a publication called Luftwaffe: Secret Jets of the Third Reich which set out to resolve some of the problems with the earlier 'projects' books by going back to the original wartime documents from which they had presumably been created.

My starting point was a document which resides in the National Archives at Kew in London – German Aircraft: New and Projected Types. Compiled by British air intelligence staff in 1945 from captured German documents and published in January 1946, it includes drawings of 174 types from the full range of manufacturers and amounts to a factually reliable 'greatest hits' of secret projects.

Onto this foundation dozens of other documentary sources, many of them apparently previously unseen, were overlaid to build up a history of German jet or 'TL' (Turbinen-Luftstrahltriebwerk) aircraft development during the Second World War. I subsequently produced a second volume concentrating on bombers – my understanding of the companies concerned, their people, their products and their histories changing and evolving as I continued to study original wartime documentation.

Where the first two volumes examined the major German aircraft design contests of the war in a loosely chronological fashion, this publication aims to look specifically at wartime flying wing or 'nurflügel' projects such as the Horten 229 and tailless projects such as the Me 163, and how they fared when pitted against conventional designs.

Above all, however, it is intended to showcase and explain some of the wildest, weirdest and most incredible aircraft designs ever produced. ●

Contents

ABOVE: The Henschel P 122 V1 high-altitude bomber prototype climbs into a clear blue sky. Art by Ronnie Olsthoorn.

FRONT COVER:
A Blohm & Voss P 215 night-fighter downs a French AAB-1. Art by Ronnie Olsthoorn. For more information about the P 215, see page 82.

INSIDE COVER:
Messerschmitt P 11 Schnellbomber drawing dated September 13, 1942. Iowa State University Library Special Collections and University Archive

AUTHOR: Dan Sharp
DESIGN: atg-media.com
REPROGRAPHICS: Jonathan Schofield and Paul Fincham
PRODUCTION EDITOR: Nigel Devereux
PUBLISHER: Steve O'Hara
ADVERTISING MANAGER: Sue Keily, skeily@mortons.co.uk
PUBLISHING DIRECTOR: Dan Savage
MARKETING MANAGER: Charlotte Park
COMMERCIAL DIRECTOR: Nigel Hole

PUBLISHED BY: Mortons Media Group Ltd, Media Centre, Morton Way, Horncastle, Lincolnshire LN9 6JR. Tel. 01507 529529

THANKS TO: Elizabeth C Borja, Steven Coates, Chris Elwell, Simon Fowler, Chris Gall, Olivia T Garrison, Carlos Alberto Henriques, Guy Inchbald, Becky S Jordan, Scott Lowther, Paul Malmassari, Paul Martell-Mead, Ronnie Olsthoorn, Alexander Power, Kay Stout, Daniel Uhr, Stephen Walton, Gary Webster, Paul Williams and Tony Wilson

PRINTED BY: William Gibbons and Sons, Wolverhampton

ISBN: 978-1-911276-44-9

© 2017 Mortons Media Group Ltd. All rights reserved. No part of this publication may be reproduced or transmitted in any form or by any means, electronic or mechanical, including photocopying, recording, or any information storage retrieval system without prior permission in writing from the publisher.

MORTONS
MEDIA GROUP LTD

High-performance

Germany's WW2 tailless and flying wing designs

An obsession with gliders in 1920s and 1930s Germany led to the pursuit of ever greater aerodynamic efficiency in powered aircraft. During the war, with piston engines reaching their limit and tailplanes causing unwanted drag, designers began to look elsewhere for performance gains…

The search for ever faster, ever more manoeuvrable aircraft reached its zenith during the life or death struggle for supremacy that was the Second World War.

Like every other air force around the world, the Luftwaffe entered the conflict operating aircraft based on a design template established 20 years earlier: piston engine-driven propellers at the front, a long central fuselage housing the crew, a large pair – or two pairs – of straight wings towards the front, straight tailplanes at the rear and an upright tail fin.

Germany differed from other nations in 1939, however, in having the world's largest concentration of aviation research and development facilities. Its aircraft builders could call upon a total of 63 wind tunnels, and the universities and research institutes that operated them, to continually test and refine new aerodynamic forms and ideas. This 'industry' had grown and developed over the preceding two decades, driven initially by the German postwar passion for gliding.

The nation's defeat at the end of the First World War had brought with it the imposition of the Treaty of Versailles which banned the manufacture and importation of all aircraft

and aircraft parts in Germany for six months. It also required that all German "military and naval aeronautical material" be handed over to the Allies. This effectively crippled the German aviation industry and left a generation

of military aviators without aircraft to fly. And the succeeding generation, brought up on tales of German pilots' wartime heroics, had no way of following in their footsteps.

Even when the ban on building small

ABOVE: Remembered today primarily for designing the Me 163, Alexander Lippisch made his name in the early 1930s with advanced gliders such as this one – the Fafnir. It was an astonishing design in 1931, when most aircraft were ponderous biplanes.

GERMAN FLYING WING/TAILLESS

• 1927	Alexander Lippisch, director of the aeronautical department at the Rhön-Rossitten-Gesellschaft (RRG), builds his first full scale manned tailless glider – the Storch I.
• June 11, 1928	Fritz Stamer makes the first manned rocket-powered flight in history on the Wasserkuppe in Lippisch's tailless Ente aircraft.
• Mid 1930	Bayerische Flugzeugwerke director Theodor Croneiss donates an engine for Lippisch's first piston engine-powered tailless aircraft, the Delta I.
• February 1932	Gerhard Fieseler commissions three new Lippisch-designed tailless aircraft from the RRG, known as the Delta IV or F 3 Wespe.
• Late 1932	The Horten brothers see Lippisch's Delta I in flight and decide to build a manned tailless glider of their own.
• Early 1933	The RRG is split up by the incoming Nazi government and the Deutsche Forschungsanstalt für Segelflug (DFS) or 'German Research Institute for Soaring Flight' is formed. Lippisch keeps his own department.
• July 1933	The Horten brothers' first glider, the Hangwind or H I glides for more than 50m – at a height of 2m.
• 1935	The technical department of the DFS is split in two – Lippisch concentrating on tailless types and his former assistant Hans Jacobs concentrating on conventional tailed designs. Lippisch works on the Delta IV, since been rebuilt as the Delta IVa, then the Delta IVc, and now redesignated the DFS 39.
• May 1935	The second Horten brothers aircraft, the Habicht or H II, makes its first flight.
• May 1936	While working on the first H V for Dynamit, Reimar Horten is conscripted into the Luftwaffe.
• Autumn 1937	The RLM commissions Lippisch to convert the DFS 39 for rocket propulsion as an experimental design.
• May-August, 1938	The Horten brothers' first H III makes its maiden flight. The RLM orders 10 examples of the H III b.
• Summer 1938	Lippisch agrees to join the Messerschmitt company.
• November 2, 1938	The Horten brothers propose their H VII design to the RLM.
• November 23, 1938	Negotiations begin for the Horten brothers to join Heinkel.
• January 2, 1939	Alexander Lippisch and his team transfer from the DFS to Messerschmitt AG at Augsburg. They form Abteilung L or 'Department L' and develop the DFS 39 as 'Projekt X' which receives the designation Me 163.
• March 12, 1939	Negotiations between the Horten brothers and Heinkel end without success.
• April 12-13, 1939	Abteilung L produces the first single turbojet designs in what will become its long-running P 01 jet and rocket fighter series for Messerschmitt.

ursuit

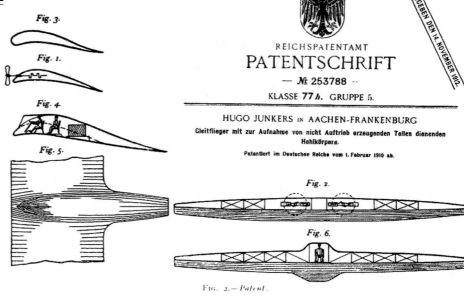

DEUTSCHES REICH

REICHSPATENTAMT
PATENTSCHRIFT
— № 253788 --
KLASSE 77h. GRUPPE 5.

HUGO JUNKERS IN AACHEN-FRANKENBURG
Gleitflieger mit zur Aufnahme von nicht Auftrieb erzeugenden Teilen dienenden Hohlkörpern.
Patentiert im Deutschen Reiche vom 1. Februar 1910 ab.

AUSGEGEBEN DEN 14. NOVEMBER 1912.

ABOVE: Perhaps the first true nurflügel or 'flying wing' design, patented by Hugo Junkers in 1910.

aircraft in Germany was lifted in 1922, and large aircraft in 1926, the country's dire economic circumstances meant manufacturers such as Junkers and Heinkel faced huge hurdles in trying to maintain and grow their businesses.

The only affordable option open to most people who wanted to experience flight was to go gliding. Starting in the early 1920s, a gliding competition was held every year at the Wasserkuppe – the highest peak in the Rhön mountains, in central Germany, and a large plateau perfect for gliding flight.

These contests rapidly grew in popularity and by the end of the decade were attracting entrants from across Europe and beyond. The relatively low cost involved in building an unpowered glider from wood resulted in a wide range of different aircraft being designed and flown by amateurs but the competitive nature of the event also spurred builders into experimentation with different aerodynamic forms in order to glide further and for longer than their rivals.

During this time hundreds of people flew on the Wasserkuppe, some of whom would later become famous in the German aviation industry – Willy Messerschmitt, Siegfried Günter, Hanna Reitsch, the Horten brothers, Heini Dittmar, Hans Jacobs and many others.

The first internationally recognised gliding organisation, the Rhön-Rossitten Gesellschaft (RRG), was established to regulate the burgeoning gliding movement and aircraft designer Alexander Lippisch was put in charge of the RRG's technical department in 1925, with the aim of producing ever-better gliders. The nearby Technische Hochschule Darmstaft or 'Darmstadt University of Technology' was also heavily involved and

came to offer training in aircraft design and aeronautics. The study of aerodynamics was becoming a science in its own right.

When the Nazis came to power in 1933, the RRG was broken up with part of it becoming a division of the Hitler Youth and the research department becoming the Deutsche Forschungsanstalt für Segelflug (DFS) or 'German Research Institute for Soaring Flight'.

The number of institutions involved in aviation research continued to grow and those who had flown on the Wasserkuppe went on to join aircraft manufacturers or became pilots in the fledgling Luftwaffe when it was formally established in 1935, in defiance of the Treaty of Versailles.

Even as the Luftwaffe grew and the German aircraft manufacturers began to receive large orders from the state for aeroplanes which pushed at the boundaries of performance, the spirit of experimentation to get better results became ever more firmly

embedded in the German aviation industry.

Veterans of the Wasserkuppe would all have been familiar with the work of Alexander Lippisch – who designed or supervised the design and construction of some of the world's most famous sailplanes, who published books concerning his theories on aircraft design and who, during the 1930s had hit the headlines of national newspapers several times with his unusual aerodynamic forms.

During the course of his work at the RRG, Lippisch had become increasingly convinced that the most efficient form for high-speed highly-manoeuvrable flight was tailless – where the aircraft has only one set of wings and a vertical fin but no horizontal tailplanes. When the DFS was formed, such was the perceived potential of tailless designs that Lippisch was able to head a department that specialised in them.

There was a precedent for tailless forms in German aircraft design – Hugo Junkers had patented a Nurflügel or ' ▶

AIRCRAFT DEVELOPMENT TIMELINE

• **August 1939**	Abteilung L begins work on its P 04 series of tailless twin-engine pusher aircraft to the same spec as the Me 210.
• **September 1, 1939**	The Second World War begins.
• **February 13, 1941**	First towed flight of the Me 163.
• **May 1941**	Walter Horten receives a staff position in Berlin as technical advisor to the Luftwaffe fighter inspectorate. Reimar completes the first H IV.
• **March 1, 1941**	Abteilung L's P 04 is substantially redesigned by Dr Hermann Wurster as a test aircraft for a large flying wing bomber.
• **April-July 1941**	One of Abteilung L's designs, the rocket-powered P 01-114, is given the designation Me 263.
• **August 27, 1941**	Lippisch proposes the 'Li P 05' interceptor, an up-scaled development of the Me 163.
• **September 1, 1941**	The P 08 four-engined flying wing superbomber is presented by Wurster as an alternative to what will become the Me 264.
• **October 2, 1941**	Heini Dittmar becomes the first man to fly faster than 1000km/h, at the controls of Me 163 V4.
• **October 1941**	The Horten brothers witness test flights of the Me 163 at Peenemünde.
• **November 1941**	Design details of the Me 163 B are finalised. All Me 163s become Me 163 As.
• **November 17, 1941**	Lippisch and Hortens supporter Ernst Udet commits suicide.
• **Spring 1942**	The Horten brothers begin designing a twin-jet flying wing, the H IX.
• **March 1942**	Drawings and proposals for the Me 163 C and Super 163 Interceptor are drafted.
• **May 19, 1942**	Lippisch designs a single-seat DB 606 pusher-prop fast bomber, the P 10.
• **May 26, 1942**	The Horten V c, intended as a testbed for a single-seat fighter, makes its first flight.
• **June 1942**	Göring instructs the RLM to award Messerschmitt a development contract for the P 10.
• **June 26, 1942**	First towed flight of the Me 163 B V1 by Heini Dittmar.
• **Autumn 1942**	Lippisch decides to drop the original P 10 and, keeping the name only, swaps it for a completely different design put forward by one of his team members – a tailless Me 210/410. The P 10 receives the designation Me 265.
• **September 10, 1942**	Willy Messerschmitt discovers what Lippisch has done with the P 10 and that the development contract has been lost as a result.
• **September 13, 1942**	The first P 11, a two-seater fast bomber powered by two turbojets, is designed by Handrick.

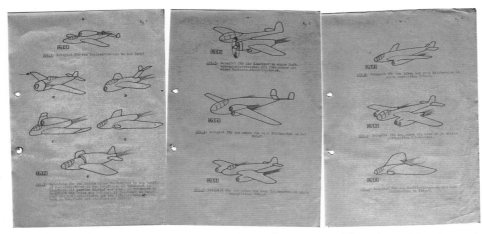

ABOVE: Illustrations showing a selection of the different German aircraft layouts considered as part of the Göttinger Programm, an in-depth research project led by Dietrich Küchemann at the AVA which studied jet engine installations and intake forms. Three of the 11 designs, slightly more than a quarter, are tailless.

all-wing' or 'flying wing' aircraft as early as 1910 – consisting almost entirely of a single large wing without fuselage or tail fin that housed the crew, landing gear and engines.

Several of the glider pioneers besides Lippisch, including Messerschmitt, had also experimented with tailless or flying wing shapes during the 1920s. The Horten brothers – Walter and Reimar – were fans of Lippisch's work but wanted to pursue the 'flying wing' shape rather than anything that involved the need for a vertical fin. They constructed

gliders and then powered aircraft during the 1930s and like Lippisch were convinced that a tailless or flying wing aircraft could be made to outperform its conventional tailed equivalent – providing the inherent drawbacks of the tailless form could be overcome.

As the Second World War began, most of the major German aircraft manufacturers were aware of the flying wing shape – Arado having even gone so far as to design a flying wing bomber during the mid 1930s – but it was Messerschmitt that took the lead by hiring

Lippisch in 1938, giving him his own design department and presenting him with a mandate to design a tailless version of whatever the company's main design office was working on.

Heinkel attempted to hire the Horten brothers later in the year with a similar aim in mind but the deal collapsed before it had been finalised. Focke-Wulf too seems to have examined flying wings and tailless designs early on but could find little benefit in them.

Other aircraft designers found the arguments put forward by Lippisch and the Hortens intriguing however, even if they were not otherwise entirely persuaded by them.

The perceived advantages of a tailless or flying wing design included a greater carrying capacity – their internal area typically being larger than that of a conventional design of a similar wingspan – low drag for better aerodynamic performance; stability in manoeuvring; a low tendency to spin; and cheaper, easier construction.

The perceived disadvantages, particularly with designs which lacked a tailfin, included often inferior flight performance in practice, potentially higher landing speeds, poor directional stability, lower permissible limits on the centre of gravity (even a small shift in the centre of gravity, for example through a bomb being dropped, could have a disproportionately negative impact on handling), a larger sweepback producing ground clearance problems for landing, wing bending oscillations in gusts,

GERMAN FLYING WING/TAILLESS AIRCRAFT DEVELOPMENT

- **November 6, 1942** Lippisch presents a talk on his Me 163 A to members of the exclusive Deutsche Akademie für Luftfahrtforschung, including Siegfried Günter of Heinkel and Hans Multhopp of Focke-Wulf.
- **December 2, 1942** A second P 11 is designed by Handrick. He makes it a single-seater.
- **February 1943** Messerschmitt produces a full technical report on the Me 329 heavy fighter, based on the P 04.
- **March 1943** The RLM orders the Horten brothers' Sonderkommando Lln 3 to cease all work.
- **March 20, 1943** The RLM orders that Lippisch's Department L should be effectively dissolved and absorbed into Messerschmitt. Lippisch leaves the company the following month.
- **April 28, 1943** Lippisch leaves Messerschmitt. He takes up his new appointment as head of the Luftfahrtforschungsanstalt Wien (LFW) in Vienna, Austria, three days later.
- **May 1943** Lippisch gives Göring his proposal for an aircraft that can fly 1000km at 1000km/h carrying 1000kg of bombs – the P 11.
- **July 1943** Lippisch receives a development contract for his P 11.
- **June 15, 1943** Arado makes its first report on a series of flying wing studies designated E 555.
- **August 1943** The Horten brothers send their 1000 x 1000 x 1000 proposal to Göring. They meet with him either at the end of the month or in early September 1943 and he provides them with a development contract for a prototype H IX.
- **January 1944** The first production batches of Me 163B-0 and B-1 airframes are completed but no engines are available.
- **March 1, 1944** The unpowered H IX V1 glider is ready for its first flight, which it makes four days later.
- **June 1944** An air raid on Lippisch's LFW headquarters kills 43 of his staff.
- **Late June 1944** Construction of the Horten IX V2 begins at Göttingen.
- **July 1944** A requirement is issued for a new single jet, single-seat fighter aircraft, an 'Ein-TL-Jäger'. Four firms, Blohm & Voss, Focke-Wulf, Heinkel and Messerschmitt, are invited to submit tenders. The design must be ready to present within eight weeks – by early September – with a mock-up ready a month later, a prototype ready to fly by December 1, 1944, and series production commencing on January 1, 1945.
- **August 31, 1944** A requirement is issued for a new night and bad-weather fighter powered by a Jumo 222 E/F, As 413, DB 603 L or DB 613 or any of these in combination with a turbojet.
- **September 1944** Dr Rudolf Goethert at Gotha begins work on a flying wing design with the intention of supplanting the Horten brothers' 8-229, which Gotha has been charged with building.
- **September 8-10, 1944** Three of the four firms invited to tender for the 'Ein-TL-Jäger' requirement present their designs. The Blohm & Voss submission is deferred since it is not yet ready. Focke-Wulf's design is largely rejected.
- **September 15, 1944** A new main development committee, the Entwicklungs Hauptkommission (EHK), led by Luftwaffe chief engineer Roluf Lucht, is established by Germany's minister for war production, Albert Speer, to oversee work on new aircraft types. Among its members are Focke-Wulf chief designer Kurt Tank, Willy Messerschmitt, Walter Blume of Arado and Heinrich Hertel from Junkers.
- **October 1944** Lippisch works intensively on his ramjet-powered P 13 rammer aircraft design.
- **October 18, 1944** A full summary of Arado's E 555 project is published.
- **October 21, 1944** Junkers is given a contract to begin development of the Ju 248.
- **November 1944** Willy Messerschmitt proposes a four-turbojet bomber design, sparking a new long-distance bomber competition – Langstreckenbomber.

difficulty landing in crosswinds, difficulty in ground-handling and drag caused by any protrusions, such as for a cockpit canopy.

Those who had written off tailless designs were forced to reconsider when the swept-wing rocket-propelled tailless Me 163 smashed the world air speed record by clocking up 1003.67km/h on October 2, 1941. This was a huge leap ahead of the previous record, set using the experimental piston-engined Me 209 V1 on April 26, 1939.

By all accounts not only was the Me 163 incredibly fast, it was also extremely manoeuvrable – the two qualities most desirable in single-seat fighters. Word of this feat, achieved in secrecy, was slow to spread but within a year most of Germany's major aircraft manufacturers were reconsidering their view on tailless types. They were also giving more thought to swept-wing tailed designs and propulsion by rocket engines, jet engines or a combination of both.

Yet while Lippisch was admitted into one of Germany's most exclusive clubs for top-flight aviation engineers, the Deutsche Akademie für Luftfahrtforschung or 'German Academy of Aeronautical Research', and rubbed shoulders with the likes of Hermann Göring and Erhard Milch, the Horten brothers struggled to gain acceptance for their flying wing ideas. They were outsiders, using whatever means they could to continue building their radical designs.

Lippisch's overfamiliarity with the highest ranking men in aviation proved to be his undoing at Messerschmitt and he left in April 1943. Almost immediately, however, he was back at Göring's door with an attractive proposal – a design that could carry 1000kg of bombs for a range of 1000km at a speed of 1000km/h. Göring gave him the funds to proceed with it but a few months later, out of the blue, received a second proposal for a design that was expected to achieve those same numbers – this time proposed by the Hortens.

Unaware of Lippisch's pitch, they had heard Göring talking about his desire for a machine that could achieve that level of performance and had drafted their own proposal. Later, Focke-Wulf assessed Lippisch's idea for itself and concluded that a conventional layout design could achieve the same performance without the risk of a tailless form.

As the war entered its final year, the German aircraft manufacturers were tasked with creating a single jet engine replacement for the Me 262 and a lengthy competition ensued, known as Ein-TL-Jäger or 1-TL-Jäger – 'Single Jet Fighter'. To begin with, the companies concerned offered conventional layout designs but by the end of the year several had switched to tailless forms for their entries. By February 1945 fully half of the designs were tailless – though Focke-Wulf never did make the switch.

As the single jet day fighter competition neared its conclusion, two further last-minute contests were begun – Schlechtwetter und Nachtjäger to produce a three-seat two-jet bad-weather and night fighter, and Langstreckenbomber to design a bomber capable of attacking bomber bases in Britain and France. Seven competing designs were tendered for the former, three of them tailless, and only three for the latter, one of them tailless and proposed by the Horten brothers. However, the front runners for Schlechtwetter und Nachtjäger were both tailless and the tailless Langstreckenbomber entry, while it was not rushed into production, was earmarked for further development.

It is interesting to note how the early enthusiasm for tailless designs, particularly in the wake of Messerschmitt's success with the Me 163, bled away as tailed designs such as the Me 262 and Me 410 continued to be chosen for further development despite tailless alternatives being offered.

The point at which Lippisch left Messerschmitt was probably the nadir for tailless aircraft design within the Third Reich but during the two remaining years of the war tailless designs continued to be examined and ultimately began to edge out their more conventional rivals. Had the war continued, it seems likely that the Luftwaffe aircraft of 1946 and beyond would have been tailless. As it was, the Allies would reap the benefits of German research into tailless and flying wing forms but the story of how such designs evolved in Germany, though replete with gaps, remains a compelling tale of passion and belief in the face of skepticism and doubt.. ●

TIMELINE

- **Mid November 1944** — A description of the Horten IX V6 is prepared.
- **November 21-22, 1944** — A meeting of the Entwicklungs Hauptkommission is told that the Ho 229 is to be developed in conjunction with Gotha and three prototypes of the H VII are to be completed. It is also stated that Lippisch's P 11 is to be developed in collaboration with Henschel. His P 13 is also briefly mentioned. It is also mentioned that the Henschel Hs 132 jet dive bomber "was to be subject to a decision on the quantity to be produced".
- **November 27, 1944** — The Horten H XIII makes its first flight at Hersfeld.
- **Winter 1944** — Work on Arado E 555 programme has come to an end.
- **December 2, 1944** — Lippisch is still attempting to obtain a pair of Jumo 004 engines for his Delta VI 2 airframe.
- **December 19-21, 1944** — Second meeting to discuss the Ein-TL-Jäger jet fighter designs.
- **January 12-16, 1945** — Third meeting to discuss the Ein-TL-Jäger jet fighter designs.
- **January 26, 1945** — A date is set for a comparison conference on the Langstreckenbomber jet bomber designs prepared by Messerschmitt, Junkers and the Horten brothers.
- **January 27, 1945** — The night and bad-weather fighter requirements are revised.
- **February 8, 1945** — The Ju 248 V1 makes its first gliding test flight.
- **February 16, 1945** — The Horten 8-229 and Gotha P 60 are compared at a DVL conference in Berlin.
- **February 18, 1945** — The Horten IX V2 is destroyed in a crash, killing test pilot Erwin Ziller.
- **February 19, 1945** — Final gliding flight of the Ju 248 V1.
- **February 20-23, 1945** — A conference is held at Dessau to compare the Langstreckenbomber designs.
- **February 26, 1945** — A meeting is held to compare night and bad-weather fighter designs by Blohm & Voss, Dornier and Messerschmitt.
- **February 27, 1945** — Technical specifications for the night and bad-weather fighter requirement are altered again, making the designs submitted so far inadequate.
- **February 27-28, 1945** — Fourth meeting to discuss the Ein-TL-Jäger jet fighter designs.
- **March 8-17, 1945** — Arado drafts nine different configurations for its entries to the night and bad-weather fighter requirement, seven of them tailless. One tailless and one conventional design are chosen to enter.
- **March 20-21, 1945** — Twin-jet night and bad-weather fighter designs by Arado, Blohm & Voss, Dornier, Focke-Wulf and Gotha are compared but the only decision made is that the latest requirement is too severe and that it should be reverted back to the January 27 spec.
- **March 22-23, 1945** — A final discussion takes place at Focke-Wulf's Bad Eilsen facility regarding the five companies' submissions to the '1-TL-Jäger' requirement. Junkers receives a development contract for its EF 128 design.
- **March 31, 1945** — Heinkel's technical design department is evacuated from Vienna.
- **April 8, 1945** — British forces overrun Focke-Wulf's Bad Eilsen design facilities.
- **April 24, 1945** — American forces overrun Junkers' Dessau headquarters.
- **April 29, 1945** — American forces overrun Messerschmitt's Oberammergau design facilities.
- **May 3, 1945** — British forces overrun Blohm & Voss's headquarters in Hamburg.

Love and rockets –
Abteilung L

When disgruntled colleagues conspired to leave him sitting on the sidelines, aircraft designer Alexander Lippisch worked his old contacts to sidestep their machinations and found himself designing warplanes for Germany's premier fighter firm.

There is little doubt that aerodynamicist, engineer and Messerschmitt Me 163 designer Alexander Lippisch was the pivotal figure in tailless aircraft design in Germany during the Second World War.

His establishment of a dedicated flying wing and tailless department at Messerschmitt in 1939, known as Abteilung 'L', would have significant repercussions for aircraft development within the German aviation industry right up to the end of the war.

Much that has been written about Lippisch charts his steady progress through a long succession of experimental tailless designs until he was eventually asked to develop a rocketplane under the implausible designation 'Project X'. Lippisch himself tends to promote this idea in his own works.

However he first made a name for himself, not to mention a successful career, designing conventional gliders – not tailless ones. After the First World War, the victorious Allies banned the development and manufacture of aero engines in Germany. Therefore, ex-military aviators grounded by the ban and young men eager to fly for the first time turned to gliders instead.

Having been a member of the aerodynamics department at Zeppelin during the war, Lippisch began to work on gliders including tailless types during the winter of 1920/21 and during 1923 he designed and built the simple open frame Hols der Teufel or 'Devil Take It', the world's first solo primary training glider. This had a conventional layout and several dozen were produced. He also designed the wing for another glider, the Bremen, which was used by his friend Fritz Stamer to help train glider pilots.

As gliding caught on and became more popular there was a growing demand for trainers and in 1926 Lippisch, now the director of the aeronautical department of the newly-formed Rhön-Rossitten-Gesellschaft (RRG), designed a follow-up to the Hols der Teufel called the R I Zögling or 'Pupil'. This proved to be very popular and plans were sold allowing gliding clubs across Germany and elsewhere to build their own versions of it.

Managed by glider research pioneer Walter Georgii, the RRG was based on the Wasserkuppe, a dome-shaped mountain that had become the spiritual home of gliding in Germany. It was set up to regulate and promote the burgeoning glider community and Stamer came on board as the manager of the RRG's training section when it absorbed his previous employer, the Martens flying school, at the end of 1925.

The following year, 32-year-old Lippisch

ABOVE: A flight of low-wing rocket-propelled fighters drawn by Alexander Lippisch to illustrate a talk he gave at to Hauptmann Oskar Dinort at Döberitz airfield in December 1934 on the military potential of tailless aircraft. Iowa State University Library Special Collections and University Archive

married Stamer's 23-year-old little sister, Katharina 'Käthe' Stamer. In between working on the Zögling and a secondary trainer to complement it, the conventional-layout R II Prüfling or 'Examinee', Lippisch was also now able to return to working on tailless designs – albeit only as models. When the Prüfling was ready, also in 1926, he finally had the time and the production capacity available to put his tailless research to the test with a full-scale glider – the Storch or 'Stork'.

Built during the spring and summer of 1927, the swept-wing monoplane Storch was first flown in the autumn. A series of test flights showed that it lacked directional stability – in other words it was hard to make it fly in a straight line. Aerodynamic changes to the control surfaces, though not to the wing itself, led to the Storch II, mostly test flown by Stamer, then the Storch III.

While this was being worked on, Lippisch continued to provide the RRG with winning conventional designs. His next, the R III Professor, was intended as the next step for pilots who were moving on from the Prüfling and it first flew in May 1928. Like the Hols der Teufel, Zögling and Prüfling before it, the Professor was designed to be easily constructed by amateurs working to drawings they had purchased from the RRG and as such it was a great success. In addition, the Professor was the first glider in the world to be fitted with a variometer for finding and exploiting lift-producing thermals.

ROCKET-POWERED FLIGHT

With these designs under his belt, Lippisch had acquired a reputation as Germany's foremost glider designer and his next task was his most unusual yet. Fritz von Opel, grandson of the founder of the Opel car company, had been working on rocket-propelled cars with Great War veteran Max Valier and the pair had decided that the time was right to try a rocket-propelled aircraft.

They approached Lippisch to see whether he could build a glider with a canard or 'tail-first' layout – so that there would be no tail structure behind the solid-fuel rocket engines when they were firing. Lippisch duly designed and had built the straight-winged Ente or 'Duck', which was test flown under rocket power on June 11, 1928, by Stamer. It was the first rocket-powered manned flight in history but would prove to be the last for some time. Stamer had a lucky escape when one of the rockets blew up and the glider caught fire, von Opel lost interest soon after and Valier was later killed in a rocket engine explosion.

Meanwhile, test flights of the latest Storch, the 'IV', in 1929 showed that the instability of earlier versions had been cured and the aircraft was much easier to fly. The fruits of this research were immediately applied to Lippisch's work on conventional gliders and the Storch IV's wing, largely unaltered, was used for the conventional-layout Falke or 'Falcon', a secondary trainer replacement for the Prüfling. The RRG's investment of time and resources in Lippisch's work had achieved a tangible, useful and above all profitable

ABOVE: The Storch experimental glider, built by the RRG in 1927 to Lippisch's design. A whole series of Storchs followed, each designed to correct the flaws of its predecessor.

ABOVE: Alexander Lippisch leans over the DKW-engined pusher prop-driven Storch V and pilot Günther Groenhoff, probably in 1929. Groenhoff was killed in 1932 while flying Lippisch's Fafnir glider. Bundesarchiv, Bild 102-13690 / CC-BY-SA 3.0

outcome. Manufactured in quantity by several professional workshops, the Falke was widely adopted as Germany's standard secondary training glider for three years and hundreds of student pilots flew it.

That same year, the RRG built Lippisch's Storch V design – essentially the Storch IV with an engine and pusher propeller fitted. It first flew in September 1929 and on the back of it, towards the end of the year, the RRG was commissioned to build a new tailless aircraft for aviation pioneer Hauptmann Hermann Köhl. The result was a high-winged experimental glider with swept leading edges and an entirely straight trailing edge – a wing shape like the triangular Greek letter 'delta'. Unsurprisingly, Lippisch called it the Delta.

As his tailless work continued to yield promising results, Lippisch concentrated much of his effort on a new conventional design the like of which had never been seen before: the Fafnir. Named after the dragon of Norse mythology, the Fafnir was a slender high-performance competition glider that was structurally strong enough for all external support struts to be eliminated and its 19m span wing incorporated the very latest aerodynamic forms. The tiny cockpit, designed around the diminutive frame of test pilot Günther Groenhoff, was hidden behind a curved plywood fairing

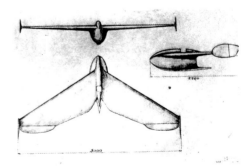

ABOVE: After his tailless Ente aircraft was used as a testbed for Fritz von Opel's solid-fuel rockets in 1928, Lippisch went on to design this rocket-propelled aircraft for him in 1929.

to reduce drag and like all of Lippisch's previous gliders it landed on a skid.

The Fafnir took a long time to build and was very costly. It had been intended to fly it competitively during 1930 but it was finished too late – shortly after the completion of the Delta in mid 1930. Testing of the Delta convinced Lippisch that the powered version would perform better with a low wing and work therefore began on another new aircraft, the Delta I, incorporating a Bristol Cherub engine donated by Theodor Croneiss, a director of the Bayerische Flugzeugwerke ▶

ABOVE: While his previous tailless designs had featured swept wings, the Delta glider of 1930 was the first to take a pure delta form – so called because its triangular shape resembled the 'delta' letter of the Greek alphabet.

ABOVE: The Delta I, built in 1931, was powered by a 30hp Bristol Cherub engine which came from Theo Croneiss, a director of Bayerische Flugzeugwerke. It was the beginning of an association with the company that would come to fruition eight years later.

(BFW) and aged just a month younger than Lippisch. This was completed in 1931 but the Cherub was damaged while flying to Berlin's Tempelhof airfield for a demonstration flight so Croneiss was approached and he donated a second Cherub. The demonstration, on September 25, 1931, was a success but did not result in any additional funding, beyong Köhl's initial investment. Croneiss, who in addition to his work at BFW was also a rising star in the Nazi party, appears to have taken a personal interest in Lippisch's work at this time.

While Lippisch had been busy with the Fafnir and the Deltas, glider manufacturer Edmund Schneider had designed and begun to build a new secondary trainer which incorporated the best features of the Prüfling and the Falke – the Grunau Baby. This became a huge hit and resulted in Lippisch's earlier designs being largely supplanted.

The Fafnir had meanwhile proven to be a huge success during 1931, with Groenhoff becoming the first man to glide further than 200km in a single flight. Now another glider manufacturer, Alexander Schleicher, decided that he wanted a similar glider for mass-production, but one that was simpler and cheaper to build. He therefore went to the RRG itself and since Lippisch was too busy, one of his apprentices, Hans Jacobs, took the job. Jacobs' design, the Rhönadler, stuck closely to the design brief and while the Fafnir remained a costly one-off, Rhönadlers were soon rolling off Schleicher's production line.

Attempting to fly the Delta I himself meanwhile, Köhl managed to break off its nosewheel during take-off and narrowly avoided a serious accident. Undaunted, Lippisch built another powered delta – the Delta II – specifically to suit Groenhoff's small size. However, problems with its Ursinius 24hp engine kept it grounded. Then the RLM belatedly decided to award the RRG a development contract based

ABOVE: The Delta I during a demonstration flight at Berlin-Tempelhof on September 25, 1931.

on the performance of the Delta I.

The new aircraft, the Delta III, would be built by Focke-Wulf at Bremen.

In February 1932, Gerhard Fieseler commissioned three examples of a new tandem seat delta aircraft, to be powered by a pair of British Pobjoy R engines with one pushing and one pulling, which the RRG knew as the Delta IV but Fieseler himself called the F 3 Wespe. Work on it commenced in April and the first machine was completed in June but attempting to fly it himself, Fieseler initially found it almost uncontrollable.

The Fieseler company itself made numerous alterations to the aircraft at Lippisch's behest, at its own expense, but eventually Fieseler managed to get out of his contract with the RRG without having

to actually buy the aircraft thanks to a technicality and left the single completed Delta IV with the RRG. Contemporary newspaper and magazine reports of the Delta IV were actually positive but less positive were allegations made in the press by Köhl about Lippisch's Delta I. Eventually the RRG had to repay Köhl's money and take back the Delta I for itself.

Disaster struck again on July 23, 1932, when Groenhoff was killed attempting to take off in the Fafnir and it was wrecked. And to round off the year, Ernst Heinkel of the Heinkel company invited Lippisch to a meeting to discuss the potential further development of his delta aircraft but then pulled out of the project.

Meanwhile, during 1932 Jacobs published what came to be widely regarded as the standard text on glider construction – Werkstattpraxis für den Bau von Gleit- und Segelflugzeugen or 'Workshop Practice for the Construction of Gliders and Sailplanes'.

Despite the setbacks he had experienced, and the not insubstantial sums he had cost the RRG, Lippisch remained highly regarded. Following the seismic political shift that occurred when Adolf Hitler became the German chancellor on January 30, 1933, the RRG was reorganised into two separate companies – the Deutschen Luftsportverband (DLV) or 'German Airsport Association' and the Deutsche Forschungsanstalt für Segelflug (DFS) or 'German Research Institute for Soaring Flight'. With fresh funding for aviation research now made available by the government, Lippisch was made head of his own department at the latter with Georgii remaining in charge overall. Stamer and Jacobs also became part of the DFS.

The formation of this new organisation involved much more than a name change however. The entire research section of what had been the RRG was moved 135km west to the old Griesheimer

Sand airfield at Darmstadt, south-west of Frankfurt. Rather than living on top of a mountain, Lippisch and Stamer moved into the comfortable Darmstadt suburb of Traisa with their families.

Lippisch also found that much of the time he had previously spent working on aerodynamic problems and building gliders was now taken up by his new managerial role. Jacobs took on many of the design duties he had previously performed and also established contracts with outside firms which could fulfil the DFS's glider construction requirements.

During 1934, Georgii led an expedition to showcase the best German gliders in South America, including a rebuilt Fafnir. When he returned, Lippisch designed his final conventional glider – the costly and elaborate but also highly advanced Fafnir II or Sao Paulo. In December 1934, Lippisch gave a talk to Hauptmann Oskar Dinort and his men at Döberitz airfield on the military potential of tailless aircraft, illustrating the presentation with a drawing of futuristic-looking rocket-powered fighters. Just over a year later Dinort would become the commanding officer of another flying wing pioneer – Walter Horten.

In 1935 the technical department of the DFS was split in two, with Jacobs taking control of everything to do with conventional gliders and Lippisch being given a separate experimental delta and all-wing division.

With the Delta III and the much-altered Delta IV airframe now under his control, and with the DFS's research budget available, Lippisch had the Delta IV rebuilt without its pusher engine as the Delta IVa. This was found to have significantly improved handling characteristics.

Towards the end of the year DFS test pilot Erich Wiegmeyer, in whom Lippisch had very little faith, crashed the Delta III and completely destroyed it – without suffering any injury himself. A few weeks later, during December 1935, he also managed to crash the Delta IVa and was asked to leave the DFS.

A technical commission was then formed from representatives of the Deutsche Versuchsanstalt für Luftfahrt (DVL) or 'German Institute for Aeronautical Research' and the technical office of the RLM to review the performance of Lippisch's delta-wing aircraft and their report concluded: "The delta type shows no promise and there is no prospect that this type of design will lead to a practical, serviceable aircraft."

However, Georgii came to Lippisch's defence. According to Lippisch himself in his posthumously-published 1976 autobiography Erinnerungen: "This situation, which would almost have led to the death of the Delta flight development, was turned around by Professor Georgii who found that he could still make a small contribution to the reconstruction of the Delta Delta.

"In fact, this point and this help from Professor Georgii was the turning point in the development of the flying-wing aircraft. After all the catastrophes, we had gained so much new experience, both theoretically and experimentally, that despite all gloomy predictions a success had to be achieved."

The Delta IVa was rebuilt as the Delta IVc – although how much of the original

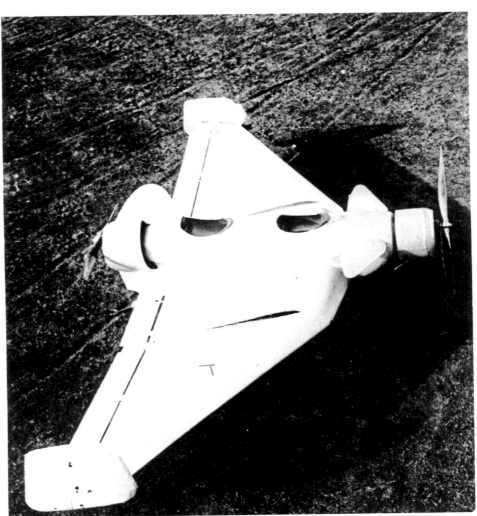

ABOVE: Lippisch built the twin-engine Delta IV in 1932 for Gerhard Fieseler, who called it the Fieseler F 3 Wespe. He found it almost uncontrollable and managed to avoid paying for it, handing it back to the RRG.

remained is questionable since it had entirely new 30 degree swept back wings, now with a swept trailing edge too, and a new fuselage made from steel tubing. Test flights made by Heini Dittmar resulted in the wings being given a less severe sweep of 23 and the rear fuselage was widened, resulting in the Delta IVc. This was put through official testing as a sports aircraft and approved, receiving the new designation DFS 39.

AN IDEAL FLYING WING
At the same time, during the winter of 1935-36, Lippisch found sufficient additional funds to have a glider with forward-swept wings built too – the DFS 42 Kormoran. This was flown but was found to be less promising than the DFS 39 and was therefore discontinued. To the surprise of everyone, perhaps even Lippisch himself, the DFS 39 now began to attract new business.

Firstly, during the winter of 1936-37 the RLM gave the DFS a research contract to work on designs for a tailless parasol-wing reconnaissance aircraft to be built by Siebel. A mock-up was built and given wind tunnel test time but this demonstrated no advantages over conventional designs and so was discontinued in 1938.

A second contract was placed at around the same time for an experimental mid-engined pusher-prop tailless design that was

expected to form the basis for a fighter – the DFS 194. And during early 1937 Lippisch also managed to find sufficient funds to build a pure all-wing pusher-prop design, the DFS 40, which he calls in his autobiography "an almost ideal flying wing test aircraft". The goal of this further substantial expense was "in order to make a decision as to whether a thin wing with an attached fuselage or a pure all-wing design was more favourable than a tailless aeroplane".

Meanwhile, in 1935 Hans Jacobs had designed the two-seat DFS Kranich or 'Crane' glider – which would go on to become the most heavily mass-produced glider in Germany right up to the end of the Second World War. One official report lists 1312 examples produced by one manufacturer alone. For the Olympic Games in Berlin in 1936, he had designed the Habicht or 'Hawk' glider which wowed the international crowds in the arena, and finally during 1937 his DFS 230 military transport glider flew for the first time – of which more than 1600 examples would be built.

With work on his DFS 194 and DFS 40 well under way, Lippisch was approached during the autumn of 1937 by RLM representative Dr Hermann Lorenz, who technically had some oversight of work carried out by the DFS, and Dr Joseph Jennisson, an RLM technical liaison officer. In a manuscript

ABOVE: After several rebuilds which changed it almost beyond recognition, the Fieseler's Delta IV became the DFS 39 in 1936.

ABOVE: The DFS 194 – although it was not a direct ancestor of the Me 163, it did contribute valuable rocket engine test data to the project.

ABOVE: The DFS 40 flying wing of 1937/38 was apparently one of Lippisch's proudest creations. He was forced to give it up when he left the DFS.

published in 2001 by Stephen Ransom and Hans-Hermann Cammann, Lippisch recalled: "Dr Lorenz and I did not get on very well. I was always doing something that was not on the agenda. Actually, it was not my fault: I was used to applying newly acquired knowledge immediately in order to get ahead quickly and, of course, this did not fit into the well-ordered scheme of things in the research department.

"In the autumn of 1937, Dr Lorenz, accompanied by Dr Jennissen, came to Darmstadt to make an inspection. I showed the gentlemen into the workshop where work was being carried out on the new DFS 194. The DFS 39 was also standing there. Dr Lorenz asked me which aircraft had the better flying characteristics. 'That's unquestionably the DFS 39, Herr Dr Lorenz.' 'Tell me, Herr Lippisch, could you build us a second aircraft of this sort with exactly the same wings but with a different fuselage?' 'Certainly we can do that.' 'We want to test a new engine and this must be installed in the rear fuselage with the cockpit forward, not like in the layout of the DFS 39.'

"As I had already heard similar talk from Fritz von Opel back in 1928 the penny dropped immediately and I replied dryly, 'You want to try out a new rocket engine?' Lorenz would have liked to have strangled me for revealing this state secret. 'What on earth made you shout that out here among all these people and how do you know anything about it anyway? This is quite outrageous!' 'I don't know anything about it at all, but we were flying with rocket power 10 years ago,' I managed to gasp when I had got my breath back. 'I must ask you not to use the word 'rocket' in public again,' Dr Lorenz said very sharply and firmly. I felt very sheepish as we retired to the privacy of my office. "After all the doors and windows had been barred, I was informed in a whisper that it

was planned to award a contract for a research aircraft for testing 'jet' propulsion at high speeds. The RLM development department had ordered such a bird from Heinkel. I was to design an aerodynamically improved DFS 39 for the research department. This design was designated Project X with the security classification 'burn before reading' and was the start of work on the project which was to become the Me 163."

Heinkel, having experience of rocket-powered flight with its He 176, was to construct the fuselage and engine installation while the DFS would supply the wings. Both fuselage and wings would be designed by the DFS. Wind tunnel testing and free-flying model tests were carried out by Lippisch, his department's aerodynamicist Josef Hubert and engineer Rudolf Rentel. The design drawings were made by Fritz Krämer. According to Lippisch's own account "ample" funds were made available for this work.

During the winter of 1937/38, work on the DFS 194 airframe was finished but installing its Argus petrol engine proved to be a "headache" due to its complicated cooling system. The DFS 40 was still under construction and the Project X was a design in progress.

A DEATH IN THE FAMILY

Just a few months into 1938, events were set in motion that would result in Lippisch leaving the DFS, an organisation in one form or another to which he had belonged since 1926, and joining Messerschmitt AG at the beginning of 1939.

The fact that he became a Messerschmitt employee, leading to the development of the Me 163, is well known. Somewhat less well known are the circumstances surrounding this critical moment in the history of Germany's tailless aircraft development. Lippisch himself gave several different

accounts of how and why it happened.

The earliest known account, from a document he prepared in 1941 while still working at Messerschmitt, states: "Because I had recognised the necessity to design the tailless aircraft specially for this new type of powerplant and that the use of swept wings for high-speed flight would only then be shown to advantage, I decided to transfer my work completely to the aircraft industry.

"My negotiations with Heinkel were almost complete when, quite by chance, I met director Croneiss and Professor Messerschmitt in Berlin and they persuaded me to join Messerschmitt AG in Augsburg."

Eighteen years later in 1959, in a letter to the editor of Flugwelt magazine correcting errors in an article published on the Me 163, Lippisch continued to state that his move to Messerschmitt was driven purely by technical concerns. Discussing the development of 'Project X' and referring to himself in the third person, he wrote: "In the course of the work, however, it became clear that the construction of this experimental model could not be carried out in the form prescribed by the requirement. For this reason, Lippisch decided to move with a number of his employees to an aircraft builder."

Another 16 years on, and 34 years after his first account, in his 1976 book on tailless flight Ein Dreieck Fliegt, he stuck to the 'technical' explanation: "Since collaboration with Heinkel appeared problematic and the continuation of the development of this experimental high speed craft was questionable at the DFS, I decided to transfer to the Messerschmitt AG in Augsburg."

Erinnerungen, written at around the same time as Ein Dreieck Fliegt, offers a far more detailed and nuanced version of events. In order to understand what happened, it is necessary to backtrack a little.

By his own admission, thanks to his workaholic lifestyle Lippisch seldom had much time for his wife Käthe. He later wrote that he had become closely connected to Fritz Stamer early on in his career, "and his sister, who knew me better from the description of Stamer than I myself, formed an ever closer union between Stamer and myself, and became my wife, who, in all the crises which always came up, was always on my side.

"She knew she could never quite possess me, which often made her sad. And I myself had probably become a stranger in many respects through experiences and events. I must admit that Käthe often did not have it easy with me."

A decade on, in 1936, Stamer was becoming increasingly dissatisfied with the way Lippisch was neglecting his sister and Hans Jacobs felt that his hard work in designing practical gliders was bankrolling Lippisch's personal interest in a dead-end field of aerodynamics. Neither of them, caught up in the wave of nationalism then sweeping Germany, was impressed when Lippisch began to actively pursue a professional relationship with aircraft designers abroad – particularly in England. He even used his influence within the DFS to set up an office where foreign works on aerodynamics

ABOVE: Lippisch, right, believed that his brother-in-law Fritz Stamer, left, was behind efforts to deprive him of his influence at the DFS in the wake of his wife's – Stamer's sister's – death. It was these machinations which evidently prompted his move to Messerschmitt, rather than anything to do with his work.

```
Projekte  1939

1.) Entwurf P01 - 113 (2x)
2.)    "      "   114 (2x)
3.)    "      "   115 (2x)
4.)    "      "   116 (2x)  Körner 13.4.1939
5.)    "      "    "  (2x)    "    12.4.1939
6.)    "      "    "  (2x)  Rentel 12.6.1941
7.)    "      "    "  (2x)    "    16.7.1941
8.)    "      "   117 (2x)
9.)    "      "   118 (2x)
10.)   "      "   119 (2x)
11.)   "      "   111 (2x)
```

ABOVE: A note from Lippisch's personal papers, presumably produced in 1941, appears to show Abteilung L's P 01 schedule. The first design in the series to be worked on was the P 01-116, rather than the P 01-111 as logic might suggest. **Iowa State University Library Special Collections and University Archive**

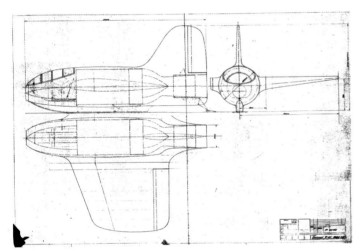

ABOVE: One of the earliest drawings of a jet aircraft ever committed to paper – Körner's P 01-116 of April 12, 1939. **Iowa State University Library Special Collections and University Archive**

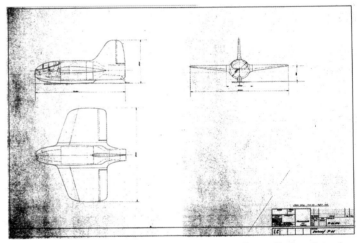

ABOVE: A full three-view drawing of the P 01-116 – the earliest version of the Messerschmitt P 01 despite the out-of-sequence '116' number – dated April 13, 1939. **Iowa State University Library Special Collections and University Archive**

could be translated into German.

He later wrote: "This gave me a lot of trouble in the family and friends circle. The supernational slogans had struck many people around me."

Matters came to a head in March 1938, just as the installation of the DFS 194's piston engine was being completed: "In the spring, my wife fell ill, was treated by a local doctor, and when it became critical, and I took her to a good professional clinic, the necessary operation came too late. A heart weakness ended her life in a few days."

Katharina Lippisch died aged 34 on March 19, leaving Lippisch himself with his 10-year-old son Hangwind and one-year-old Jürgen-Günther to look after.

He recalled: "We had a second son, Jürgen-Günther, who was now a motherless baby in the nursery and had to get a nurse for a quarter of a year. I put a last bouquet of roses on her coffin and said good-bye to such a changeable life, which had now found such an abrupt end."

Far from taking a break to spend time

with his children and mourn the death of his wife Lippisch, now 43, redoubled his efforts and threw himself into the development of new smoke-tunnel technology. He also became increasingly friendly with a young female colleague – 23-year-old Gertrude Knoblauch.

For Stamer in particular, this appears to have been the last straw. During the summer of 1938, together with Jacobs, he persuaded Professor Georgii that it was time to put Lippisch in his place.

Unaware of what was going on behind his back, Lippisch continued to work on preparing the DFS 40 for test flights and refining the aerodynamic form of Project X – which he had now discovered was to be a research aircraft capable of gathering data while flying in the high subsonic range.

At the same time, it was decided that the whole DFS organisation should be moved east to Ainring near the Austrian border. With war in the west becoming an increasing possibility, the DFS's base at Griesheim, west of Darmstadt, was strategically vulnerable.

Now Stamer, Jacobs and Georgii saw an opportunity. They drew up plans for a restructuring of the DFS, coinciding with the upheaval of the move, which would see Lippisch's role dramatically decreased.

According to Erinnerungen: "Thus a shift and a reorganisation of the DFS was worked out, but I was not a little attracted to it because my former friends Stamer and Jacobs now convinced Professor Georgii that my all-wing division would no longer be of any interest at the outbreak of the war.

"They had stripped me out of the organisation and left me only a small model building department. This plan was to be concealed from me, but the secretaries still had so much character that they could not take part in this ignoble contempt for my work.

"So I learned through back-channels of all these machinations and had nothing more to do than to put myself in my car and drive the 1000km to Rechlin in one go, to get in touch with my friends from the Darmstadt group and from the gliding flight and I then went ▶

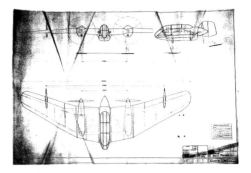

ABOVE: Lippisch appears to have mapped out many of his projects as concepts in advance then worked on them out of sequence. His team's work on the P 01-116, their first project for Messerschmitt, was followed by the P 04. The P 04-106 illustrated here was a tailless fighter-bomber to the same specification as the Me 210, dated August 1939.

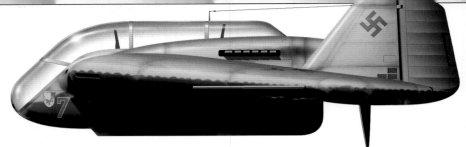

ABOVE: Messerschmitt P 04-106. Art by Daniel Uhr

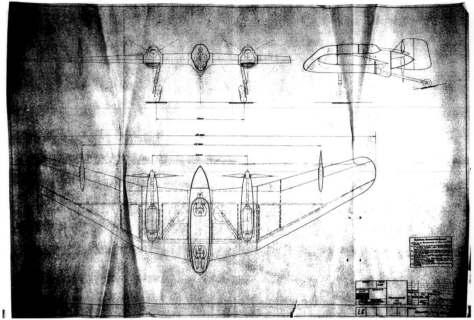

ABOVE: A trainer version of the P 04, the P 04-107a, was worked on alongside the fighter-bomber version. It was powered by a pair of 459hp Argus As 410s. The drawing is dated August 26, 1939.

to Berlin, where the attitude was 'thank God for your work', something that I thought was quite different from the DFS organisation.

"At first I contacted Heinkel, but soon found out that he was really interested only in the order to test the high-speed aircraft, not in me and my co-workers. So I went to Messerschmitt, whom I knew quite well from the years on the Rhön. There was also director Croneiss, who was very much in our favour and helped us with the Delta l.

"So I agreed with Messerschmitt to move from the DFS to Messerschmitt AG in Augsburg at the beginning of 1939, and to take a number of my best employees into a newly founded department. All this I did without the knowledge of the clique at the DFS, and I then submitted the final plan, sanctioned by Berlin, to them. There were long faces, for such a move had not been expected on my part."

After the war, Lippisch seems to have forgiven Georgii and blamed Stamer and Jacobs for "strongly influencing him". Nevertheless, Lippisch had neatly sidestepped an attempt to derail his career with the help of Messerschmitt director Theo Croniess and chairman Willy Messerschmitt himself. By this time Messerschmitt was riding high on the success of the Bf 109, which was becoming the Luftwaffe's standard fighter. The company was in line for some very lucrative contracts and could afford to make an investment in some additional research and development muscle. But whether it was Messerschmitt's decision to hire Lippisch, or Croniess' is unclear.

Georgii allowed Lippisch to take his DFS 39 and DFS 194 away with him, but not the DFS 40 – which Lippisch said he left behind "with a heavy heart".

He recalled: "On January 2, 1939, at 8 o'clock in the morning, I arrived at Messerschmitt with my car from Darmstadt, where a group of my co-workers were already waiting for me. So we were first stamped in as Messerschmitt employees with many signatures on forms, all possible examinations, and finally we were correct members of Messerschmitt AG in Augsburg-Haunstetten.

"Now we were a sort of secret department, because we were supposed to build and test

the rocket-driven experimental aircraft, whose aerodynamics we had already worked on at DFS. Of course the rocket propulsion was strictly secret, so that the whole department had to be housed in a special part of the building and secured by appropriate positions at the doors. Since no other room was available at the moment, we moved into a large screening room on the top floor of the main building."

The newly formed Abteilung L or 'Department L' was given special treatment at first too: "In the morning a waitress with a large tray would be admitted to our secret room. We would then have the Bavarian-style quite-rich breakfast. This went on so well until the commercial director, Mr Kokothaki, accidentally rode with the same elevator with the waitress, with the large tray full of treats for Abteilung L. This resulted in a somewhat excited discussion and my gentlemen then had to eat their breakfast in the canteen."

Lippisch was also pleased that he no longer had to deal with Dr Lorenz at the RLM, now being allocated Hans-Martin Antz, an advisor seconded to Section LC 2/III of the RLM's technical office.

FIRST AMONG EQUALS?

The arrival of a whole new team at Messerschmitt, dedicated to working on tailless aircraft designs, meant the company now had two separate project departments – the other being the company's projects team headed by Robert Lusser. Lippisch

had walked out of one 'conventional vs tailless' arrangement and straight into another – although there is no evidence to suggest that Lusser and the others felt any animosity towards the newly arrived former DFS men. In fact, Lusser left the following month to be replaced by Waldemar Voigt.

Lippisch's first order of business was to scrap all the existing drawings of Project X and start again, since it had been decided that the aircraft's rocket thrust would be increased. Secondly, it was decided that since data on the performance of aircraft fitted with rocket engines was practically non-existent, a test vehicle was needed. The DFS 194 was a suitable candidate for conversion so this work too got under way – though there was no engine yet available to fit. Thirdly, Lippisch began to work on a series of designs for a new fighter.

It seems likely that this third project, designated P 01, was prompted by a study contract Messerschmitt had received a month earlier, in December 1938. The actual specification for this was only received on January 4, two days after the arrival of Lippisch and his team. It called for a single seater powered by a single turbojet engine in two roles – high-speed fighter and interceptor.

In either configuration it was to be armed with two MG 17 machine guns and one MG 151/20 cannon. Top speed was to be 900km/h (559mph) and landing speed was to be not more than 120km/h (75mph). Flight duration was one hour as

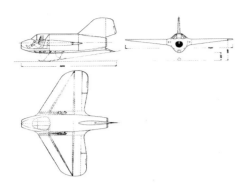

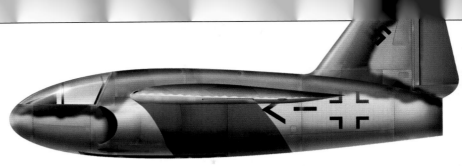

ABOVE: The single-turbojet P 01-111 was first drafted in November 1939, seven months after the P 01-116. The space left for the engine is large and undefined since the precise dimensions of the turbojet likely to be used were unavailable.

ABOVE: Messerschmitt P 01-112. Art by Daniel Uhr

fighter and 30 minutes as interceptor.

It appears that Lippisch began by writing out a list of potential configurations, engine options and other features and allocating each one a different number from 111 to 119. Then, rather than having his department work through the different concepts in numerical order, he started work on the design designated P 01-116. Where many of the other ideas featured rocket engines in one way or another, the initial concept of P 01-116 was that of a single-seat fighter powered by a single turbojet engine. The concept designated 111 was also a single-seat single turbojet fighter but work started with 116 – which might have been seen as the concept most closely matching the January 4 specification.

The first drawings were produced by Körner, one of the less well known members of Lippisch's team who had followed him over from the DFS and remained with Abteilung L until it was dissolved. Lippisch's only comment on it was "this design was based on the first available data for a turbojet".

The P 01-116 of April 12 and April 13, 1939, was a remarkably small tailless aircraft – measuring just 5.48m long and with a wingspan of 6m. A large tailfin gave it a height of 2.715m. By way of comparison, the diminutive Me 163 B-1 was 5.98m long by 9.33m wingspan and 2.75m high. The P 01-116's fuselage was cylindrical and its wings were extremely broad and almost rectangular in shape, with only a slight sweepback to the leading edge. Take-off would have presumably involved a wheeled dolly and landing was to be accomplished on a long skid with a small additional skid at the extreme end of its tail.

It is uncertain precisely which turbojet Lippisch had received data on, although it is unlikely to have been the Heinkel HeS 3 which would power the Heinkel He 178 during its first flight four months later – the first flight by any jet aircraft – on August 27, 1939. Unlikely, because Ernst Heinkel was unwilling to offer his jet engine designs for use in other manufacturers' aircraft at this stage.

While Lippisch got started on a single-jet design as P 01, so did Voigt's department under the designation P 65. Their first designs evidently had a similar twin-boom layout to the de Havilland Vampire but

by June 1939 it had been abandoned in favour of a twin engine design.

Meanwhile, Lippisch had married Gertrude Knoblauch in May 1939. He wrote: "We lived in a suburb of Augsburg and since all private motor vehicles were shut down, I went by bicycle to the Messerschmitt factory. We got half the wing of the newly constructed experimental building, a large hall with side-mounted office buildings, which ended out in a round porch that now became my office."

The first towed gliding flights of the DFS 194 took place on July 28, 1939, with further flights taking place in August. Work on the P 01 continued, if there was a P 02 all information about it has been lost and Lippisch himself never seems to have mentioned it. Work was also begun on the P 03 – the intended next-step development of what had now become known as the Me 163.

In his memoir, Lippisch wrote: "The name '163' was also a camouflage name, because Messerschmitt had previously designed and tested a slow-flying aircraft as competition to the Fieseler 'Storch', which, however, was not good enough and was supposedly to be improved. If then our drawings with the 163 number on them went to the workshops, so did the new parts for the improvement of this slow-speed aircraft. And so the work we did on the 163 and then on the converted airframe of the DFS 194 remained astonishingly secret."

Also in August 1939, designer Rudolf Rentel made the first drawings of yet another project, designated P 04. The earliest known example, P 04-106, shows a two-seater 16m wingspan tailless aircraft powered by a pair of DB 601 E engines driving pusher propellers, with a small fin on the trailing edge of each wing outboard of the engine. This was apparently intended to be a fighter-bomber or bomber aircraft and the drawing shows it armed with two cannon and two machine guns facing forwards. A relatively capacious bomb bay is also depicted, housing what appears to be a pair of 500kg bombs.

There is no suggestion of a rear-facing armament, but the back seat crewman is shown facing to the rear and also lying prone in a bomb-aimer position. The undercarriage consisted of a pair of mainwheels that retracted into the inner wings and a very long tailwheel leg that protruded way out to the rear when extended.

A second drawing dating from around this time, P 04-107a, shows a different version of the 106 design, with the DB 601 Es replaced by Argus As 410 engines. Lippisch states that this was a trainer version and looking closely at the drawing it is possible to see that the pilot appears to be wearing a suit jacket.

It could be argued that the P 04 was designed for no particular reason, but it is also

difficult to ignore the similarities between it and the Messerschmitt Me 210, which made its first flight in September 1939. The latter two-seater had a 16.34m wingspan, was powered by a pair of DB 601 Fs (effectively the same engine as the DB 601 E) and carried a forward armament of two MG 151 cannon and two MG 17 machine guns. Its maximum internal bomb load was a pair of 500kg bombs.

This appears to be the first example of Lippisch putting his tailless ideas directly into contention against the 'conventional' designs of the original Messerschmitt project office, although it is equally possible that the study was initiated by Messerschmitt himself. It is unknown whether the P 04 designs were actually formalised at this stage or whether they were simply an exercise to see what a tailless Me 210 spec aircraft might look like. It seems more likely to have been the latter, since at this point in time there was every reason to believe that the Me 210 would soon take its place as the successor to the outdated Bf 110.

A TAILLESS ME 262

The Second World War began in September 1939 and the Messerschmitt company came under massive pressure to step up production and development of the Bf 109 and Bf 110. Resources were diverted away from Abteilung L's work on the Me 163 but the engineless DFS 194 was transported to the testing facility at Peenemünde and began to undergo further glide testing on October 16, 1939.

Work also continued in earnest on the P 01. The next design in the sequence, first drafted in November 1939, went back to the numerical beginning – P 01-111.

This was a development of the P 01-116 in every respect, being larger at 6.6m long with a 7.5m wingspan. The pilot sat higher up in a slightly larger cockpit with a nose intake for the single-jet engine positioned in front of his feet. The P 01-111's skid design was improved and a pair of cannon were even shown buried in its wing roots. A sharper sweepback was applied to the wings, including a swept trailing edge, the tailfin was also more swept and the rudder was enlarged.

The 'conventional' Messerschmitt design department had by now been working on exclusively twin-engine layouts for its P 65 jet fighter – which would eventually receive the designation Me 262 – for nearly six months and had reached the mock-up inspection stage by December 1939.

It would seem that further data on the early jet engines was received around this time, since the next Abteilung L design, the P 01-112, featured a pair of turbojets buried within its fuselage. A full brochure

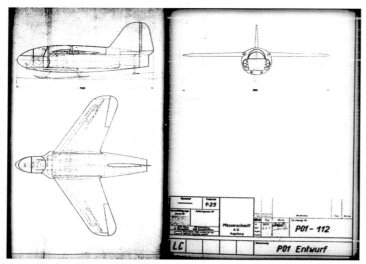

ABOVE: The original broad fuselage P 01-112 fighter, drawn up on January 31, 1940.

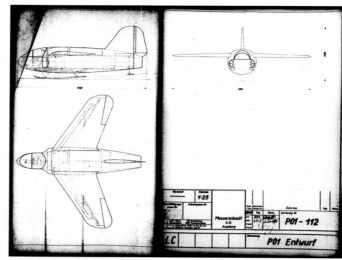

ABOVE: The broad fuselage P 01-112 as an experimental aircraft, dated January 31, 1940.

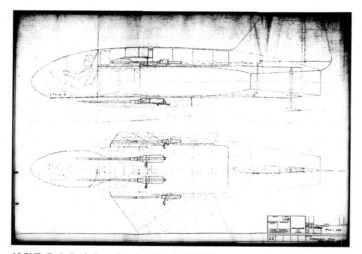

ABOVE: Detailed view showing the P 01-112's armament of two MG17 machine guns in the upper fuselage and two cannon below the engines. The drawing is dated February 1, 1940.

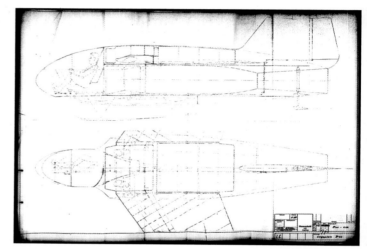

ABOVE: The P 01-112 as an unarmed experimental aircraft, as drafted on February 1, 1940.

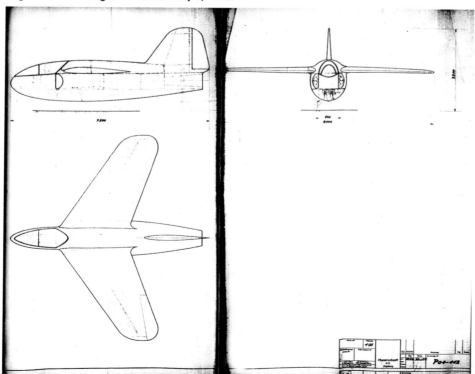

ABOVE: The final-form twin-jet P 01-112 with narrow fuselage, wheeled undercarriage and straight leading edge wings, dated February 12, 1940.

on this design was issued in February 1940 and just as the P 04 had with the Me 210, the P 01-112 appeared to 'shadow' the work of the conventional design department.

But where the P 65 had thin straight wings, the P 01-112 had a 35 sweepback on its thin wings. And where the P 65's engines were carried in wing-mounted pods, the P 01-112's were fitted within its fuselage – fed by a pair of curved intakes, one either side of the pressurised cockpit.

As the foreword of the P 01-112 brochure notes: "The drive is carried out by two jet engines (Jumo), which are arranged in the fuselage under the wing. This eliminates any negative influence of the engines on the flow on the wing.

"The pilot's seat, arranged in front of the wing and the engines, offers the best visibility and allows the formation of an armoured pressure booth which can be designed independently of the static structure of the fuselage.

"A central runner and spur, both retractable, are provided as the main landing gear. The take-off takes place on a jettisonable trolley. For the initial unarmed version without equipment, fuel is provided for half an hour's flight time. The space for armament and fuel tanks for one hour flight time will be available however."

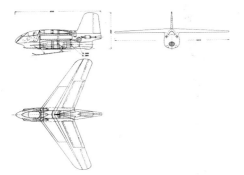

ABOVE: The mixed rocket/turbojet propulsion P 01-113 of July 1940 – five months after the P 01-112. The whole P 01 sequence was spread out over a considerable period of time.

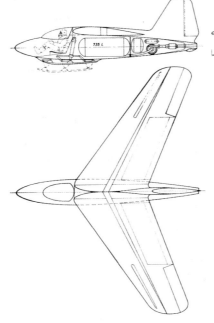

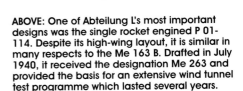

ABOVE: One of Abteilung L's most important designs was the single rocket engined P 01-114. Despite its high-wing layout, it is similar in many respects to the Me 163 B. Drafted in July 1940, it received the designation Me 263 and provided the basis for an extensive wind tunnel test programme which lasted several years.

The fuselage was to be made of a load-bearing light metal shell with the skid in a box under the floor along the centre. The wings, built as a single piece, were to be fitted onto the fuselage over the engines, with the fuel tanks then fitted on top of that. The engines themselves were to be separated by a central partition and could be accessed or removed by taking off the upper portion of the fuselage.

There would be space for weapons both beneath the cockpit and the wing roots next to the fuselage.

Another advanced feature was a system for blowing air over the upper wings to improve lift during landing: "A suction line runs through the wing from the suction chamber in front of the engines, which can be switched on, in particular, during landing and sucks the boundary layer on the outer wing through slots arranged behind the main hoop.

"The installation of a slat is therefore not planned. Also, an extensible slat would interfere with the sensitive upper side of the outer wing at high flight speeds. The thickness ratio of the profiles in the direction of flight is 8%."

Furthermore: "The air sucked in by the engines flows in through large openings in the fuselage. The exhaust line is branched off from the vacuum chamber located in front of the engine to one wing each. The normal air supply to the engine is throttled by flaps, which are attached to the rear edge of the pilot's compartment, so that in particular the engines are used only for suction during landing. The extent to which the exhaust can also be used for take-off and climb requires testing."

This may be the earliest example in history of a variable geometry jet engine intake. Unfortunately, the P 01-112's design was being hampered by the lack of information from Junkers about the engines: "Since details of the engines are not yet available from the manufacturer, they can only be made later. The design provides that the exhaust jet of both engines is discharged through an extension nozzle on the fuselage tail."

Four weapons were to be fitted – two MG 151s under the pressure cabin with 500 rounds each and two MG 17s, one in each wing root, with 1000 rounds each.

The performance figures provided suggest a clear advantage over those provided in a late September 1939 report on

the P 65 – albeit powered by Junkers engines rather than the BMW ones then being considered for that design. Maximum all up weight of the P 01-112 was to be 3840kg, compared to 4325kg for the P 65. Top speed at 4000m was 1080km/h (671mph) compared to 975km/h (606mph) at 3000m. Landing speed was 125km/h compared to 150km/h.

BACK TO ROCKETS

By now Lippisch had found that progress on turning Abteilung L's freshly made Me 163 drawings into a working aircraft had slowed dramatically. He wrote: "Our scientific work on the creation of the high-speed aircraft 'Project X', now called Me 163, was practically stopped by the outbreak of the war and the design office had to provide assistance in all possible places". With practical design and development work on tailless projects all but halted during the early months of 1940, Lippisch busied himself with theoretical work on transonic and supersonic flight, calling on the talents of another recently recruited Messerschmitt employee, mathematician Dr Friedrich Ringleb.

A few months later, "apparently at the Ministry of Aviation was the realization that the planned Blitzkrieg could not be brought to a rapid conclusion and that, as far as possible, one had to resume and carry forward promising developments". Now there was an engine ready for the DFS 194 – a Walter unit capable of producing 400kg of thrust – and it was installed at Peenemünde's own workshops. The DFS 194 made its first rocket-powered flight on June 3, 1940.

According to Lippisch's own account: "In the summer of 1940, a series of experimental flights with a rocket drive began, with Heini Dittmar taking over this task, which was not without danger, and carried out with great success.

"Since the fuselage was comparatively large, we were also able to install an Askania quadruple recorder and the performance measurements that resulted from it gave us very valuable new insights. The original

fuselage of the DFS 194 was not designed for high speed, so we had to abort our experiments at 550kph because otherwise the loads exceeded the permissible limit."

With this exciting work now taking place, Abteilung L returned briefly to the P 01 series in July 1940 – designing two more concepts which unsurprisingly each featured rocket propulsion – the P 01-113 with a single turbojet plus a rocket engine, and the P 01-114 which had the same wings as the 113 but a new slender fuselage housing only a rocket engine.

In fact, according to the design brochure, the P 01-114 was intended simply as an experimental vehicle to assess the features of the P 01-112 and P 01-113 designs – rather than being a prototype for a production aircraft in its own right.

It states: "The model P 01-114 is a single-tail tailless aircraft which is used to test the design at very high speeds and high gradients with respect to the patterns P 01-112 and 113. The structure perfectly corresponds to the wing provided for the heavily armed designs, while the fuselage was simplified with regard to simple and fast manufacture. The HWK engine, which is provided for the drive, permits a step-by-step test with different thrusts, so that the properties can be flown out at very high speeds."

The wings were to be adjustable so that different angles of sweepback could be tried and a device was to be fitted which could alter the sensitivity of the elevator control to make it easier to use at very high speeds.

"The fuselage was designed as a rotationally symmetrical body in order to ensure the simplest design of parts, so that only a few devices are required for producing the fuselage shell," it states. "The cockpit is pressure-tight. A normal chassis was dispensed with. The take-off takes place on a jettisonable roller train, while the landing takes place on the retractable skid and the spur. The experimental testing of a crawler roller is planned."

Despite its intended use, the P 01-114 would later go on to have a second life as first the P 03 and then under the official designation Me 263. But in the meantime, with work recommencing on the construction of the first two Me 163 prototypes and promising results already having been obtained from flight testing the DFS 194, Abteilung L suspended almost all project design work for nearly a year to carry out what Lippisch later described as "intensive work on the DFS 194 and the Me 163".. ●

Outsiders

The Horten brothers to 1942

After Alexander Lippisch, the greatest proponents of tailless aircraft in Germany during the war were two brothers – Reimar and Walter Horten. Their enthusiasm and persistence resulted in a string of flying-wing gliders and a handful of powered aircraft.

ABOVE: The Horten brothers' first attempt at a manned aircraft, the Hangwind.

ABOVE: The Horten H Vc flying wing, powered by a pair of Hirth HM 60 R engines, in flight during 1942.

Walter and Reimar Horten were born into an independently wealthy family in Bonn, western Germany, in 1913 and 1915, respectively. Their father Max had three PhDs – in philosophy, culture and languages – and their mother had studied geography at Oxford University.

When the First World War ended, Max Horten lost most of his money during the economic strife and hyperinflation which followed, but he retained the family's three-storey house plus living quarters at the University of Bonn, where he was a professor.

The boys grew up with their elder brother Wolfram, a year older than Walter, and little sister Gunilde, born in 1921. In 1927, as members of the Bonn young flyer group, the brothers were each asked to make a model aircraft to fly at an exhibition in Düsseldorf. Walter was to make one with a rubber band propeller but Reimar's was to be a glider.

Having already been taught some of the rudiments of model aircraft construction by a neighbour who was a former Junkers employee, Franz Wilhelm Schmitz, Reimar designed and built his 1.8m span model from sheets of plywood and old cigar boxes.

At the exhibition, Reimar's model flew 270m - more than two football field lengths – and won first prize. This success prompted him to build more models and soon both he and Walter were test-flying them every morning before school, then again when they got back from school at 1pm, and then making adjustments to them every evening.

Their parents bought them woodworking tools and encouraged them to keep at it. In 1929, their father took up a new teaching position at Breslau on the opposite side of Germany and moved over there with his wife and Gunilde, leaving the three brothers, then aged 17, 16 and 14 to look after themselves in the family home.

Reimar was now able to stay up all night working obsessively on his models and his schoolwork suffered. But he was soon preparing for model flying competitions at the Wasserkuppe – first participating with Walter's help in 1930, then again in 1931 and 1932. During this time, Reimar became convinced that shifting an aircraft's centre of gravity was the key to stability in flight

and began to build models without tail fins.

Towards the end of 1932, the brothers saw Lippisch's Delta I in flight and decided it was time to make a full-scale manned glider of their own. When Hitler came to power on January 30, 1933, all Germany's schools closed for two months so that the teachers could be screened for political suitability.

This left Walter and Reimar with nothing to do for two months, so with their parents still away, but apparently with their blessing, the brothers began to build parts of their first aircraft, dubbed 'Hangwind' after Lippisch's nickname of the time, on the ground floor of their home.

The design was even more radical than that of the Delta I, with no fuselage at all – just a wing with enough room for the pilot in the centre section and a skid to land on.

Enlisting the help of friends, they eventually managed to complete the Hangwind by the late summer – too late to be entered for the Wasserkuppe gliding contests in August. Walter participated in flight tests of the glider during September and October 1933 before joining the German army on April 1, 1934.

Reimar was barely able to get out of school for the 1934 Wasserkuppe competitions and Walter had to take leave. Both of them flew the Hangwind but then Walter had to leave to rejoin his unit. Eventually everyone else was packing up to leave but Reimar had no way of getting home with the Hangwind. He later told historian David Myhra: "I knew that I wouldn't be able to keep it at the Wasserkuppe now that the Nazi party was conducting a soaring school. I called to Bonn to the aerodrome to see if they would send me a towing plane to the Wasserkuppe. I'd have to pay them for at least three to four hours of flying time.

"They wouldn't help and they told me to call Essen for some assistance. I called there and told them that I'm in the Wasserkuppe. If you come and get me I'll give you the plane. Well, they teach soaring instruction, however, this instruction does not include tailless planes, therefore, they had no need for the H I [as Hangwind would be retrospectively designated later].

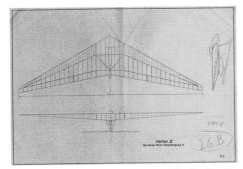

ABOVE: Contemporary drawing of the Horten H II, also known as the Habicht. The drawing has their home address, Venusbergweg 12, Bonn, printed on it.

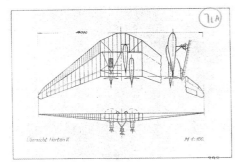

ABOVE: A drawing showing the H Vb – redesigned so that the two crew could both sit upright, each under his own canopy.

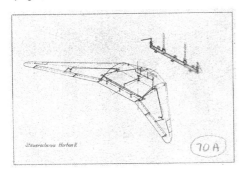

ABOVE: A diagram showing the controls of the H Vb.

ABOVE: The Horten H V without its plastic skin.

ABOVE: With its plastic skin applied, the H V gleams. The sparse cockpit for the two reclined crew is just visible in the nose.

ABOVE: The Horten H V (top) is posed alongside the powered H IIm.

Thanks anyway but they could not come and tow me back. We have no order to do it.

"I was willing to offer the plane for nothing if they'd come and get me. They said the only authority was the DFS in Darmstadt. Well, I called Lippisch at DFS and told him I'm here at the Wasserkuppe. I'll give you the H I if you'll send me a towing plane. Lippisch said that he didn't have the possibility of sending me a towing plane.

"For six months in the winter time Lippisch had been in Bonn, had been in my house, had spoken with my father and saw the Hangwind and told my father that if I had my degree, he would take me to Darmstadt. Now, talking to him on the telephone he told me that it was impossible to come to the Wasserkuppe and get me. I was there and now couldn't do anything. I couldn't find anyone to give me a tow."

Wolfram was able to pick up Reimar on his motorcycle but there was nothing they could do with the Hangwind so they broke the tips off its wings by standing on them, stripped the fabric off it, dragged it out of the hangar and burned it.

Myhra asked Reimar exactly what

Lippisch had said to him on the phone when he rang him. Reimar said: "Lippisch told me that he didn't have any possibility of helping me. He had changed his mind. I don't know why he all of a sudden did not want to help me. He did in fact have the possibility to help me for he could have asked Georgii, the director of DFS, for permission to send a tow plane after me.

"If he had told me that he'd come in a day or two I would have waited. But he gave me no reason why he could not help me. Well, I did not say anything to Lippisch for I was only 14 or 15 years old. Later Lippisch was in Bonn and discussing his lift distribution and he was at the hotel and I was there. Could you give me a copy of your speech and I'll return it the next day.

"This he did do and the next day I returned and spoke with him. I told him I did not fully understand some of the things he was writing about and he explained them to me. I saw then that I could learn. This surprised

and pleased me for I didn't think that I'd ever sit side-by-side with Lippisch. And I wanted to learn from him. But it did not happen.

"So I decided that it would be only possible for me to learn if I built my own sailplanes and learned through trial and error. Lippisch was not going to give me any instruction nor did it appear now that

ABOVE: Two views of the twin-canopy Horten H Vb – a new aircraft but with the engines salvaged from the wreck of the H V.

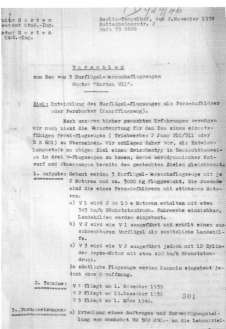

ABOVE: The first page of the Horten brothers' November 2, 1938, proposal to build the advanced Horten H VII.

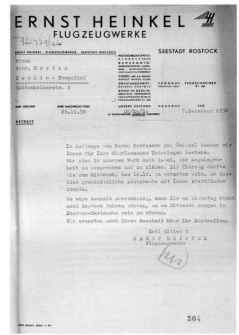

ABOVE: The letter sent to the Horten brothers by Heinkel on December 7, 1938, while contractual negotiations between the two parties were ongoing.

he wanted me to join him after I earned my degree in Bonn at his workshop at DFS in Darmstadt. So I'd build my own aircraft and learn and show him and the others that I could build and design better sailplanes than them in the form of an all-wing."

Reimar had hoped that when he had free time Walter would help him work out the correct wing profile for his next glider, the Habicht, later known as the H II. He said: "After completing the H I, I was really busy in seeking to come up with the correct wing profile for the H II and I was totally preoccupied with this work. I had no time for any other things.

"Walter spent more time with girls for although he helped me on the theory of wing lift distribution, he was not as preoccupied on the topic as I was. Frequently I was angry that he would not help me but instead wasting his time in the company of girls."

In April 1935, Walter asked to be transferred from the army to the Luftwaffe and was sent to various aviation training schools before being posted to the newly created Fliegergruppe Giebelstadt (later KG 155), equipped with Dornier Do 23s medium bombers, at Giebelstadt, near Würzburg, in October.

Meanwhile, the family home was again pressed into service as a makeshift workshop by Reimar but now Max, Elizabeth and Gunilde had returned, Max having decided to retire, and with Walter often away the Habicht took 5000 hours spread across nine months to complete – five times longer than the Hangwind. Its first flight was in May 1935, a month after Reimar started a course in mathematics at the University of Bonn.

DYNAMIT STEPS IN

Later it was decided to fit the Habicht with a borrowed Hirth HM 60 engine and pusher propeller, enabling much longer flight times and allowing the brothers to gather more valuable flight experience in a flying-wing design until the engine had to go back after overheating.

Reimar then persuaded the Hirth company to give him another engine. During one flight of the Habicht towards the end of 1935, a representative of IG Farben plastics subsidiary Dynamit AG approached Reimar and offered to supply him with materials to make another flying-wing with the aim of helping to sell those materials to the aviation industry.

They struck a deal and in February 1936 work commenced at Troisdorf, between Bonn and Cologne, on building a set of wings for a Hol's der Teufel primary glider out of composite materials as a trial run for the plastic flying wing. The latter was to be a twin-pusher engine flying wing with positions for two crew reclining on their backs housed within a transparent section of the wing's leading edge. The nosewheel of the tricycle undercarriage was retractable.

The Hol's der Teufel trials were completed in May 1936 and Reimar was

engaged in attempting to build the flying wing itself, dubbed the H V, when he was conscripted into the Luftwaffe.

Dynamit was annoyed at this turn of events and tried to get Reimar back so he could continue with the project. The factory's director contacted IG Farben in Berlin and strings were pulled so that after completion of his basic training Reimar was allocated to the Luftwaffe's inactive reserve and allowed to return to Troisdorf later in 1936.

Walter petitioned Luftwaffe chief of staff Walther Wever to be allowed to join a fighter unit close to Cologne so he could help Reimar and got his wish in early 1936, joining JG 134 at Lippstadt, near Cologne. At the time the

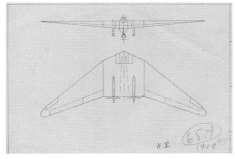

ABOVE: Slightly more detail of the H Vc's canopy arrangement is shown in this contemporary drawing.

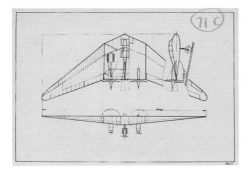

ABOVE: Drawing from a report showing plans for a single-seater Horten H V, the H Vc.

unit was equipped with Arado Ar 68s and Walter's commanding officer was Hauptmann Oskar Dinort – the same Hauptmann Dinort who had been briefed on the potential of flying wing aircraft for military use by Lippisch just over a year earlier.

Reimar was now in the odd position of being a member of the Luftwaffe but without belonging to any particular unit. He later recalled: "I was liberated of all the duties for the military, only that I had to work in Troisdorf. In this form I could continue with my studies at the University of Bonn."

The fact that the plastic flying wing was the H V begs the question – what happened to

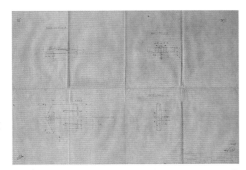

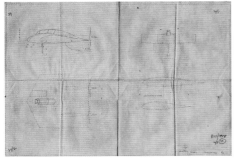

ABOVE: Design drawings for a display model of the H Vc's centre section, dated October 1941.

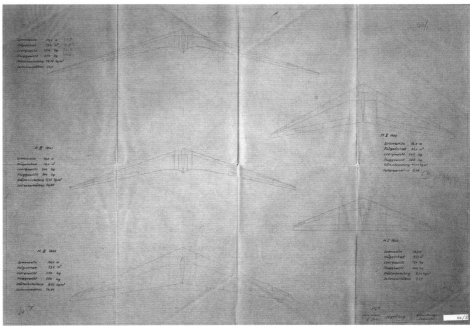

ABOVE: This drawing, dated November 28, 1940, shows the Horten brothers' gliders up to that point.

the H III and IV? Reimar explained to Myhra that at this stage they did exist albeit only as concepts; the H III as a 16m span design and the H IV with 20m. But these were all gliders, "if I came to build the twin-engined plane, what number should I give it"?

"Well, we were in our thinking in the H III and H IV but the twin-engine was very different from the whole. I had to give it a new number and I called it H V. Therefore in Troisdorf had been the H V and the H III and H IV were not built."

With both brothers now located in Cologne, Dinort asked Walter if he and his brother could build three new H IIs for him, powered by Hirth engines. According to Reimar: "This Major Dinort said that he had material and men in the workshop and we can build three examples and the three of us will fly them. 'I will fly one, Walter one, and your brother Reimar can fly the other'. Thus in 1936 he was hoping to participate in some demonstrations in Germany all with the Horten all-wing planes.

"Walter told this to me and I thought that, well, if he'll have three H IIs, the drawings I have, we can make some variations of the H II which I think that they should be, for instance, make them for aerobatics and give them a little more strength plus a few other changes – I will do it."

Dinort told Reimar that his unit's headquarters at Cologne were not yet ready so he would set up a workshop at Lippstadt where Dinort's own men would build the H IIs. "Weekly now I was driving over there to speak with these men in the workshop and see how things were going," said Reimar.

The H V was completed in the spring of 1937 and Reimar and Walter took it up for its first flight together in June. Almost as soon as the aircraft left the ground Reimar realised that its centre of gravity was in the wrong position and told Walter to land. Walter decided to bring the aircraft around but a wingtip hit the ground and it crashed – injuring both brothers, Walter's front teeth were knocked out, and the H V was destroyed.

Dynamit was philosophical about the loss, telling the brothers it had invested 40,000RM in the project but had received three patents and a lot of experience in working with the new plastics in the process.

Dinort suggested that the H V could be repaired by his men and the first new H II made its first flight around this time. With Reimar's arrangement with Dynamit at an end, Walter arranged for him to be assigned to Dinort's workshop, under Dinort's command.

Two of the H IIs were completed by July and were taken to the Wasserkuppe to participate in the competitions but Dinort himself was unable to attend, having left the unit on April 1, 1937. However, he vowed to take part in 1938 and ordered the Hortens to build him two H IIIs – the 20m span design, which was otherwise largely the same as the H II.

On leaving, Dinort had told Ernst Udet about the brothers and he had them transferred to Ostheim airfield, also near Cologne, where their work continued. The brothers started working on a new H V made from conventional materials with the idea that it would make a useful aircraft for the military, while also finishing Dinort's third and final H II before getting to work on his H IIIs.

The new H V, known as the H Vb, differed from the plastic original in having two conventional seats, each under its own canopy, rather than two reclined crew positions. Its wingspan was also enlarged by 2m, its control surfaces were altered and its tricycle undercarriage was fixed in place. The undamaged Hirth engines from the first H V were transplanted into the H Vb.

The first H III made its maiden flight on May 7, 1938, and the second followed a month or two later – both being ready in time for the Wasserkuppe competitions in July. Both were then destroyed on August 6 when they were flown into a thunderstorm. One of the Hortens' regular pilots was killed and the other suffered severe frostbite from flying too high but the RLM evidently placed an order for 10 further examples at this time.

During the year, alongside the 16m span H IIIs, the Hortens built another 12m span sailplane, like the H I, with an entirely rounded leading edge – the Parabola – but at the end of the year this was put into storage for the winter having never been flown.

HEINKEL AND THE H VII

A demonstration of the H Vb for RLM officials at Berlin in the autumn failed to result in an order, so the brothers formulated a proposal for an upgraded version they called the Horten VII and presented that to the RLM on November 2.

It began: "Proposal. For the construction of three all-wing experimental aircraft. Pattern: 'Horten VII'. Objective: Development of the all-wing aircraft as a remote reconnaissance aircraft or long-range bomber.

"According to our experience so far, we are not yet in a position to assume responsibility for the construction of a ready-to-operate front-line aircraft (engines: 2 x Jumo 210/211 or DB 601). We therefore propose to build as a development stage to the above objective an intermediate type in mixed construction in three V-planes whose aerodynamic design and dimensions already correspond to the set goals.

"1. Task: 3 x flying wing test aircraft with 2 x engines each and approx. 3000kg flying weight are to be built, the dimensions are those of the remote reconnaissance aircraft, which will have stronger engines.

"A) V1 will get 2 As 10e engines with about 343km/h maximum speed. Landing gear can be retracted, landing aids are installed. B) V2 is designed like V1 and is given a swing-out slat as an additional landing aid. C) V3 is executed as V2 but with 12 cylinder Argus engine with approx. 400km/h maximum speed. All the airplanes are without weapons equipped.

"2. Dates: V1 flies on 1 November 1939, V2 flies on 15 December 1939, V3 flies on 1 March 1940. 3. Prerequisites (a) to issue an order and to provide 500,000 RM for the necessary construction materials."

Within three weeks, Udet had read the proposal and suggested that the brothers meet with Heinkel (sometimes referred to as EHF – Ernst Heinkel Flugzeugwerke) to discuss getting the H VII built. A meeting was held on November 23 between the Hortens and a Heinkel representative called Kapp.

Heinkel later prepared a summary of

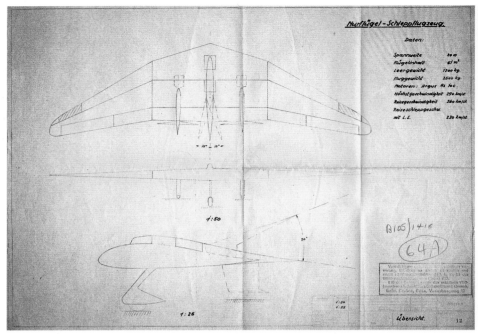

ABOVE: One proposed version of the H Vc was as a towing aircraft for gliders. This drawing shows the movement range of the rear attachment point as well as the type's fully fixed undercarriage.

what was discussed at the meeting and it begins: "The purpose of the cooperation between EHF and the Horten brothers is to bring the development of tailless aircraft carried out by the Horten brothers to a broader base and to prepare and carry out a series production starting from it technically, commercially and factory-wise.

"The development and construction of the two-engine aircraft is under the Heinkel company. Three ways of cooperation were discussed.

"Way 1: The Horten brothers have a 600m sq working space, which is to be used both for the construction and the assembly of the three test aircraft. For the production of the individual parts and whole assemblies, many companies are available to the Horten brothers. EHF would accelerate the development by design engineers and carry out the entire operation commercially.

"Way 2: The Horten brothers are reinforced by Heinkel designers. The design work will be carried out until the end of March, 1939, and the entire construction of three test specimens will be carried out within the EHF, Rostock-Marienehe.

"Way 3: The custom-made parts

are produced as usual by external companies and in the workshop Berlin-Tempelhof. The assembly of the test aircraft is, however, in Marienehe.

"All three ways are considered by the Horten brothers as viable."

Regarding patents, the brothers would get a one-off lump sum for assigning all the important ones to Heinkel: "There are 15 basic patents as well as some additional patents, which pass from the Horten brothers to the Heinkel company. The Heinkel company would implement the patent application."

Further contract points discussed included the number of hours the Hortens would require for planning, licensing fees, commercial confidentiality and the external suppliers Heinkel intended to use: "From the constructions to be developed outward, the following was established: a) engine development could be carried out either by EHF together with Argus, or by Professor Lürenbaum of the DVL, which promised the development of the project. b) Undercarriage. The chassis design would be either by Dr Eisbein of Elektron, or EHF could carry out the design itself. c) The development of an adjustable propeller would eventually be carried out by VDM at Heddernheim together with DVL."

ABOVE: The H Vc from the rear.

ABOVE: The completed Horten H Vc as seen from the roof of a nearby building. It is painted in RLM 71 dark green on top and RLM 65 light blue underneath.

ABOVE: Two shots of the Horten Vc in flight.

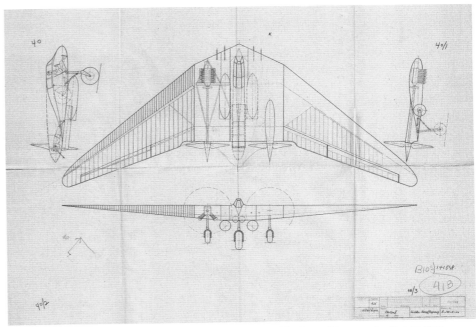

ABOVE: A variety of different configurations were proposed for the military production version Horten H Vd. This drawing of March 19, 1942, shows it as a light bomber with rear turret.

Two days later, Reimar sent the following letter to Ernst Heinkel himself: "Dear Professor! With reference to the discussion held on 23.11.38 with your dear Mr Ing. Kapp, we will present an overview sketch with measurements and performance data of one of our planned new constructions. This draft has already been approved by General Udet in great detail.

"We also add a spreadsheet and we note that when the hour numbers were fixed, we have assumed maximum values based on the experience of the buildings of our last engine and glider aircraft.

"We may point out that, at your request, the documents will be made available to you exclusively as a basis for negotiation with regard to the cooperation between the Heinkel aircraft works and us, as contemplated by the RLM, and must be considered as our intellectual property."

The Heinkel company sent back a brief note on December 7, 1938: "On behalf of Professor Dr Heinkel, we would like to thank you for your documents. We are still in the process of discussing and clarifying the matter. The clarification should be expected by Wednesday, 14.12, so that a basic discussion with you could take place.

"It would therefore be appropriate if you were going to Rostock on Tuesday evening to be in Rostock-Marienehe on Wednesday morning. We are waiting for your arrival."

Two days later, on December 9, Reimar sent a letter back which might be described as brusque: "We received your letter of 7 Dec. Unfortunately, at the present time we have not yet received into our possession the promised copy of the conference of 23 Nov. 38 with your dear Mr Ing. Kapp.

"In the coming week, we will be waiting on the acceptance of components for our currently under construction 10 flying airplanes, Horten IIIb model, from various of our delivery companies. A meeting in the next week is unfortunately not possible for this reason.

ABOVE: Walter Horten climbs aboard the H Vc. The aircraft was eventually written off after a crash during the spring of 1943.

"In the above-mentioned discussion, three possibilities of cooperation between the Heinkel aircraft works and us were exhibited. In order to avoid further time losses we ask you to submit your offer in the meantime within the scope of these three possibilities."

The Heinkel response, sent on December 13, explained that further face-to-face discussions were necessary: "In order to be able to make the best possible agreement on the nature of the compensation, it would be necessary for you to bring along documentation about your development work, i.e. patentable proposals and innovations, in order to be able to find a better estimate of the amount of the compensation. We would welcome it in all circumstances if you could come to Rostock-Marienehe at the beginning of the next week, in any case before Christmas, so that we can come to a further clarification by means of a joint debate."

Reimar wrote back on December 16 agreeing to meet at Rostock-Marienehe on December 19 at 11am.

On the 19th, Reimar and Walter sat down with Heinkel representative Heinrich Hertel and worked out eight points of agreement with which to form the basis of a binding contract.

The document, evidently typed up on the day, is addressed to Reimar Horten and starts: "We confirm the agreements you have made with you as follows:

"1. They act with immediate effect as advisory engineer to the EHF with the task of processing the development of flying wing aircraft. With this transition to the EHF, you are giving us the results of your previous development work.

"2. Since no patents have been registered for the ideas you have elaborated and realised, EHF immediately provides a competent patent engineer who will prepare the patent applications. These patents on your development work should be in the name of Professor Dr Heinkel, but with the appointment of Reimar and Walter Horten."

Point three is a one-off payment of 10,000RM to the brothers "as a recognition for the development work of your results". Further "one-time bonus" payments, point four, would be made with the completion of each for the experimental Horten VIIs – 4000RM for the first one and 2000RM each for the second and third.

In point five it is recognised that Walter, as a serving officer, cannot enter into a contractual relationship with Heinkel "but will continue to work with you in the most intimate terms on the development of fly-wing aircraft exclusively in our factory, as you will".

For the sixth point, each brother would get a monthly salary of 600RM but also, point seven, "of the patents to be registered and transferred to Professor Heinkel, you will receive a 20% share of the licence net income for both domestic and foreign sales".

Finally: "The start-up of the work is designed so that until March 1, 1939, you complete your preparatory work in Berlin so far that you will move your work to Marienehe on 1 March. The execution of your work in the factory is planned so that its pre-construction office is formed in which you carry out the construction's preparatory work."

In other words, the brothers would both be given jobs working on the development of flying wing aircraft at Heinkel with salaries and incentives, plus a share of income via their patents. On January 16, 1939,

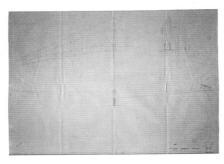

ABOVE: Drawing showing the powered Horten IIId.

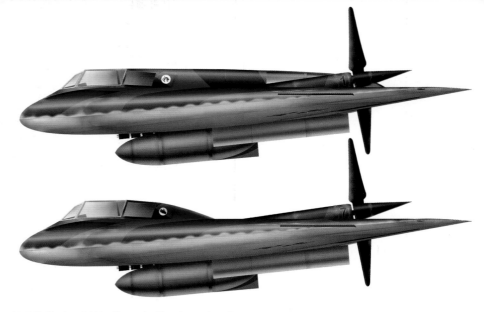

ABOVE: Horten H Vd with and without rear turret. Art by Daniel Uhr

the agreement was formalised into a contract but with a new ninth point: "The duration of the contract shall end with the completion of the third test aircraft; But no later than 1 October 1940. Exceptions to this rule is Section 7, which remains legally valid for the duration of the patents."

On February 8, Reimar sent another personal letter to Heinkel including a list of requested amendments to the contract intended to prevent Heinkel from reassigning their patents to a third party, requiring that the brothers be paid travel and other expenses for their work, denying Heinkel any patents on gliders or aircraft with engines up to 100 PS, and requiring that Heinkel continue to register patents on behalf of the brothers following the expiry of the contract in October 1940 at no cost to the brothers.

The letter itself read: "In the appendix I am sending to you, as discussed, the wording of our agreements of 19.12.38 proposed by us. I kindly ask for the return of a receipt. On 1.3.39 we will then move to Rostock and continue our work in your plant."

This was about as close as the Hortens got to the establishment of an 'Abteilung H' at Heinkel – which Reimar later stated had been his ideal outcome of the negotiations. Further communication between the brothers and Heinkel continued until March 12, 1939, when Reimar sent Ernst Heinkel a letter marked 'Personal!' in which he stated that his last meeting with Heinkel personnel on March 6 "took a rather unpleasant course" which "strengthened in us the far from encouraging impression which your contract draft of 14.2.39 left behind". This had essentially rejected the brothers'

amendments intended to protect their patents.

Reimar could "unfortunately see no possibility" to proceed unless his patent-related amendments were accepted, stating: "We would like to emphasise that the essential difference that did not allow us to come to an agreement is that you would acquire the result of all our work so far for a relatively small sum of a total of 20,000RM, and to secure ourselves along with our patents. What would become of us and our work including the patents after expiry of the contract?

"The payment of 20,000RM you have offered does not yet replace our cash outlays, which we had previously had to pay for our insurances. They are therefore not a compensation for our service. It is crucial for us that we do not leave you forever after the course of a short-term contract having registered the patents in your name with our current and above all future life's work."

He finished by stating that dealing with Heinrich Hertel had been "very unpleasant" and said: "We therefore see the negotiations with you as completed and ask you to return the preliminary design of our trial machine."

The Hortens had successfully negotiated themselves out of a contract which might have been the making of their careers

primarily on the basis that Heinkel would not pay them enough money. From their perspective, however, they had Udet's support and believed that their work ought to be worth Heinkel's while paying for. Heinkel, like the brothers themselves, seems to have been primarily concerned with acquiring patents for their work under the most favourable possible conditions.

There is some evidence to suggest that not long after the deal fell through, Heinkel went and patented some of their ideas in the name of Ernst Heinkel anyway, since the brothers themselves had not bothered to do so. A Heinkel patent drawing for a flying wing design was published in Flugsport in 1943 – presumably some time after the original patent was filed.

THE WILDERNESS

Early in 1939, it was discovered that the Parabola had warped badly over the winter and was now ruined so it ended up being burned without ever having been flown. Reimar continued with his university studies while working on the 10 new H IIIs – some of which were entered at the Wasserkuppe during the summer of 1939 – and Walter was sent to study at the Technical University at Berlin-Charlottenburg by Udet.

After that year's gliding contest, Reimar began thinking about making the H IV he had planned several years earlier as an entry for the 1940 contests. The H VI had already been sketched out as a 24m wingspan glider before the advent of the H VII, but this was still a long way from becoming a reality. As the prospect of war in Europe loomed closer, Reimar also came up with the idea for what would become the H VIII.

He told Myhra: "The political situation was changing and I heard on the radio that war could break out at any time. I thought at this moment that we had many engines from the old Bf 109 B and the Junkers 210 of 550hp and water-cooled inverted V and 12 cylinders. And also there were good engines.

"I believed that we could build an aircraft with two times the span of 20m. We then could have 150sqm of wing surface and we

ABOVE: The Horten H VII outside its hangar.

ABOVE: The straight leading edge of the Horten H VII is visible in these shots of it in flight.

could arrange for this aircraft to fly around England and over the ocean. I thought that the aircraft could fly for 24 hours with a crew of three men. It could be used as an observation and bomber plane."

When the war came, Walter rejoined I./JG 26 as technical officer under the command of Adolf Galland while Reimar was eventually assigned to a flying school at Halberstadt as an auxiliary instructor before being sent to a pilot school himself to learn fighter tactics.

On May 20, 1940, the eldest of the three Horten brothers was killed in unusual circumstances. Wolfram was a Heinkel He 111 pilot flying missions to drop 1000kg mines in the English Channel. Reimar told Myhra: "They started about midnight in the North Sea to fly to London and in the first light of day they get there. At a height of two or three metres lay their mines. This was his task during the entire winter of the war.

"Then when the war began with France during May 1940, he was called to go to Dunkirk and he had to do that same task there. But something happened and he was told that three of the mines in one of the He 111s were accidentally activated and were ready to explode due to bad handling. They wanted volunteers to fly the plane off and drop these mines into the sea and Wolfram volunteered to do it. Starting the aircraft everything went okay until they took off then the aircraft exploded and Wolfram including his crew were lost."

Towards the end of 1940, a pair of H IIs and five H IIIs were brought together in readiness for the planned invasion of Britain – Operation Sealion. The H IIs were later swapped for two more H IIIs. The Horten aircraft, along with 80 Kranich gliders, were to fly ammunition supplies to front line infantry units as they advanced into the English countryside. Reimar began modifying some of the H IIIs to carry a 400kg load of ammo but this work was abandoned with the cancellation of the operation in its entirety.

In May 1941, Walter was given a staff position in Berlin as the technical advisor in Luftwaffe Inspektion 3 (LIn 3) – the Luftwaffe fighter inspectorate. At first he served under General Kurt-Bertram von Döring, then later in the year under General of Fighters Werner Mölders, then following his death in November 1941 under his replacement, his old unit commander, Adolf Galland.

Meanwhile, Reimar had been transferred to Königsberg in December 1940 where he continued to work on the H IV high aspect ratio glider, the first example of which was finished during May 1941.

At around this time, Walter persuaded Udet that the H Vb, which had been left out in the open since the winter of 1938/9 ought to be repaired and modified to become a single-seater military design – the H Vc. The weathered aircraft was taken to Minden in north-western Germany where the repair contract was awarded to Peschke Flugzeugbau, a small former furniture manufacturing business run by Otto Peschke. Walter had by now become friendly with Udet's secretary, a woman who was able to sign off official documents on her boss's behalf and who would do favours for Walter when he asked for them.

Walter therefore used his newfound influence to put Reimar in charge of a new unit of his own creation, Sonderkommando LIn 3, to oversee the work on the H Vc.

H VII RESURRECTED

Overseeing Peschke required very little direct involvement from Reimar so he went back to his studies at the University of Bonn. While he was there, he was able to arrange for a second group of workers to construct yet another H III, but this time equipped with a 48hp Walter Micron engine positioned centrally and to the rear. This was designated the H IIId.

Reimar now realised that he had the resources and the opportunity to build the long-planned H VII at the same time, if only Walter and his girlfriend could see to the necessary paperwork. He had three draftsmen at Minden by this time and all of them were now set to work on the H VII. He later said: "I had spoken with Peschke and they would like to make the H VII for us but he needed an order to construct it. Walter then organised or arranged for the construction of the H VII by Peschke."

The order Peschke needed was a long time coming, however. Yet during the winter of 1941 to 1942, Peschke and his men still managed to not only rebuild the H Vb as the H Vc, but also to construct a pair of new unpowered H IIIs. There was no room to keep them at Minden, however, so Walter obtained an order to move part of Sonderkommando LIn 3's operation to Göttingen, near the AVA, where there was hangar space available. Not only that, he had an order issued via the RLM to recruit new workers for the Göttingen facility.

Since the order to have Peschke build a prototype H VII had not come through, Reimar simply began building it himself using these new workers. In October, Walter took Reimar to witness a rocket-propelled flight of the Me 163 at Peenemünde, which both men found encouraging since it served to demonstrate the value now being placed on tailless aircraft designs elsewhere in the industry. Eventually Peschke did receive his order – despite Udet's suicide on November 17, 1941 – and began work on the centre section of the H VII, with the wings being built by Reimar's men at Göttingen.

With Udet gone, the flight of the Me 163 still fresh in their minds, the first H VII under construction, the H Vb being rebuilt as the H Vc and with several new H IIIs on the way, Walter made a discovery which would have dramatic repercussions for the brothers going into 1942. Through his work as a technical advisor he had learned that Junkers was working on a revolutionary new powerplant – the turbojet. ●

ABOVE: While all earlier Horten designs had some form of fixed undercarriage, the H VII's was fully retractable, giving it a very slender profile in flight.

Faster than a Messerschmitt

Abteilung L – 1940 to 1942

Having started his new career at Messerschmitt almost unable to believe his good fortune and happy to shadow the company's main design team, Lippisch's old self-confidence soon began to reassert itself. Everything changed again when his team achieved a spectacular career-defining coup…

Above: The Messerschmitt P 06 as it appears in the project brochure. The design was intended to help experienced pilots retrain on tailless types.

By the end of 1940, Abteilung L had been part of the Messerschmitt organisation for nearly two years. The company continued to enjoy large contracts as Germany's main supplier of fighter aircraft – working on substantial upgrades for the Bf 109 while readying the Me 210 to replace the Bf 110.

The firm's main project office continued to be shadowed by Abteilung L, even as much of the latter's attention was devoted to the DFS 194 and Me 163. While most of its work on other projects had been suspended, Abteilung L nevertheless managed to complete one design which was deemed essential if a rocket-propelled tailless type was ever to reach front line service – a trainer.

Projektbaubeschreibung P 06 was published on November 4, 1940, bearing the standard disclaimer on its title page:

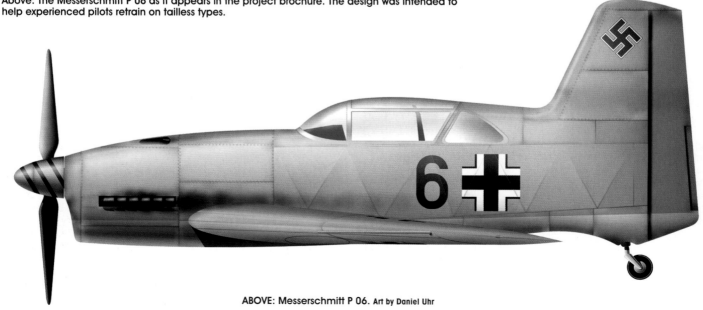

ABOVE: Messerschmitt P 06. Art by Daniel Uhr

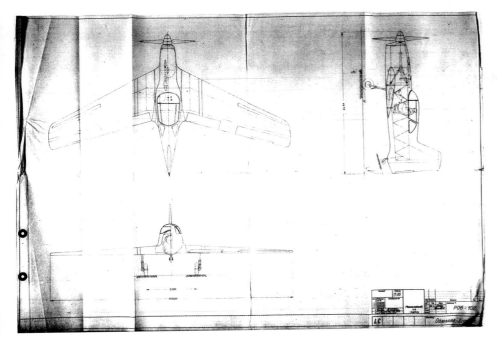

ABOVE: Three-view of the Messerschmitt P 06.

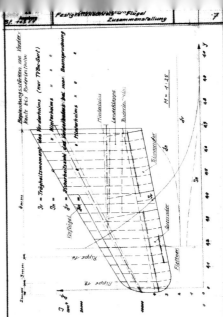

ABOVE: A wing design drawing for the Me 163 dated February 24, 1941. The project's original 'camouflage' name, Bf 163, appears in the top left corner of the page below the Messerschmitt AG logo.

"If changes or modifications are made, the company reserves the right to make these changes. Messerschmitt AG, Augsberg."

The introduction began: "The P 06 project is a two-seater tailless retraining aircraft that can be used with an MG 17 as a fighter aircraft trainer. In order to be able to compare flight characteristics as well as performance, the engine power was matched to that of existing fighter trainers and an As 410 engine is to be installed. The propeller is three position and adjustable in flight. The fuel supply is rated for three hours.

"The occupants sit side by side; a duplicate set of controls, which can be activated by the flight instructor, is provided for the flight student. One set of flight monitoring and navigation devices are arranged in the centre of the instrument panel, and the engine monitoring units are doubled, one on the right and one on the left. For the occupants, height and length-adjustable standard seats for seat cushion parachutes are provided."

The P 06 was to have a steel tube fuselage with a firewall in front of the occupants. The forward section would have metal skin but the rear would be covered with cloth. The Plexiglas cabin featured an ejectable rear section so the instructor and student could quickly bail out in an emergency.

The undercarriage was hydraulically retractable, folding into the wing centre section, and where the tail was concerned: "Elevators and ailerons are, as is customary for tailless aircraft, located at the rear edge of the outer wing. Under the fuselage, an expansion flap is located in the region of the wing front edge and in the inner part of the outer wing flaps, which are used as trims and landing flaps."

The outer part of the wings, removable for rail transport, were to be made of wood with plywood skin. The wing centre section, however, would be made of steel tubing with metal ribs covered partly with fabric and partly with duraluminium.

The Argus As 410 A-0 engine would be fitted on welded steel mounts with built-in shock absorbers. Its single control lever would be mounted in the cockpit "on the bench between the seats". The fuel tank would be located in the wing centre section.

In many respects, the P 06 was to be a mechanically unremarkable aircraft – a simple two-seater to help experienced pilots get used to the idea of flying a tailless machine. However, it would never be built and Abteilung L had other work to keep it occupied.

The final flight tests of the DFS 194 were conducted at Peenemünde on November 30, 1940, and the first towed flight test of the newly completed Me 163 took place at Augsburg on February 13, 1941, with Heini Dittmar at the controls. Lippisch's father Franz died nine days later on February 22.

In the meantime, Abteilung L had been joined by a new recruit – Dr Hermann Wurster had previously been Messerschmitt's chief test pilot, conducting many early tests involving the prototype Bf 109s and the Bf 209 speed record aircraft; now he switched to designing aircraft rather than flying them.

Wurster's first job, while his new colleagues were busy elsewhere, was to pick up the P 04 project and revamp it. The purpose in doing this was twofold: firstly the P 04 was to continue as Abteilung L's tailless alternative to or replacement for the Me 210, which was already somewhat delayed by the end of 1940, and secondly as a scaled down experimental prototype version of a large long-range bomber.

At this time, Messerschmitt's main project office was working on conventional-layout designs for just such a bomber under the designation P 1061, which would eventually go on to become the Me 264. But at the point when Wurster began his revisions of the P 04, mid-to-late 1940, the P 1061 was still just Messerschmitt's entry for the Fernkampfflugzeug competition.

The work seems to have taken Wurster longer than expected since his completed

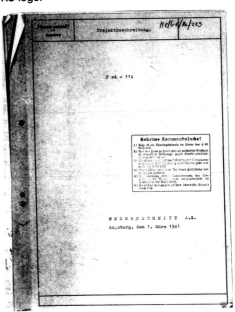

ABOVE: Title page of Hermann Wurster's project description for the revised Messerschmitt P 04.

report, Projektbaubeschreibung P 04-114, was not published until March 1, 1941. According to the introduction: "The P 04-114 is a prototype aircraft for the development of a tailless two-seater heavy fighter or fighter-bomber, as well as a tailless long-range bomber. These tailless types have the following general advantages compared to today's design: 1) Smaller wetted surface and therefore low drag. 2) Best propeller efficiency because of propeller arrangement. 3) Greater manoeuvrability. 4) Lower set-up weight, or greater range with the same flying weight. 5) Unimpeded defence weapons and better visibility to the rear. 6) Free passage through barrage balloons, due to continuous arrow shape."

Wurster's proposal was for a test aircraft with Argus As 10 C engines – but which would otherwise be the same as the production version heavy fighter with DB

▶

601s. However, "The test aircraft is statically dimensioned in such a way that the wing ends can be lengthened to increase the lateral ratio in order to produce similar conditions to the long-range bomber.

"This experimental aircraft is intended to clarify all airworthiness issues, in addition to the stability, especially the rudder forces and rudder effects, turning flight, tipping, take-off and landing characteristics with landing aids of differing strength and at different centres of gravity.

"The experimental aircraft is also simultaneously a flying mock-up. It is intended to clarify the visibility conditions for pilots and radio operator guns in flight in connection with combat tactics. The visual conditions can be changed if necessary. In order to produce the optimum flow characteristics, a great deal of flexibility in rudder and Flettner sizes, in the size of the landing gear and in the V-shape of the wing is provided."

In contrast to much of the German aircraft industry during the Second World War, Lippisch was seldom content to rely on complex calculations or even wind tunnel test results alone to provide data on an aircraft's likely performance and handling characteristics. He preferred to conduct practical experiments either with flying models or full-size prototype aircraft and it would seem that Wurster felt the same – not so surprising given his background as a test pilot.

He wrote: "Recognising that the flying characteristics of the freestanding aircraft cannot be clarified, especially in the case of such types in the wind tunnel, we consider this work to be the most urgent task. This is all the more so since the aircraft can be constructed with the most appropriate design and operating equipment in the construction used here and using already existing complete engines and standard undercarriage and control parts."

The P 04's fuselage was to be made of welded steel pipes with wooden frames and skin while the wings were to be constructed in three sections: the inner section was to feature a twin steel spar with wooden ribs and fabric covering, the outer section which was all wood, and the slim centre section where the engines and undercarriage connections were located. The engine's steel tube support rack would be attached to the front and rear steel spars and its outer cowling would be made of duraluminium. For maintenance, the engine could simply be lifted out vertically on its rack.

Cooling air for the engines came from a slot in the wing leading edge and the two 160-litre fuel tanks were located in the wings in front of the spar.

The hydraulically-actuated tricycle undercarriage featured main landing gear positioned aft of the centre of gravity. "The standard tailwheel and spring strut of the Me 210 is used as the nose wheel, the standard wheel and shock absorber of the Me 109 is used as main gear. The nose wheel and the main gear are only pivoted about an axis when retracting." Most of the P 04's pilot controls were to come from the Me 109 too and no weaponry was to be

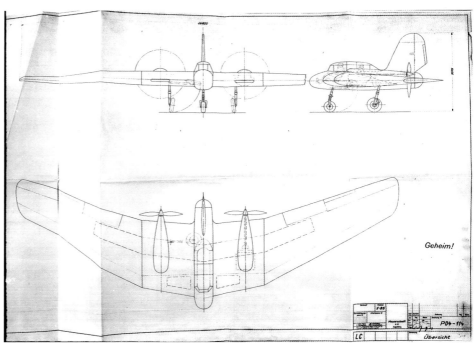

ABOVE: Drawing of the Messerschmitt P 04-114, an experimental sub-scale prototype for a large flying wing bomber, dated June 30, 1941, and signed by both Wurster and Lippisch.

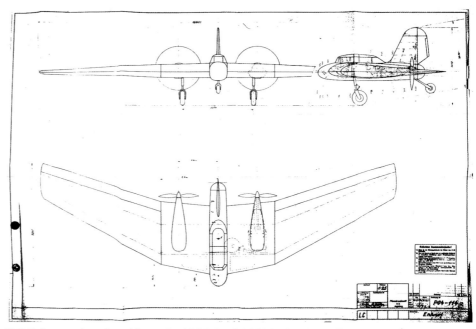

ABOVE: A second version of the revised P 04, the P 04-114a, this time with a tail-sitter undercarriage.

installed – though space for them to be fitted retrospectively was to be provided.

The long-range tailless bomber for which the P 04 was to be a subscale experimental version – the P 08 – does not appear to have been detailed at this point and just five days after Wurster's report was published the P 1061 was chosen as the winner of the Fernkampfflugzeug competition. It received the RLM designation Me 264 and a contract was placed for six prototypes and 30 production examples.

THE FIRST ME 263

A month later, in April, the Aerodynamische Versuchsanstalt (AVA) at Göttingen, working as a contractor, commenced a wide-ranging series of wind tunnel tests on Messerschmitt

P 01 designs with a variety of different fuselage and wing forms, taking the P 01-114 as a starting point. These tests must have been hugely expensive, since the work lasted from around April 21, 1941 to at least October 6, 1942, and generated a vast amount of aerodynamics data for Abteilung L.

At some point between the start of the tests in April and July 7, 1941, what had been the P 01-114 was given the official RLM designation Me 263 – copies of the original P 01-114 report dated August 1940 then having '263' retrospectively added to them. Lippisch himself later refers to it as both the P 03 and the Me 263, although the AVA reports go from being marked simply 'P 01' briefly to 'Me 263 (P 01)' then finally to 'Me 263' without P 03 appearing. It is worth pointing out here too that the aircraft which eventually bore the designation Me 263 in 1944 – itself originally designated Ju 248 – was unrelated to the P 01-derived 1941 design.

Having previously been suspended, P 01 now recommenced as the third ongoing strand of the department's work alongside the Me 163 tests and Wurster's continuation of the P 04.

Fittingly, the first design drawing to emerge for the 'new' P 01 series, on June 12, 1941, was given the designation P 01-116 and like its namesake of over two years earlier was a single jet fighter. This out-of-numerical-sequence reboot of the series left a gap at P 01-115 which was filled on July 2 with the creation of a mixed propulsion single turbojet and rocket-propelled design – the same day that Heini Dittmar made

his last unpowered flight in the Me 163 V4 before it was moved to Peenemünde so that its Walter rocket engine could be fitted.

According to Lippisch: "In the summer of 1941, we moved into our quarters at Peenemünde and the people from Walter installed the engine. Heini was familiar with the aircraft's characteristics because of the gliding tests he had carried out and, therefore, the initial flights got off to a good start. Seeing him fly this bird was a wonderful sight. After take-off, the aircraft stayed close to the ground while gaining speed and then climbed steeply to an altitude of 4000-6000m.

"The flying characteristics were excellent and when, more or less as a spectator, I watched the bird disappear into the clouds, trailing smoke, my thoughts went back to

the beginning, to our creation's childhood and adolescence, and I was very glad that, in the end, we had managed to overcome the many, almost insurmountable problems."

A couple of weeks after this important phase of the Me 163's development began, on July 16, another new P 01-116 was drafted. This was another pure rocket-propelled design. For years, Lippisch's odd way of numbering the P 01 series had caused confusion but looking at the sequence and the design details together, his thinking becomes slightly clearer.

The sequence began with P 01-116 because that was the design he wanted or perhaps needed to tackle first out of a set of pre-determined concepts for P 01. This was followed by P 01-111, P 01-112, P 01-113 and P 01-114. Then the series

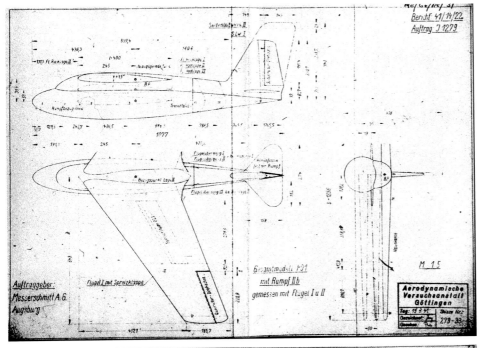

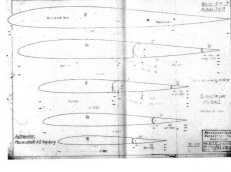

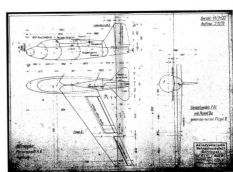

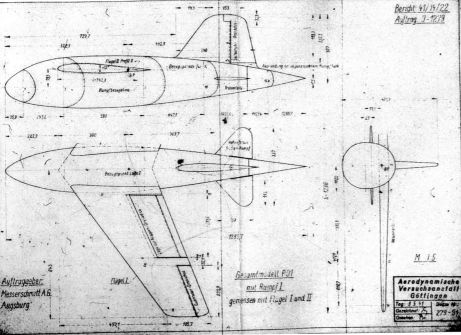

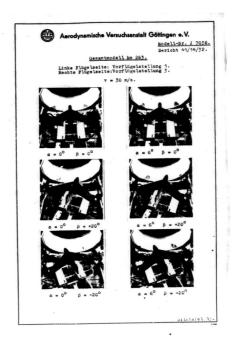

ABOVE: Extensive wind tunnel tests were carried out on various different configurations under the project heading P 01. Both tailed and tailless configurations were tried with a variety of fin and fuselage shapes over a period of more than a year.

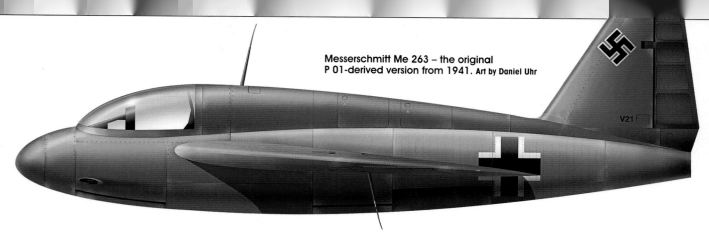

Messerschmitt Me 263 – the original
P 01-derived version from 1941. Art by Daniel Uhr

ground to a halt for around nine months. When the series began again, Lippisch deliberately chose to skip over the next number and went back to P 01-116.

This 'new' P 01-116 retained the squared-off tailfin of the P 01-114 and the amorphous P 01 wind tunnel models being tested by the AVA, making it a natural next step in the sequence. The P 01-115 which followed had a new rounded tailfin and this feature was carried over to the P 01-116 which came next, indicating that the latter was the only one of the three P 01-116s to fit correctly with the numerical sequence.

Within three weeks, the last trio of P 01 designs were produced – the P 01-117 on July 22, the P 01-118 on August 3 and the P 01-119 on August 4. The first featured a cockpit where the pilot was expected to lie flat on his belly in a prone position, the second boasted a novel tilting seat arrangement to improve the pilot's visibility during a steep near-vertical climb, and the third had a pressure cabin for high altitude operations. Each of them was to be powered by a single Walter rocket engine for the initial climb to altitude, but the P 01-118 also featured a second rocket engine for cruising to provide greater endurance. From this point on, all mention of the P 01 ceased and the project continued as the Me 263.

Then, on August 13, 1941, Heini Dittmar made the first powered flight in a Messerschmitt Me 163. The outcome of this and further tests seems to have been twofold – firstly it demonstrated to any doubters that the concept of a highly manoeuvrable rocket-powered interceptor was sound and an avenue worth pursuing. Secondly, the start of practical testing freed up Abteilung L's design staff to concentrate on whatever might come after the purely experimental Me 163.

At this stage there was no 'Me 163 A' since there was no 'B' – it was simply known as the Me 163. Lippisch himself believed that a combination of the practical Me 163 tests and the theoretical and wind tunnel-tested P 01 series would produce a single-seat combat aircraft. It would not necessarily need to embody the features of the Me 163 or any of the P 01s up to that point since their collective purpose was gathering data.

ABOVE: One of the various late-series P 01 designs, the P 01-117, which featured a prone pilot position. The drawing is dated July 22, 1941. Iowa State University Library Special Collections and University Archive

LIPPISCH P 05

With this in mind, on August 27, 1941, Lippisch unveiled his first proposal for a military design based on Me 163 flight experience – the P 05 Interceptor, drafted by Rudolf Rentel.

The title page of the P 05 brochure, bearing Lippisch's signature, is revealing. The standard disclaimer seen previously on the P 06 brochure has changed a little. It now states: "If, during the course of the further flight testing of the Li 163, comparative engine changes are necessary, the manufacturer reserves the right to carry them out. Messerschmitt AG, Augsburg."

Lippisch is now referring to 'his' creation as the Li 163. Indeed, the brochure is headed 'Projektbaubeschreibung Li P 05 Interceptor' even though it is printed on a standard Messerschmitt-headed form.

The foreword states: "On the basis of

ABOVE: An Me 163 fuselage under construction. Once design work on the experimental Me 163 was completed in early 1941, work on building the first prototypes advanced rapidly.

ABOVE: A view under the starboard wing of Me 163 V5, GG+EA, in high gloss finish. Its leading edge slot, landing and control flaps are visible.

other two engines were on either side of it but set further back. The 750kg engine was set just above the former.

The P 05's three main fuel tanks were positioned behind the pressure cabin and two of them fed the launch engines. The third tank, armoured and sandwiched between the others, was for the cruise engine. The brochure notes that there is space in the wings available for the installation of further fuel tanks. Landing involved a sprung skid actuated using compressed air and a brake parachute, while armament was four MG 151/20s with 100 rounds each.

COMPLETE AGREEMENT

The publication of the P 05 brochure headed 'Li P 05 Interceptor' and making casual reference to the Li 163 on August 27 seems to have been followed on August 28 by a pre-arranged meeting between Willy Messerschmitt, Lippisch, Theo Croneiss, Messerschmitt production director Fritz Hentzen and RLM representative Oberst-Ing Gottfried Reidenbach.

Up to this point, Abteilung L had

the flight experiences and characteristics test of the Me 163 V4 the present project was developed as a massive enlargement of the tried and tested pattern.

"In accordance with the intended use, the rocket engine propulsion interceptor achieves the shortest climbing time at the application altitude and on the other hand ensures superior speed and climb performance compared to normal combat and fighter aircraft.

"The drive type allows only a short operating time because the fuel consumption of the currently developed engines of this type is many times higher than in Otto engines with a propeller drive. The superior climb and speed performance combined with a strong armament still make the interceptor a weapon effective for air defence."

This last point is reiterated in the technical section of the brochure which describes "usage: daytime use as a local guard with strong armament and high climb and flight speed".

As with most of Abteilung L's other creations, the P 05's wings were to be made entirely from wood except for the rudders, while the fuselage was a steel tube and light alloy construction. The pressure cabin cockpit was to be assembled separately then attached to the fuselage as a single piece.

Unlike the Me 163 with its single 1500kg thrust HWK rocket engine, the P 05 was to have no fewer than four engines – three of them with 1500kg thrust each. According to the brochure: "The three climb engines are not controllable, they are started one after the other by means of a common throttle lever, so that a certain thrust graduation of 1500 to 3000 to 4500kg thrust is possible."

The fourth engine was for level flying once operational altitude had been reached and could be throttled back if necessary: "The cruising device is infinitely adjustable within the limits of 200-750kg thrust."

One of the 1500kg engines was set at the extreme rear of the aircraft and the

ABOVE: Wooden Me 163 wings under construction. The central spar would be deleted from the design for the Me 163 B.

ABOVE: Completed Me 163 V4, KE+SW, in July 1941 at Peenemünde – later that year it would be flown to 1003km/h by Heini Dittmar.

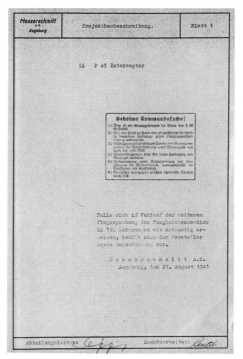

ABOVE: The title page of the P 05 project brochure shows changes afoot at Abteilung L. It appears to be the first attempt by Lippisch to use his personal prefix 'Li' for one of the department's designs. Iowa State University Library Special Collections and University Archive

spent more than two and a half years as a productive and integrated part of the Messerschmitt organisation but all that was about to change. At the meeting, several points of disagreement

concerning the future of the department and its work were discussed.

Evidently Lippisch wanted it clarified that his project office had equal status to that of Woldemar Voigt, while Ernst Udet, possibly at Lippisch's instigation, had decided that Abteilung L should be transferred to its own separate facility at Obertraubling and that Lippisch's type designations should bear his 'Li' prefix rather than the Messerschmitt 'Me'.

At another meeting on August 29, again attended by Croneiss, Hentzen and Reidenbach but this time accompanied by RLM Flugbaumeister Hans-Martin Antz, minutes from the August 28 meeting were read out by Croneiss: "Oberst-Ing Reidenbach accepted Professor Messerschmitt's objections to moving Abteilung L to Obertraubling and agreed that Abteilung L should remain in Augsberg. He asked whether Lippisch and Voigt's project offices would have equal status within the organisation under Professor Messerschmitt and whether the design office and prototype workshop would support both project offices to the same degree.

"Brigadeführer Croneiss and Direktor Hentzen answered both questions in the affirmative. Oberst-Ing Reidenbach said he was satisfied with this solution."

Now it was Reidenbach's turn to read out another set of minutes, from a recent meeting held by Udet and attended by his adjutant Max Pendele, Antz and Heini Dittmar, who had presumably just climbed out of the Me 163 V4's cockpit at the time: "At the meeting, which had taken place after a

demonstration of the Me 163 at Peenemünde, General-Oberst Udet had decided that: 1) the Abteilung Lippisch should be transferred to Obertraubling, 2) the aircraft designed by Lippisch should bear his name 3) the manufacture of the first batch of aircraft should be accelerated so that the aircraft can become operational next year 4) Lippisch should be provided with the personnel he requires to undertake this task.

"Oberst Ing Reidenbach added the following comments to these minutes: to 1) he would inform the General-Oberst that he should reconsider this decision, since, after re-examining the reason for transferring Abteilung L to Obertraubling, Professor Messerschmitt and Lippisch had reached an agreement on this point at a meeting held on the 28th of this month. To 2) Oberst-Ing Reidenbach did not have the authority to decide this point and recommended that Professor Messerschmitt discuss the matter directly with Generaloberst Udet. Brigadeführer Croneiss and director Hentzen pointed out that an earlier decision made by the RLM technical office required aircraft types to be prefixed by the name of the manufacturer. Oberst-Ing Reidenbach did not accept this argument but still thought Professor Messerschmitt should discuss this point personally with Generaloberst Udet.

"To 3) Brigadeführer Croneiss handed over the description of the enlarged version of the Me 163 to Herr Antz for further attention, to 4) this will be the subject of a discussion at Augsburg on September 4."

In short, Lippisch and Abteilung L

ABOVE: A perspective drawing of the scaled-up Me 163 – the P 05 interceptor – from the project brochure. Iowa State University Library Special Collections and University Archive

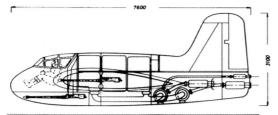

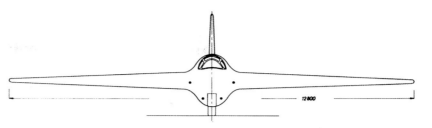

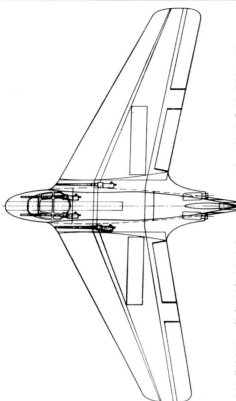

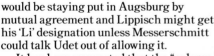

ABOVE: A three-view drawing of the P 05 showing the positioning of its four rocket engines – three for take-off and one for cruising at altitude.

would be staying put in Augsburg by mutual agreement and Lippisch might get his 'Li' designation unless Messerschmitt could talk Udet out of allowing it.

It has been suggested that the "enlarged version of the Me 163" mentioned here refers to the Me 163 B - but this had not yet been designed, whereas Lippisch had only published his description of the P 05 the day before. It seems likely that this is what was handed to Antz for "further attention". Indeed, graphs exist, dated September 10, 1941, which show that a revised version of the P 05 was still being worked on at that time.

Continuing with the August 29 meeting: "Herr Antz informed the meeting that the Project Office chief Voigt had submitted a project closely resembling that from Abteilung L. He had received a drawing of P 1079/13a, dated August 11, 1941, and an accompany description of an aircraft, which although not tailless, had a sharply sweptback wing and was powered by a jet engine. Herr Antz remarked that when Herr Voigt had handed over this information he had said that if this project were developed it would not be necessary to build the Me 163 and the interceptor.

"Direktor Hentzen remarked that Professor Messerschmitt had considered it necessary to fit high-speed aircraft with sweptback wings after learning of the

investigations made by Professor Betz and had, therefore, issued instructions for this project to be so designed. Croneiss added that, at a meeting held on the 28th of this month, Professor Messerschmitt had expressly forbidden Herr Voigt to investigate tailless designs, since these were and would remain the responsibility of Abteilung L."

Voigt's drawing, extracted from the wide-ranging P 1079 series of studies, would end up providing the basis for the later pulsejet-powered Me 328 – albeit in much modified form and without the swept wing.

In the meantime, Lippisch had won the backing of Ernst Udet and clearly had a degree of support from within the RLM, particularly from Antz. His new assertive attitude did nothing to endear him to Willy Messerschmitt, however, and it is likely that Croneiss was acting as an intermediary at this point.

FROM P 04 TO P 08

During the summer of 1941, Messerschmitt suffered the first of a series of blows to its reputation as a company. The RLM, while carrying out due diligence checks on the P 1061, now the Me 264, discovered that Messerschmitt's numbers did not add up. It was apparent that the aircraft would be unable to fly 15,000km nonstop, let alone the 20,000km Messerschmitt had originally claimed it could manage.

According to a summary written on May 12, 1942, by Generalleutnant Eccard, Freiherr von Gablenz: "Because Messerschmitt lacks experience in building heavy aircraft, and also because, in the opinion of the RLM technical specialist, the Me 264 plan-form was too narrow, the design could not be adopted as the standard long-range bomber for the Luftwaffe and other firms had to be invited to tender."

The order for 30 Me 264s was put on hold and the number of prototypes was reduced to five while a new set of requirements for a re-run of the Fernkampfflugzeug competition were drawn up. Messerschmitt would have to re-tender and now ran the risk of another firm being given the contract. It was a disaster, but it also presented Abteilung L with a new opportunity.

Hermann Wurster's revival of the P 04 had always been intended as a sub-scale test aircraft for a large long-range bomber but his report had been delivered too late for consideration as a basis for Messerschmitt's official entry to Fernkampfflugzeug. Now he had been handed a second chance – the deadline for submission of designs for the competition's re-run was in December, 1941, so a new report was swiftly prepared on the P 04's full-scale

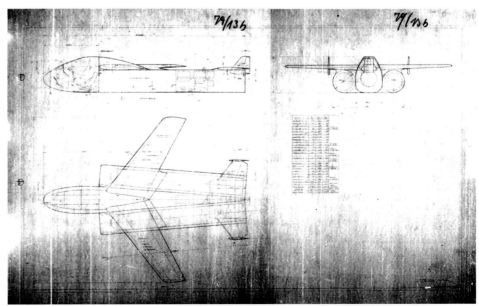

ABOVE: Woldemar Voigt of Messerschmitt's conventional project office offered the RLM his team's P 1079/13a as an alternative to the Me 163 and interceptor. The 'a' is lost but the 'b' gives some idea of how the twin-pulsejet design may have looked. Radically altered, the design would provide the basis for the Me 328.

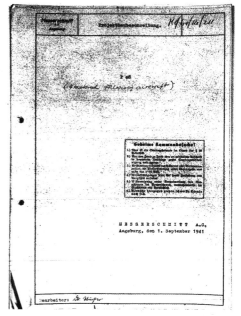

ABOVE: The title page of the Messerschmitt P 08 project brochure, signed by Hermann Wurster.

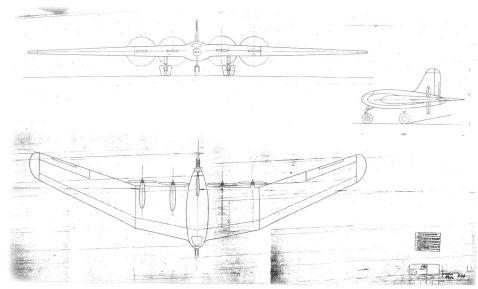

ABOVE: Drawing of the Messerschmitt P 08 from the project brochure, dated September 1, 1941, showing its armed configuration. The P 08 was intended as an alternative to what became the Me 264.

long-range bomber development – the P 08 – and published on September 1, 1941.

There was no 'Li' or standard disclaimer on this report and it was simply headed 'Projektbaubeschreibung P 08'.

Rather than having an introduction or foreword, the report begins with a section entitled 'Purpose' which states: "In the case of previous Fernkampfflugzeugen [long-range bombers], it appears that the ratio of the bomb load and resulting fighting force to the value of the crew and equipment deployed is low. It has also been shown that bombs of 500 to 1000kg are insufficient when attacking battleships or other powerful targets. Attacking heavily fortified large targets will require bombs of the most extreme calibre.

"In addition, it is a necessary requirement that such a valuable long-range aircraft should be adequately protected against fighters by means of appropriate defensive weapons. The present project fulfils these tactical requirements to a certain extent, as is not possible with Fernkampfflugzeugen of the hitherto customary design.

"The project is also reaching far-reaching tactical possibilities. The aircraft has sufficient space and weight reserves to cope in the event of a sudden development of heavy artillery weapons with systems for glide bombs or defence weapons.

"The project is designed in such a way that the surface loading during take-off and landing moves within proven limits.

The start to the long-range flight can also take place without start aids on existing runways. A further increase in the surface load can be reserved for later.

"Another special point of view is the possibility of adapting the aircraft in a matter of minutes by replacing the bomb chassis with the various possible applications, as the specialisation of such heavy aircraft is undesirable."

The report then gives seven possible applications to which the P 08 could be put. Firstly, it could be a Fernkampfflugzeug with a 15,000km range carrying 20,000kg of bombs, secondly a maritime aircraft able to carry four 5000kg glide bombs or the equivalent in torpedoes up to 6.5m long, thirdly a 2500km range bomber carrying 50,000kg of bombs, fourthly a reconnaissance aircraft with a 27,000km range.

The fifth option was to use it as a 15,000km range transport carrying up to 22 tons of armoured fighting vehicles or other field weapons and equipment, sixth was as an unpowered glider carrying a staggering 100 tons of kit, and finally and most outlandishly as an enormous night fighter fitted with a quartet of 88mm anti-aircraft guns.

A list of the design's general advantages compared to a conventional layout type followed, including lower weight because of the lack of a fuselage and tail,

more efficient propellers because of the giant wing 'smoothing' the air before it reached them, better manoeuvrability and better fuel economy.

Military advantages included: the ability to have payload and fuel making up 60% of total flight weight, high speed in horizontal flight, the ability to drop bombs at any angle of attack between 0-90°, good visibility to defensive weapons, the ability to pass through barrage balloon cables unhindered, fully armoured fuel tank and good protection for crew and payload, no possibility of the enemy shooting off a vulnerable tail, longer floating time in the event of ditching in water, and easier dispersal of hot air from the engines for deicing.

Inside the P 08's all-metal hull, there would be separate pressure cabins for the pilot and crew, while the payload space could be swapped out depending on which role the aircraft was needed for.

The tricycle landing gear was hydraulically retractable with compressed air available for emergency retraction and the main gear featured pneumatic brakes. The control surfaces would be actuated using a differential pressure system, supplied by Siemens.

Power would come from either four DB 613s or four DB 615s driving adjustable four-bladed metal propellers, which could be used as dive brakes, tactical brakes or landing brakes. For maintenance

Messerschmitt P 08. Art by Daniel Uhr

purposes, the engines would be installed or removed as required from below with the propeller drive shafts pulling out to the rear.

Defensive weaponry, if required, was to consist of two MG 151/20s or MG 131s in the nose and another two at the rear of the wing. Further weaponry could be fitted if necessary. Evidently complete equipment for night-fighting would be installed.

RECORD BREAKER

The idea that the P 08 could supplement or even supplant the Me 264 as Messerschmitt's Fernkampfflugzeug entry seems to have been rather a stretch – particularly given the huge sums of money the company had already invested in commencing construction of the first prototype. The P 08, therefore, went no further. Wurster, however, continued to refine the P 04 throughout 1941 and into 1942.

During September, as planned, discussions took place about the P 05 Interceptor during which it appears that the project was effectively split in two. Rather than having a single large aircraft that could climb extremely fast then cruise along at altitude engaging in dogfights, two projects emerged which each took up part of the P 05's role. One was a fast-climbing, short endurance rocket fighter and the other a version of the P 05 with a conventional undercarriage and powered by two turbojets.

In Ein Dreieck Fliegt, Lippisch wrote that the Li P 05 "was a true-to-scale enlargement of the Me 163 V4 to ensure the design of an aircraft of known characteristics, good weaponry (four machine guns), and great range. However, since it was feared that in this aircraft of 12.8m wingspan the control forces would be too high, it was decided to return to the smaller size.

"On September 14, 1941, we produced a smaller design, the Li 163 S (S for series production) with a wingspan of 9.2m that was to be armed with four machine cannons."

The Li 163 S fighter was to be a fairly straightforward development of the experimental Me 163 and was given the designation Li 163 S in the confident expectation that Messerschmitt would be unable to persuade Udet that Lippisch should be denied his 'Li'.

Rudolf Rentel took on the task of turning his own rocket-propelled P 05 design into a similarly scaled twin-turbojet fighter – a task which evidently took a little longer than the swift makeover which had resulted in the Li 163 S.

In the meantime, on October 2, 1941, Heini Dittmar became the first man to fly faster than 1000km/h in the Me 163. Lippisch wrote: "Our success in 1941 was crowned by Heini flying faster than 1000km/h. At just over 1000km/h the shock wave caused the outer wing to separate suddenly and the aircraft pitched nose down, the instruments registering a negative acceleration of 11g. Heini pulled the throttle back quickly, the aircraft slowed down and he was able to take control again. In the evening the Askania theodolite measurements were evaluated: the final result revealed a speed of 1003km/h!

"After it had been reported to Berlin, the significance of our progress began to be recognised. When I returned to Augsberg, Messerschmitt did not speak to me at first: he first had to digest the fact that my aircraft was faster than his."

Rentel's first completed design for the turbojet P 05, now designated the P 09, was produced on October 28, 1941. The type of turbojets to be used for this new fighter was unspecified and its wingspan was reduced from the P 05's 12.8m down to 11.6m, while its length was reduced by 50cm from 7.6m to 7.1m. Its undercarriage consisted of two mainwheels which retracted into the wings and a tail skid.

Ernst Udet committed suicide on November 17, 1941, and with him died Lippisch's hopes of having his Messerschmitt type designations prefixed with 'Li'. It would be the Me 163 from this point on.

By now, the Li 163 S had been superseded by another new design which received

ABOVE: In September 1941, it was decided to split the P 05 Interceptor project in two – a simple rocket-powered interceptor which became the Me 163 B and the P 09 – a twin-turbojet design on roughly the same scale as the P 05.

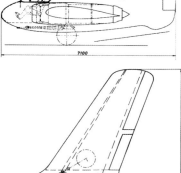

the designation Me 163 B. The original Me 163 was retrospectively renamed the Me 163 A and plans to build the 'B' in series had got under way with an order being placed for 70 examples.

The final new Abteilung L design of 1941 was a ground-attack spin-off from Rentel's P 09, given the unusual designation P 010, presumably to indicate that it was more of a P 09.5 rather than the P 10, a designation which would not be applied until May of the following year. The P 010, dated November 26, 1941, was substantially increased in size from the P 09 fighter, having a 13.4m wingspan and being 8.15m long. This resulted largely from the need

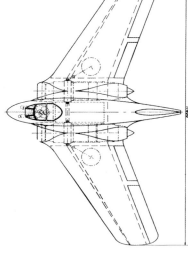

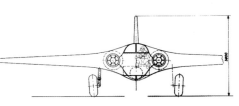

ABOVE: The P 010, dated November 26, 1941, a ground-attack aircraft based on the P 09.

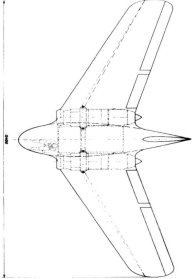

to provide space for a capacious bomb bay in the central portion of the fuselage.

On December 1, construction of the first Me 163 B prototype was commenced and later in the month the deadline for design submissions to the rerun of the Fernkampfflugzeug competition passed. There were two entries from Messerschmitt – but neither of them was the P 08. Instead two different versions of the Me 264 were submitted, one with four engines and one with six.

However, despite all this productivity there were storm clouds gathering on the horizon for the Messerschmitt company. Work on the long-awaited Me 210 was not going well and Udet's successor would be less inclined to tolerate Messerschmitt's seemingly endless delays. ●

The tailless super-aircraft

Heinkel and Focke-Wulf designs 1942

The flying wing and tailless work carried out at Messerschmitt during the early years of the war is relatively well known but designers at the firm's main competitors had also spent time assessing these new aerodynamic forms…

While Messerschmitt remained the only company to have a whole design office devoted to working on tailless and flying wing aircraft projects, Junkers had a long history of working with tailless concepts. Heinkel had been interested in them since at least the early 1930s and Arado had looked at them during the mid 1930s.

Focke-Wulf came to study them in detail during 1942. On May 13, 1942, Focke-Wulf chief executive Kurt Tank sent a memo to the firm's top four men in aircraft development – production manager Willi Kaether, project office head Ludwig Mittelhuber, head of aerodynamics Hans Multhopp and chief engineer Herbert Wolff – telling them: "Since the ongoing development work on large aircraft already has a weight of 120 tons per our discussion, it is appropriate to consider the issue of the flying wing aircraft again.

"The following investigation should therefore be made: at moderate surface loads (200kg per square metre), which still allow a sufficiently high speed, especially in the case of the all-wing type, it is necessary to investigate the weight of the wings as much as the dimensions of the wing, with loads including fuel for very great range in the wing.

"Due to the wide distribution of the loads along the wing span, care must be taken that the bending moments during the flight are reduced to a minimum. In order to keep the impact on the ground as small as possible, it is advisable to distribute the landing gear in the same way as the two Grosstransporter projects along the span in individual bogies, so that the weight is evenly distributed among the wheels on the ground."

He said that there should be no protrusions from the wing either for cockpit visibility or defensive armament during flight "in order to avoid additional harmful resistances. The ideal shape of a wing is to be aimed for as far as possible".

He went on: "Since realising such an aircraft type will require a longer development time, engines such as the BMW 803 can be expected. For installation in the wing, the development of the flat counter-piston motors, which starts at Cologne – Deutz, must also be well suited. When installing six such units of 5000hp, the total power of 30,000hp would allow a flying weight of approximately 200 ton.

"The wing required at the given surface load with a relative wing thickness of 20% at the root would have to be sufficient for the required space. In carrying out these investigations, I ask for ongoing information, if necessary to improve the project, to change the task in this or that direction. The basic task of this type is the transport of large loads over very large distances at moderate speed."

The full extent of the work then carried out is unclear and few documents or drawings have surfaced to shed further light on it, but tantalising evidence does exist – along with evidence of work done by Heinkel and Arado.

One of the great strengths of the German aircraft industry during the war was the ease with which news of the latest scientific accomplishments was spread between those who needed to know about them.

The numerous aviation-focused research organisations continued to function and none was more prestigious than the Deutsche Akademie für Luftfahrtforschung or 'German Academy of Aeronautical Research', which had been founded in July 1936 by Adolf Baeumker with Hermann Göring as president, Erhard Milch as vice-president and Baeumker himself as chancellor.

From the outset, it was meant to be composed of just 60 regular members with 100 additional associate, honorary,

ABOVE: This page from a Heinkel report is dated October 8, 1942, but was amended on November 5, 1942 – the day before Lippisch's talk to the DAL on tailless aircraft. It details different layouts for fast bombers, including an otherwise unknown tailless single engine pusher prop design.

sponsoring or outstanding scientific members. However, it never had more than 45 regular members at a time and during its nearly nine year existence only had an overall total membership of 218.

It was, effectively, an elite gentlemen's club which only the most important figures in German aviation research were invited to join.

Alexander Lippisch, a Messerschmitt representative and a regular member himself, presented a lecture to the ninth scientific meeting of regular members on November 6, 1942, entitled The Evolution of the Tailless Aircraft. In the audience were Heinkel chief designer Siegfried Günter, Multhopp from Focke-Wulf and Lippisch's old boss Professor Walter Georgii, head of the DFS, among others.

The talk itself began with Heini Dittmar's record-breaking flight in the Me 163 V4 more than a year earlier, then went back to the beginning, mentioning the tailless developments and ideas of Englishman John William Dunne, Austrian Igo Etrich and Hugo Junkers before going on to discuss his own Storch and Delta series.

Towards the end Lippisch said: "Developments performed throughout these years aimed primarily at improving the flying capabilities of tailless aircraft to such an extent that they would compare well with normal types. This point has already been passed and despite all contrary predictions, the tailless aircraft has succeeded in attaining a superiority over normal aircraft.

"This argument against this type of construction may be dropped, but there is still discussion on the question of whether a considerable increase of performance is to be expected by changing from normal types of aircraft to tailless types."

He then argued at length that such an increase in performance could indeed be expected from tailless types.

Professor Franz Nikolas Scheubel, chairman of aircraft and flight technology at the Technischen Hochschule Darmstadt, asked a detailed question, to which Lippisch gave an equally detailed answer, then Günter said: "Such an important construction as the tailless aircraft has naturally also been considered by us. We thought which parts of the aircraft had to be omitted as there was only a part of the fuselage and the tail unit, i.e. the elevator. The fuselage itself could not generally be reduced."

He then outlined why be believed that drag created by the fuselage remained the same whether the aircraft was tailless or not – mainly due to the engine nacelles and the wing assembly – and highlighted problems with lateral control.

"The centre of gravity movement is the next problem, as already mentioned by Herr Scheubel," he said. "The problem of the available range and centre of gravity position is closely connected with the arrangement of the propellers. The achievement of 10-15% permissible movement of the centre of gravity on aircraft with tractor propellers is of much more significance than for an aircraft with pure jet propulsion."

The next to speak was Multhopp: "We also have been thoroughly occupied with this problem, because the industry has been continuously approached with the project of tailless aircraft.

"With regard to the flying performance we, as well as Herr Günter, obtained different results from those of Herr Lippisch. We were less interested in the tailless fighter aircraft than in the tailless super-aircraft and particularly in the all-wing aircraft. The all-wing construction is extraordinarily difficult for large aircraft which are built either for the transport of very heavy and bulky goods, or for long-range flying.

"This is particularly based on the difficulties of lateral control, as also already mentioned by Herr Scheubel and Herr Günter. It is, however, repeatedly said, that on the all-wing aircraft no extensive movements of the centre of gravity along the chord were desired, but owing to the high angle of sweepback required, the shift of a load along the span also involves a shift in the direction of the chord.

"It is, therefore, difficult to trim the wing efficiently. On large aircraft of the usual construction the wing is by no means empty, because this space is nowadays utilised for the accommodation of a large amount of the total load, and at least houses the engines and fuel. The distribution of all the load and equipment in the wing leads to considerable contradictions.

"The yawing moments when one engine cuts forces the engineer to concentrate the engines either entirely in the middle section of the wing, or to connect them with each other and with the propellers by means of complicated couplings under application of free-wheel clutches, a solution generally disapproved of by the flight engineer.

"As the inner wing is on the other hand required for the crew and usually also for the [illegible] of the maximum height of the inner wing, and as the adjacent space is used for housing the undercarriage, there is then only the outer wing of the all-wing aircraft for the stowage of fuel. This solution is quite efficient as the fuel is out of the way, but the fuel is then too far behind the centre of gravity, thus entailing more than the permissible movement of the centre of gravity for all aircraft of higher range.

"For this reason we can practically put no load into the outer section of the all-wing. This has then the effect that the all-wing aircraft is growing too large, owing to the amount of fuel which it would have to house, and this involves further drag. It must be observed that the incorporation of a fixed volume in a fuselage takes with the most efficient utilisation of space only a quarter of the resistance than the accommodation in a wing of normal span.

"Moreover, the stress in the wings and thereby the weight are growing unpleasantly high, as particularly with large aircraft, we are very much resorting to the reduction of the supporting structure by housing the load in the wing.

"Finally from our consideration of the performance it followed that the longitudinal control was reducing the maximum lift to a large extent. It is obvious that the tail unit, i.e. the elevator, does not act on a considerably long lever just for fun, but principally to prevent any loss of lift. For landing we must have a certain moment which depends on the position of the centre of gravity and this is achieved in the best way by a force on the surface of the tail unit which is at a great distance from the centre of gravity.

"Reduction of this distance must cause the corresponding increase in the force which naturally has a bad effect if a part of the wing must be used as elevator. If it is necessary to keep forward shifts of the centre of gravity within a normal range on the all-wing aircraft we get very remarkable losses of lift, even if we do not consider high-lift devices such as fowler wings and other arrangements of tabs, which

cannot be considered for tailless aircraft.

"These were the essential facts which resulted from the investigation into the all-wing construction."

Lippisch's RLM supervisor on 'Projekt X', Hans-Martin Antz, an invited guest rather than a member, then introduced a film showing the first test flights of the Me 163 A at Peenemünde.

When the film was finished, Lippisch stood up again and said: "In principle, I quite understand that the other gentlemen have quite a lot of hesitation and that one must have hesitations if one has no practical experience in the field of tailless aircraft. In that case, things always acquire a more difficult aspect than they have in practice.

"One must evidently have experience and evidently one must have built aircraft to possess the necessary knowledge on the subject. I should like to emphasise again that it does not suffice to establish a comparison solely by calculation. It really does not suffice. Wind tunnel measurements, which are in many cases restricted by the Reynolds numbers, are also not sufficient for giving a clear picture of this type of aircraft. If I had proceeded from such ideas, these aircraft would never have been built.

"One had to advance by a different route. One had to construct the flying model, one had to gather experience on the flying model itself. Such a project, however, must

"We are still at the beginning of our work, whereas you with your normal aircraft have practically reached the end"

be approached with a certain optimism and I believe that this is essential with every new project. If we do not have this optimism and steadiness ourselves, which enables us to keep smiling in moments of failures so that all the others carry on with their work, then any further work is impossible

"This is a decisive fact. I know quite well that certain difficulties exist. This is absolutely clear and self-evident, as we are still at the beginning of our work, whereas you with your normal aircraft have today practically reached the end. But it is therefore even more necessary to enter the new land and not to look about and not to get the essential knowledge, which makes further work possible. It is a work which has to be accomplished by many and not only by the individual, otherwise there will be no progress in this direction."

He then went on to address each of the individual points raised by Multhopp and Günter before Georgii gave a summing up to close the lecture. Exactly what form Focke-Wulf's 'tailless super-aircraft' took is unknown but it appears that it underwent detailed design work. Since most of Heinkel's project documents are lost the precise form of that firm's early work also remains a mystery – but it is clear that both firms were considering tailless and flying wing designs long before the better known late-war projects were drafted.

What little is known of Arado's early work on flying wings is discussed elsewhere in this volume.. ●

Machinations

Abteilung L – 1942 to 1943

Messerschmitt was in trouble at the beginning of 1942 and it only got worse. A chain of events had been set in motion that would result in the dissolution of Abteilung L after more than four years and the departure of Alexander Lippisch from the Messerschmitt company.

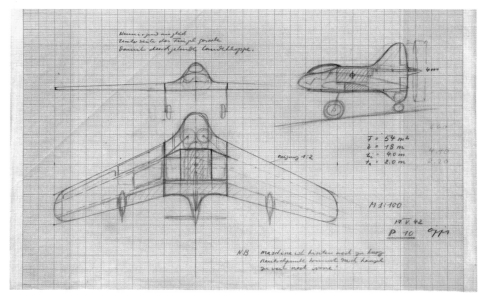

ABOVE: The original Messerschmitt P 10, as sketched by Alexander Lippisch on May 17, 1942. Controversy resulting from this design would ultimately lead to Lippisch leaving the company. Iowa State University Library Special Collections and University Archive

A bteilung L spent the first four months of 1942 fully engaged in design work on the Me 163 B rocket-powered interceptor. In reality, the Me 163 B was almost a completely new aircraft – the fuselage being entirely different from that of its predecessor.

Lippisch himself, however, seems to have had little direct involvement with the detail design of the Me 163 B. In his memoir Erinnerungen, he writes: "On October 2, 1941, Heini Dittmar succeeded in increasing the top speed of this trial aircraft to 1003km/h. Then there was a sound that drove the plane into a dive, but Dittmar managed to get the machine back into the air and smoothly landed on the airfield.

"Actually, like all the others, this flight was a pure test flight and should have been tested several times at different altitudes, but it was unthinkable, because the speed we had achieved triggered an enormous activity at the Ministry of Aviation."

One side effect of this increase in activity was a rise in the number of meetings Lippisch was invited to attend at the RLM in Berlin, some of them involving Hermann Göring himself. Lippisch also became

increasingly conscious that despite his tailless aerodynamic ideas having now been 'proven', none of the new aircraft designs being created by Abteilung L were being chosen for development.

He wrote: "Our advocate, General Udet, had chosen suicide and despair about the leadership of the Luftwaffe and his successor, Milch, had nothing more to do than to reduce our programme. Udet had no longer been able to watch with what true dilettante measures the air war was carried out.

"None of the new machines, the single-seater fighter Me 209, the two-engine destroyer Me 210 of the Messerschmitt AG and the big bomber He 177 of

**BELOW: Messerschmitt Super 163.
Art by Daniel Uhr**

Heinkel, were used. They were complete mis-constructions and better types were not in sight. How should the German Luftwaffe, with its now obsolete types of aircraft, face the newly created types of their opponents?"

He bemoans the delays at rocket engine manufacturer Walter which resulted in the Me 163 failing to reach front line service until January 1944, then continues: "Leaving the universally enthusiastically acclaimed features of the Me-163, we also made parallel designs for tailless fighters with turbojet and piston engines, so as not to be reliant on the unsafe rocket.

"We also made designs for fast tailless destroyers and bombers with turbojet or piston engines. These, however, often only reached mock-up stage and none of them were built, since comparisons made with other designs were corrupted and tainted for different reasons.

"In addition to these machinations, all sorts of personal differences had taken place which had a profound effect on productive work. The whole mishap of the aircraft and many other things was already apparent in 1941. In 1941 I often had to go to Berlin, where I noticed many things in the RLM, which did not appear in the press under Goebbels, about the fact that we had lost the war and that it was only a question of preventing a total collapse as far as possible."

It seems unlikely that Lippisch was noticing "many things" at the RLM which indicated that the war was lost in 1941, but nevertheless he was spending more and more time in Berlin while his team got on with their work on the Me 163 B at Augsburg.

He did, however, still find time to muse on what the successor to the Me 163 B might look like. In a notebook bearing his signature and dated January to February 1942, he penned drawings of what he called the 'Super 163', a low aspect ratio interceptor based on the Me 163 with a short and wide delta wing, a longer flatter canopy and a sharply swept tail fin with substantial under-fin. Alongside this, he jotted down calculations on an Me 163 C.

It was the latter that became the subject of a full report on March 23, 1942 – the Super 163 evidently proceeding no further than a handful of calculations and sketches. However, the Me 163 C (Nahaufklärer) or 'Me 163 C (Close reconnaissance)' report

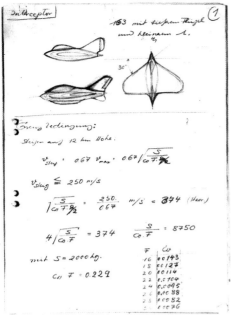

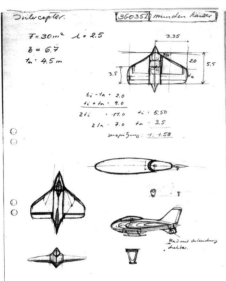

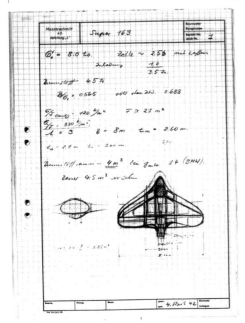

ABOVE: Lippisch's designs for a low aspect ratio interceptor, from a sketchbook dated Jan/Feb 1942 but including work up to April. Earlier designs are labelled simply 'Interceptor' but this later becomes 'Super 163'.

ABOVE: Messerschmitt Me 163 C. Art by Daniel Uhr

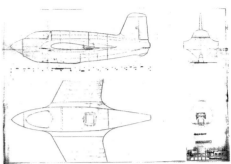

ABOVE: Drawing from the original report on the Me 163 C, dated March 1942. It was to be a reconnaissance version of the Me 163 – with an extended fuselage, camera and small second rocket engine for cruising.

was a stark contrast to the Abteilung L reports which had preceded it. Gone was the 'Abteilung L' headed notepaper, and in its place the standard Messerschmitt AG form complete with title page Messerschmitt logo.

It begins: "Task: To examine the performance of a fuselage of the Me 163 B pattern modified for the purpose of close reconnaissance. In this case, it is assumed that the fuselage is designed without armament and armour and without fuel tank protection. An FK 50/30 camera is to be installed. The aircraft is equipped with a pressurised cabin.

"Constructive measures: The unchanged fuselage of the Me 163 B is unsuitable for the installation of an FK 50/30. By extending the fuselage without changing the wings and tailpiece, i.e. by inserting two sections at the thickest point of the trunk, the space is created."

The aircraft's internal fuel tanks were to be shuffled around to create room for the camera and in addition to the usual 1500kg thrust rocket engine, in this case to be supplied by "BMW (Zborowski)", a second much smaller rocket engine of just 100kg thrust was to be provided to extend the aircraft's cruising range.

In operation, the Me 163 C would climb rapidly to 20,000m (65,616ft) before gliding over its target and then back to base. The maximum possible range would be 900km, though launched from a standing start on the ground using only its own internal engine range would be just 500km.

Summing up, Lippisch writes: "The provision of such an aircraft can take place in the autumn of 1942, if the construction work on the Me 163 B, ending in April 1942, is immediately switched over to this pattern." This was the first appearance of the Me 163 C and would be by no means the last but for now the project went no further.

Lippisch's burden was eased by a new recruit who joined Abteilung L on April 1, 1942 – Walter Stender, a Latvian who had moved to Germany in 1918 with his parents when he was 13. Stender's career began in 1927 when he joined the DVL in Berlin to work as an air accident investigator. This led him to investigate problems associated with 'flutter' and to freelance as an aircraft design consultant before moving to Sweden in 1933 to work on aerobatic aircraft design.

He joined the research department at Hamburger Flugzeugbau, later Blohm & Voss Flugzeugbau, in 1935 and spent the next seven years making a name for himself with his involvement in designs such as the BV 222 and BV 238.

In short, Stender was a very capable engineer and seems to have deputised for Lippisch by undertaking some of the visits to Berlin in his stead. He evidently also met Göring and gained his trust to the point

where the Reichsmarschall would later ask for Stender by name when ordering Willy Messerschmitt to send over a representative to talk about the future of the Me 323.

THE P 10 DISASTER
The Me 210 was a huge failure for Messerschmitt. The chosen successor to the Me 110 heavy fighter, its development had been subject to a string of delays and the aircraft that had been completed proved to be flawed – fatally so in some cases where their pilots were concerned.

Yet there had been such confidence in the conventional twin-engine design that vast quantities of components had been produced and delivered to Messerschmitt's factories in anticipation of full production being given the green light. The expense involved was immense and the company was required to pay all of its suppliers in full.

Production of the Me 210 was cancelled on April 14, 1942, and within a month Willy Messerschmitt had been removed as chairman of the board and managing director of his own company. Even his personal aircraft, Bf 108 D-IMTT, was taken off him.

However, he stayed on at the company as chief designer – giving him direct day-to-day responsibility for both Abteilung L and the conventional project office and making him effectively Lippisch's line manager. In the meantime, Abteilung L had been busy.

Up to the completion of the engineless fuselage of the first Me 163 B prototype in April 1942, the department's project design work had concentrated on single-seat fighters and two-seat heavy fighters – with a few spin-offs including a piston-engine trainer, a long-range heavy bomber and a ground-attack aircraft.

Now Lippisch and his team turned their attention to the 'fast bomber' category. What prompted this change is unclear but the resulting designs are contemporaries of, for example, the Blohm & Voss P 170 fast bomber design so it is possible that

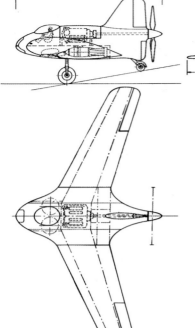

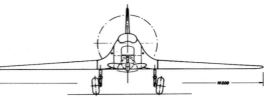

ABOVE: The Messerschmitt P 10 as it was presented to Hermann Göring in mid 1942. He awarded the company a development contract based on this layout.

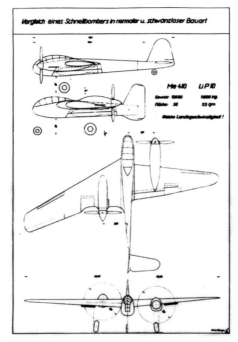

ABOVE: Criticism of the original P 10 prompted Lippisch to swap it for an entirely new design, effectively a tailless Me 410, while retaining the P 10 designation.

an RLM requirement was issued.

The first attempt was a large delta-wing design powered by two rocket engines which was apparently a continuation of Rudolf Rentel's P 09 work. Indeed it was given that same designation, which had previously been applied to its twin-turbojet forebear.

On May 20 another, substantially larger, high-speed bomber was drawn up and given the designation P 10. In Ein Dreieck Fliegt, Lippisch credits Dr Hermann Wurster as the designer of the P 10 – yet a sketch exists, dated May 19, 1942, showing more or less the same aircraft but signed by Lippisch himself.

The P 10 was to be powered by a single 2700hp Daimler-Benz DB 606 – a pair of DB 601 engines joined together – and measured 9.85m in length with a wingspan of 16m. The engine was positioned centrally in the fuselage and drove a single pusher propeller via a long driveshaft. The P 10's pilot sat in the nose under a large bubble canopy which would have afforded excellent visibility in all directions. The tail-sitter undercarriage arrangement was one that Wurster was moving away from in his own designs, having already favoured a tricycle layout for both his revised P 04 and the P 08.

During June 1942 Lippisch appears to have taken the P 10 directly to Göring, and as a result received a contract to build an experimental example of the machine. Perhaps still struggling to adjust to his new circumstances, Messerschmitt himself appears to have been aware of this contract but not the means by which it was obtained.

However, the RLM's own specialists were sceptical about the P 10 and the following month produced a four-page report on it entitled Stellungnahme zum Schnellbomberprojekt Lippisch or 'Opinion on Fast Bomber Project of Lippisch'. This reviewed the design's advantages and drawbacks – the latter including a lack of stability, the central location of the engine's exhaust, the difficulty inherent in accessing

the engine for maintenance and the limited amount of weapons it was able to carry. Taken together, according to the report's anonymous author, these were "found to outweigh the aerodynamic advantages obtained".

This appears to have been enough to convince Lippisch to drop DB 606-powered P 10, but the same designation was then applied to a concept put forward by Stender – converting the Me 210 or 410 into a tailless design –the Me 410 being essentially the same as the Me 210 but fitted with DB 603 engines rather than DB 601s – thereby retaining as much parts commonality with the original as possible. Incidentally, though it may have been abandoned at this point, Lippisch's

own P 10 would soon come back to haunt him. At around this time it seems as though the designation Me 265 was expected to be applied to the 'new' P 10 when it was built.

Discussions were held at Messerschmitt on August 28 about whether Stender's P 10 might offer superior performance to the conventional layout Me 210/410 and a few days later, in early September, Stender produced a 10-page report entitled Warum fliegt das Schwanzlose Flugzeug schneller? or 'Why does the Tailless Aircraft Fly Faster?' in which he argued that his P 10 would outperform the Me 210/410 by virtue of its wing design and having pusher, rather than tractor, engines – allowing the wing to act as a sort of airflow straightener.

This elicited an indignant response from Willy Messerschmitt a few days later – tempered by the knowledge that there was at least a contract to build the P 10. He wrote: "As a result of the discussion on August 28 about the tailless projects for a high-speed bomber, I have stated my opinions regarding the performance of the said projects and proposed that, to clear up once and for all the question of whether such a large aircraft would produce an advantage in performance relative to a conventional aircraft similar to the 210 or 410, wind tunnel measurements and calculations should be put in hand, to which I will come later.

"From wind tunnel measurements which were carried out with models of the 163 and the 210 and 262, it can be concluded that the drag coefficient per unit area is probably smaller for the tailless machine, but by a simple multiplication by the wing area, the drag relative to the same speed will not be smaller for the tailless projects if account is taken of the additional drag which must necessarily occur because of 1) perturbations which are structurally unavoidable e.g. doors of retractable undercarriages, cabin glazing

ABOVE: Concept artwork for the new P 10, which Lippisch claims was designated Me 265. The RLM refused permission for the original P 10's development contract to be reapplied to this new design.
Iowa State University Library Special Collections and University Archive

strips etc. 2) the necessary bulges which occur due to the engine installation 3) the additional drag from the presence of the radiator.

"I am aware that an exact comparison cannot be made on the basis of the calculations since there are some unknowns present, which are not explained in any wind tunnel nor in any flight test, such as, for example, the question of the greater efficiency of a propeller situated at the back.

"In any case the experts here are not yet unanimous as to whether the pusher propeller really has an appreciably higher efficiency than the tractor, since the losses from the rotating slipstream from the tractor propeller are partly alleviated by the wing which acts

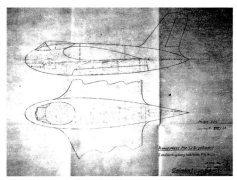

ABOVE: Dr Wurster's Me 329 design from a drawing dated September 24, 1942. It was to be compared against the Me 410 and tailless P 10.

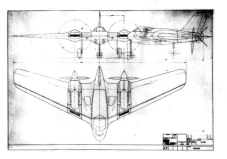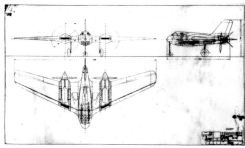

ABOVE: Three-view drawings of the Me 329, believed to be ultimately the development of the P 04, showing it with and without a bomb load.

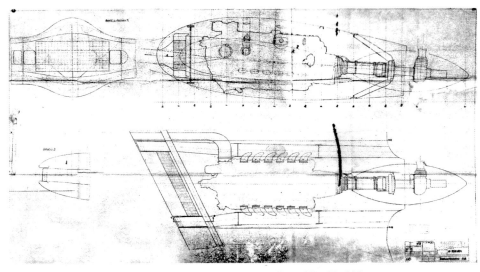

ABOVE: Drawing showing the engine and radiator installation of the Me 329.

as a flow straightener, which is not the case with a tractor airscrew lying behind the wing with no additional flow straightener; this again would mean more drag.

"Now as ever, I am of the opinion that an advance can be achieved in some circumstances with a tailless aircraft but that it is necessary to weigh up carefully how small this tailless aircraft can be built in order to realise the advantage of the missing tailplane and the shorter fuselage.

"To clarify this point, I have proposed that, in a joint effort between the aerodynamicists of Abteilung L and the aerodynamicists of the Project Office, the drag coefficients should be built up separately and not just on the basis of wind tunnel tests and aircraft which do not exhibit any of the perturbations of the type mentioned above.

"I consider this co-operative work and the accurate explanation of the individual drags, in so far as it is possible by calculation, to be absolutely necessary before the tailless aircraft is finally built. The weights of the 210 and 410 have been clearly determined by weighing. The landing speed of the 210 is roughly achieved with the wing loading required for the high-speed bomber.

"How important a low landing speed is has been shown by experience to date, since the Luftwaffe would rather have a higher

landing speed than a lower maximum speed because the maximum speed is the 'weapon'.

"If now the result of the weight estimate for the tailless aircraft shows that its weight is so much higher than the weight of the 210, the reason certainly cannot lie in the equipment, since it is by no means more extensive than that for the 210, but only in the excessively large layout of the tailless aircraft. The main thing to check here is how the weight of the airframe on a tailless

machine must not be greater than that of a conventional machine with a tail unit.

"Naturally, it is true of both aircraft that all the latest experience, the possibility of using jet engines, the improved installation of radiators and the reduction of interference drags, are made use of. It should be noted, however, that by a new arrangement of the whole tail unit the drag of a conventional machine with a tail can probably be reduced by 10%. ▶

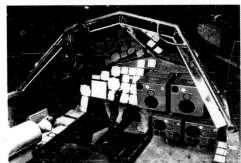

ABOVE: A full-scale mock-up of the Me 329 was constructed. A surprising amount of time, effort and money was invested in the design.

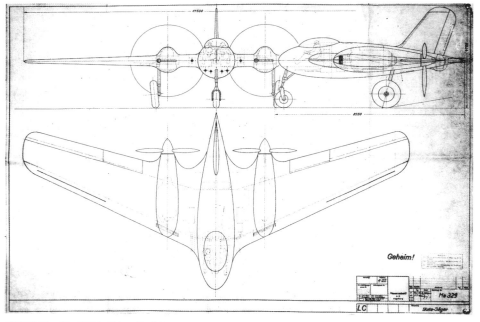

ABOVE: The Me 329 in its earliest form as a fighter-bomber, from Wurster's brochure dated March 15, 1942. It differs from the later form in having an undefined canopy, a different engine installation and heavier armament.

"I therefore propose that Herr Lippisch declares himself ready to join in on these detailed investigations to avoid any comeback later, because the results of the investigation can in no way speak against the tailless machine but can only serve to ensure the success of the tailless aircraft or to make it appear as great as possible."

Messerschmitt went to see Georg Pasewaldt, the head of the development section at the RLM's technical office, on September 10, 1942, and was disturbed to be told Göring was unaware that the original DB 606-powered P 10 had been abandoned. He was doubly disturbed to discover that the contract associated with the original P 10 could not be transferred on to Stender's P 10 and was therefore effectively cancelled.

Writing to his fellow Messerschmitt AG directors after the meeting, Messerschmitt stated: "On that occasion, Pasewaldt spoke to me about the above matter and explained to me that Herr Lippisch had presented to the Secretary of State some time ago a project for a high-speed tailless bomber with the engines arranged in the middle. In the meantime, Lippisch has withdrawn the project from the experts in the department as being impracticable. The Secretary of State [Göring] still knows nothing of this, however.

"In answer to my question as to why this had not been passed on to the Secretary of State, Pasewaldt explained that this was a matter for Lippisch and our company, since Lippisch had bypassed the official channels and personally given the project to the Secretary of State. The responsibility for this was carried by the company, naturally. I took note of this and agreed that the matter will be straightened out by the company.

"The new P 10 projects were familiar to Pasewaldt. He stated that he and his experts had doubts about this layout. I then told Pasewaldt that there was a contract from the RLM for the design and construction of a flying experimental aircraft, whereupon Pasewaldt explicitly stated that this contract related to the original project under the obvious condition that everything was in the open.

"In no way did this contract relate to further projects. These must first be examined by the department and be approved for design and construction if satisfactory. The work must, therefore, be stopped immediately in so far as it went beyond the project work and what pertained to it. Also, the demand for personnel and accommodation by Lippisch personally was inappropriate in so far as the project was not approved.

"On this matter I discovered yet again that Lippisch and/or Stender are making visits to the RLM without informing the Berlin office and involving Urban. As the matter stands at the moment, I consider an immediate intervention to be necessary. Lippisch is giving project schemes with performance figures to the ministry and the company then has to take the responsibility for them.

"As the responsible leader of the whole technical department, I must insist that this is conducted along properly controlled lines. As I have already demanded some days ago, I must have the opportunity to check all information before it is sent to the ministry. I propose, therefore, that the whole matter is aired at a meeting of the board and that Lippisch gets an instruction as to how he has to fit into the company."

ME 329 TO THE RESCUE?

The revelation that the P 10 contract was now lost seems to have resulted in some internal recriminations between Lippisch and Stender, with Wurster also entering the fray by attempting to rescue the situation with a new design of his own devising – yet another Me 210/410 competitor derived from the P 04 studies. It was a tailless fighter-bomber with twin wing-mounted engines in a pusher configuration. A broad fuselage allowed space for the pilot and radio operator to sit side-by-side and defensive weaponry was installed in a small remote-controlled turret beneath the central fin at the rear. Stender appears to have publicly dismissed this latest P 04 relative as "amateurish".

Again writing to his fellow directors in late September, Messerschmitt noted: "I have not closely studied the sketch but I propose to wait for the investigation already under way. I must only point out that a tailless aircraft designed for the same landing speed could not be faster than a conventional aircraft for the same state of the engineering art.

Messerschmitt Me 329. Art by Daniel Uhr

"The investigation which I have put in hand has the intention of clearing up basically whether aircraft for a specified application, if built tailless, would be faster or more capable than aircraft with a tail and how much the higher capability amounts to.

"I consider this investigation to be absolutely necessary so that a picture is obtained of how big the tailless aircraft can be designed with capabilities considerably higher than those of the developed 210. In this respect, care must essentially be taken to ensure that the landing speed of the 210 is not exceeded. If the investigation should show that the tailless aircraft is a good bit faster than the developed 210 but the landing speed is lower than that of the 210, that would be a further gain and an advantage for the tailless machine.

"By this investigation I only want to prevent an aircraft being built whose most important performance figure, namely speed, is no higher than that of the developed 210, since otherwise the problem would not be properly solved.

"I would like to avoid going in detail into the comparison of Herr Stender, since the investigation already set up will clarify all these questions. Nevertheless, I consider it important that these reciprocal reproaches between Lippisch, Stender and Dr Wurster be eliminated, particularly as they are not well founded. The proposal from Dr Wurster is certainly not amateurish but has a number of advantages relative to the other proposal which are undeniable. I am certainly capable of forming an opinion on the basis of my many years of practical experience."

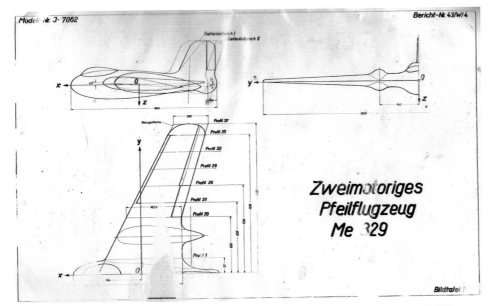

Modell Nr. J-7062

Bericht-Nr. 43/W/4

Zweimotoriges
Pfeilflugzeug
Me 329

Bildtafel 1

ABOVE: A damaged drawing of an Me 329 wind tunnel test model, showing a potential tail fin variation.

ABOVE: Poor quality photographs show a model of the Me 329 used for wind tunnel tests.

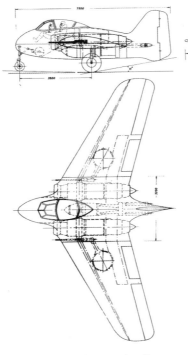

ABOVE: Abteilung L's P 11 two-seater twin-jet fast bomber, dated September 13, 1942.

Wurster's new design, its designation unknown today though it may have been referred to as the P 04, appears to have been favourably received by Messerschmitt and later the RLM. However, Lippisch and Stender continued to push the P 10.

On November 16, 1942, Lippisch produced a 22-page report entitled Vergleich eines Schnellbombers normaler und schwanzloser Bauart or 'Comparison of a Fast Bomber of Normal or Tailless Design' which directly refuted Messerschmitt's letter of early September, arguing that Stender's P 10 was almost identical in weight to the

Me 410 and had the same landing speed.

It was a lost cause, however, and on December 8, 1942, the first Messerschmitt Me 410 was delivered. And in the meantime, there had been another political shift at Messerschmitt – on November 7, 1942, Theo Croneiss died aged 47. Croneiss, though a great friend, colleague and supporter of Messerschmitt himself, had also been a supporter of Lippisch since 1931, as previously related. His loss may have contributed to the deteriorating relationship between the two men. Then Lippisch's surviving parent, his mother Clara, died on December 31, 1942, which must have resulted in further personal business to attend to.

On January 29, 1943, Messerschmitt wrote to Lippisch: "I have heard yet again that you have been discussing projects with the RLM's technical office and, once more, must insist that you stop doing this and, in

the future, discuss all projects with me before visiting the RLM. I can no longer accept that you, as a member of Messerschmitt AG, undertake steps which have not been previously approved by the board of directors.

"In addition, you must always take a member of the Berlin office with you like everyone else when visiting the RLM's technical office."

In the meantime, Wurster's P04-related design, first presented as the Me 329 in a March 15, 1942, brochure, was gaining traction both at Messerschmitt and the RLM. A full scale mock-up was constructed and wind tunnel testing of models was commenced.

A full report on the project, complete with photographs of the mock-up, was published on February 5, 1943. Unusually, the report bears no author's name or signature and there is no mention of Abteilung L anywhere either. Under "intended use" it says: "This project design is a destroyer. The aircraft can be used as: heavy fighter, escort, night fighter, stuka, bomber or armed reconnaissance aircraft. The tailor-made design chosen for this project is superior to the corresponding aircraft of the usual design in flight performance, flight characteristics, armament and vulnerability."

The report offers the usual Abteilung L arguments to support this bold assertion: lower drag, better propeller efficiency because of air being 'smoothed' by the wing before it reached them, lower weight and ease of passage through barrage balloons.

It throws in a few attractive extras too, unique to the Me 329: "In this version, the aircraft is likely to have the strongest bow and stern armour. In addition, the project also takes into account the possibility of installing further, even stronger shooting and launching weapons. There is the possibility to install two 8.8cm cal. or two 3.7cm anti-aircraft guns to fight heavy tanks and light naval forces. The use of thicker calibre than MG 151/20 for the rear weapon is also possible.

"As a launching weapon, all calibres between 0 and 1000kg can be suspended internally and calibres between 0 and 2500kg, also the Marinetorpedo, outside. For the use as a pathfinder, accompanying fighters or night fighters, an additional tank with 1000kg fuel can be accommodated in the bomb bay to increase the range.

"As a particularly great advantage, we consider the arrangement of the crew next to each other, which ensures a better cooperation and communication possibility for the crew. For both crew members, sight-free visibility is achieved according to the latest guidelines for destroyers. The possibility of such close co-operation between the crew during the whole mission reduces the burden of the individual and increases the fighting power considerably."

ABOVE: Two views of Messerschmitt Me 163 BV2, VD-EL, photographed at Augsburg in September 1942 before being fitted with four 20mm MG 151s for firing trials in October.

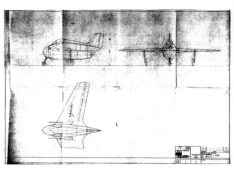

ABOVE: The final Abteilung L design – the Me 163-derived P 20 jet fighter. This drawing is dated April 16, 1943, and shows an early version of the design.

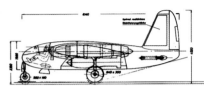

ABOVE: Lippisch evidently realised that the concept of a twin-jet bomber had potential and stuck at P 11, evolving it into this aerodynamically cleaner version, dated December 2, 1942.

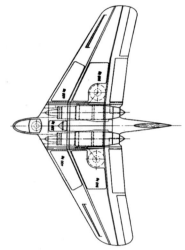

The forward section of the Me 329's fuselage was to comprise a pressure cabin for the crew with four fixed forward-firing weapons installed under their feet. In the centre was the bomb bay with a large fuel tank directly above it and to the rear was the defensive turret.

The tricycle landing gear was hydraulic and structurally the Me 329 strongly resembled the P 04, with the wings divided into inner, outer and engine supporting centre sections. The engines themselves would be DB 603s – making the Me 329 still more of a competitor with the Me 410 – or Jumo 213s but where the P 04's would be lifted out, the Me 329's would be unscrewed and dropped out for even easier access.

As 'standard' the Me 329 was offered with two MG 151/20s and two MK 103s in the four forward-firing positions, with an FHL 151 rear turret controlled by the radio operator/navigator via a periscope.

Bomb options suggested for use in the internal bay were one SC 1000, two SC 500s or four SC 250s. The report notes that externally the Me 329 was ideal for "bombs with jet thrust and rail guides fixed to the lower fuselage".

The crew would be protected from incoming fire up to 15mm from the front by armour plating and from fire to the rear by the fuel tank behind them. The engines combined oil and water coolers would have 20mm armour to prevent damage

from the front and would be protected from the rear by the engines themselves and the aircraft's steel wing spar.

As a final argument, rather than a prose summary the report provides details of comparative wind tunnel tests carried out on models of the Me 210, Me 410 and Me 329 by the AVA at Göttingen. These apparently concluded that in performance terms the Me 329 and Me 410 were on a par but it was expected that in practice the pusher configuration of the Me 329 would give it the advantage – an idea evidently difficult to conclusively demonstrate or debunk in a wind tunnel.

Nothing further on the Me 329 seems to appear after this point and with the Me 410 now in production it seems clear that the time for Wurster's design had passed.

ALL GOOD THINGS

While the P 10/Me 329 drama was being played out with Lippisch, Stender and Wurster arguing for the various designs, other members of Abteilung L had continued to work on designs to suit the high-speed bomber role. Rudolf Rentel's P 09 and P 010 twin-turbojet high-speed bombers had been followed up by another Abteilung L designer, Handrick, with a third refinement of the design on September 13 – the P 11. This was presented as either single-seater or a two-seater where the others had been purely single-seaters but now the tail-sitter arrangement of the earlier pair was replaced with a tricycle layout.

Over the next three months, the P 11 was still further refined. The two-seater option was abandoned and the engine intakes were tidied up considerably.

At the same time one of Lippisch's longest serving staffers, aerodynamicist Josef Hubert, was working in parallel on the P 12. Two versions of this high-speed bomber, apparently intended as a turbojet revival of the original long-abandoned DB 606 P 10 appeared on September 30, 1942. Its unusual

shape was dictated by the sheer size of the BMW 3303 jet engine intended to power it.

And Hubert produced another, final, DB 606 P 10 alternative on November 25 with the P 13. This took the basic concept of the centrally mounted 'twin engine' DB 606 and imagined how the type might look with two entirely separate piston engines – one centrally mounted and driving a pusher prop, like the original P 10, but the other fitted in the nose to drive a tractor prop in a tandem push-pull arrangement.

Abteilung L's P 12 went nowhere and neither did the P 13 but Lippisch seems to have become increasingly convinced that Handricks' P 11 had potential.

Stender left the company during early March to take up a new position with the aircraft construction department at the Zeppelinwerke in Friedrichshafen, specifically to take charge of the Me 323's ongoing development, which had been passed on to Zeppelin.

A meeting was held on March 26, 1943, attended by Lippisch and Messerschmitt's managing director Friedrich Seiler. According to the minutes: "Herr Seiler informed Herr Lippisch of the order of Oberst Pasewaldt dated March 20 in accordance with which Abteilung L is to be entirely incorporated into the overall organisation of Messerschmitt AG. Herr Lippisch stated that he was in agreement with this action. As a result Herr Seiler informed Oberst Pasewaldt that this order had been carried out.

"It is now agreed that Herr Lippisch will give up his position as an employee of the Messerschmitt company and take up a professorship in Vienna. In accordance with a proposal of the Messerschmitt company, Herr Lippisch will conclude a consultancy agreement with the Messerschmitt company. The draft of such an agreement submitted to the Secretary of State was presented to Herr Lippisch and received his basic approval.

"As far as it concerns the ownership of the patents which are taken out because of the collaboration of Herr Lippisch within the framework of this agreement, Herr Lippisch proposed that all these patents, even if they were attributable to his own inventions, should belong to Messerschmitt AG and that he himself is not interested in their industrial exploitation. Only the free right to joint use is to be belong to Herr Lippisch.

"Herr Lippisch was given a copy of the draft of the consultancy agreement. He will give his opinion on this, if possible

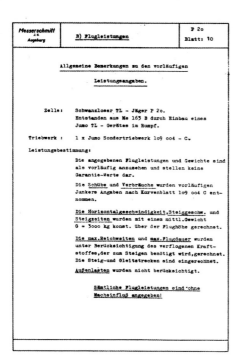

ABOVE: The April 19 report on the P 20 gives surprisingly scant details about the design.

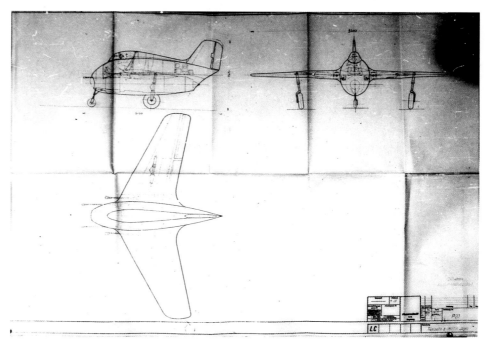

ABOVE: The post-Abteilung L P 20 of June 23, 1943. The design has grown 37cm longer and 18cm tall though the wingspan is the same.

before April 2, particularly regarding the amount of the indemnification, about which he would first like to speak when he knows what income he is to expect from the research institute in Vienna.

"Herr Seiler declared that Herr Lippisch's salary from the present contract with Messerschmitt AG would in any case continue to be paid until Herr Lippisch was enjoying the salary from the research institute. Herr Seiler asked Herr Lippisch explicitly about the wishes that Herr Lippisch might have in connection with the termination of the present contractual conditions with Messerschmitt AG. He emphasised in this respect that Professor Messerschmitt recognised the services of Herr Lippisch in the field of aeronautical research and estimated highly the value of his work.

"He placed great importance on the need

to completely reconcile the differences with Professor Messerschmitt evoked by Herr Lippisch's letter and insisted that the departure of Herr Lippisch should take place in a friendly spirit. The financial demands of Herr Lippisch had been treated by Messerschmitt AG in such a way that they would in no way become an impediment to a complete agreement.

"Herr Lippisch only made the request that five of his closest colleagues whose names he has already given to Herr Bley, should be allocated to him for his future work. Herr Seiler stated his agreement to this. As far as the financial requirements are concerned, Herr Lippisch will make his views known after discussion with the research institute."

Abteilung L still had one last card to play, however. On April 19, 1943, a report was produced on the P 20. The design itself was for a stubby single jet fighter or bomber. The report lacks an introduction – commencing on Blatt 1 or 'Page 1' with a graph showing only the performance of the Jumo 004 C – and is produced on 'Messerschmitt AG Projektbüro' standard forms.

The only text given in a total of 11 pages is almost a series of bullet points: "General comments on the provisional performance specifications. Fuselage: Tailless jet fighter P 20. Originated from Me 163 B by installing a Jumo jet device in the fuselage. Engine: 1 x Jumo special engine 109 004 C.

"Power determination: The indicated flights and weights are to be regarded as provisional and do not constitute guarantee values. The thrusts and consumptions were taken from preliminary Junkers data according to curve sheet 109 004 C.

"The horizontal speed, climbing speed and climbing times were measured with an average speed. Weight = 3000kg. No external loads were taken into account. All flight performances are without Mach influence!" The exclamation mark at the end seems to speak volumes for the incredulity of the report's author, presumably a member of Messerschmitt's conventional project office, concerning the performance numbers being claimed for the P 20. The drawing attached, dated April 16, is by Wurster.

Finally, a memo dated April 27, 1943, shows the 86 remaining members of Abteilung L, including nearly all of the men who had followed Lippisch from the DFS, being divided up between the project office, stress office, design office, flight test department, workshops and administration office of Messerschmitt AG. Lippisch officially left the company the following day, April 28.

Abteilung L might have been gone but several of the projects it created lived on – most notably the Me 163 and its derivatives but also the P 11 and the P 20, the latter if only for a little while. ●

ABOVE: The P 20 survived long enough to be compared against the Me 262 and two conventional layout designs in a July 3, 1943 report but appears to have been dropped at that point.

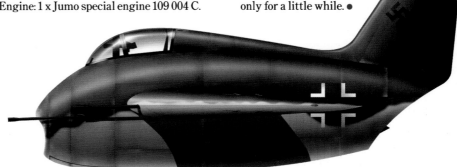

ABOVE: Messerschmitt P 20. Art by Daniel Uhr

All-wing jet

The Horten IX

Conceived simply as a jet-propelled flying wing in 1942, the Horten IX has gone on to rank among the most controversial aircraft projects of the Second World War.

During the winter of 1941-42, Walter Horten gave his brother Reimar rough copies he had made of documents showing the projected performance and physical dimensions of an entirely unfamiliar type of engine – the turbojet.

Specifically Walter had managed to gather information on the Junkers Jumo 004 being developed by Dr Anselm Franz

ABOVE: The undeniably magnificent Horten H IX V1 glider. It was completed at the beginning of March 1944 and flew shortly afterwards.

at Dessau, but at this stage the new invention seemed little more than a high-tech curiosity. However, a few months later Walter brought his brother some more exciting news – it might soon be possible to lay hands on the real thing.

Reimar later recalled: "It was in the first months of 1942 that we began thinking in turbojets and Walter found out that we could obtain two of them from Dr Franz at Junkers. Walter first told me about these turbojet engines in November or December 1941, however, but it was only after learning that we could actually get two of them in about six months, did I get down to some serious thinking."

Unfortunately, Walter's hastily hand-drawn copies of the original document proved to be inaccurate: "Walter had copied the thrust curves of a Jumo 004 by placing

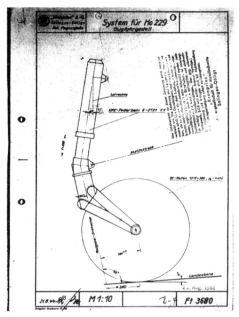

ABOVE: One of the earlier known 8-229 (rather than H IX) design drawings is this nosewheel by Kronpriz AG, a company which still exists today, dated August 21, 1944.

ABOVE: Another view of the H IX V1 with the man walking alongside giving a sense of scale.

ABOVE: The H IX V1 is rolled out of its hangar at Göttingen for another flight.

the original sheets up to a window and made a tracing. But they had been wrong. They were 600kg where I thought that they had been 900kg. So I calculated that what we needed for gliding was not clear yet."

Nevertheless, Reimar began to sketch out ideas for what might be done with a single turbojet or two.

"First I thought to place a single turbojet engine on the H VII, outside the circle of the propellers," he said. "Thus we would have two piston engines as well as one turbojet. But there was a thing about weight. The H VII was designed to take off and land on grass. However, if we placed two Junkers turbojets on the H VII too, it meant that this aircraft could no longer land on grass. It would be too heavy and it meant that it would only be able to land on concrete runways.

"This I thought would be bad for it would limit the use of the turbojet-powered H VII to only hard surfaced runways. Plus, I figured that the air intakes for the turbojets would have to be fairly high up from the runway to avoid the picking up of dirt, rocks and other items. The higher, I thought, the better."

The most difficult problem to overcome, however, was the need to strengthen the H VII's structure. Reimar calculated that

the covering of the wings would need to be 7-8mm thick, compared to 2.5mm of the existing design. The internal spars would need to be significantly strengthened too.

Reimar said that when he broke the news to Walter, his brother quickly came up with a solution: "I told Walter that we could not use the H VII as we first had planned. We'd have to leave the H VII as it is. For the turbojets, we would have to design a whole new plane.

"At this moment he made a model of a twin-engine turbojet all-wing aircraft. The engines were placed partially in the wing, however, we now had a form which the H IX might take. Later on I calculated that the aerodynamics were not good and so I found that I had to give the H IX another shape. Thus, step by step, we went through a series of designs to come up with the final H IX planform.

"This first model which Walter built did not have a number, however, he had shown them this model in the RLM, how our proposed all-wing turbojet-powered fighter would look once it was built. So while he was showing this model I had come up with another."

Having worked out that his brother's concept was flawed, Reimar reasoned that

ABOVE: The H IX in gliding flight.

▶

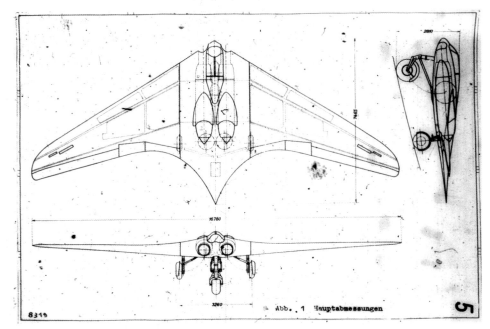

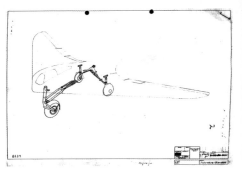

ABOVE: The 8-229's tricycle undercarriage arrangement.

ABOVE: A three-view drawing of the 8-229 from an unusual document published by Gotha on November 22, 1944, entitled Vorläufige Baubeschreibung or 'preliminary building description'. It gives a full description of the 8-229 without naming it once.

it would be better to have what he was now calling the H IX's engines entirely above the wing: "The first model of the proposed turbojet-powered aircraft of ours had the turbojets mounted fully above the wings. Later on I designed the two engines to be fully enclosed in the interior of the wing. But the turbojets above the wings was my first thinking and we in fact changed the design several times before settling on what was to become the H IX."

No drawings of the early H IX concepts appear to have survived but another potential version was outlined by Reimar when discussing Rudolf Göthert's Gotha P-60 design with David Myhra. Myhra asked him: "What do you think of Göthert's placement of a turbojet on top and one on the bottom?" He replied: "Oh, that could

not be. That arrangement we had for the first time with the H IX. If a turbojet is placed on the lower side it will pick up all the sand and dirt from the runway and its life will be shortened considerably.

"Placing the turbojets on the outside along is the same form we had for the delta also, however, the turbojets were all to be placed above the wing. That could not be then because we did not have clean runways during the war."

The H IX design evolved during the course of 1942 as Sonderkommando LIn 3 continued to work on the brothers' H V and H VII projects.

Reimar told Myhra: "I believed that I would need about six months building time to construct the H IX. Later on I expected to have the first drawings of

the proposed H IX within three months. Then later on in the workshop I could continue the drawings but at least we would have the H IX under construction.

"This aircraft was not one in which I could say to my workers 'well, tomorrow we go into the workshop and begin'. Therefore I figured I'd need about 12 months to complete the drawings, start construction and get the aircraft ready for flight. I thought that the H IX prototype would be flying by the summer of 1943.

"Several components of the H IX we started building right away. However, Walter kept telling us that all the parts of this aircraft would have to be very strong because this would be a very fast aircraft. I answered that if it will be faster, then I need more men to build it.

"Therefore I soon received more men, draftsmen, engineers and others to help me. Also these extra men included welders to construct the centre section etc. Now we had grown to between 80 to 100 men in the workshop at Göttingen. Well, Walter was organising all this at Göttingen from Berlin and the Air Ministry did not know anything about it.

"Then when the work was going and started and we still had no order to build the H IX, somehow the Air Ministry found

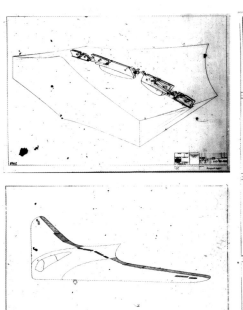

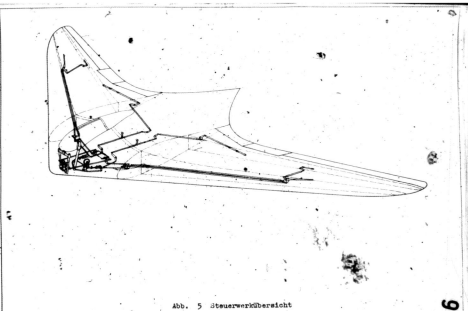

ABOVE: Drawings showing the 8-229's control system, air brakes and control surfaces.

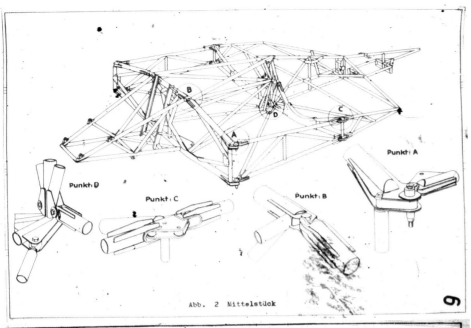

Abb. 2 Mittelstück

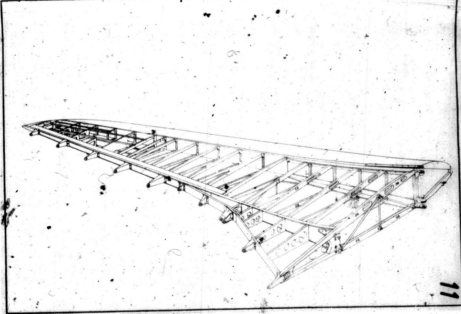

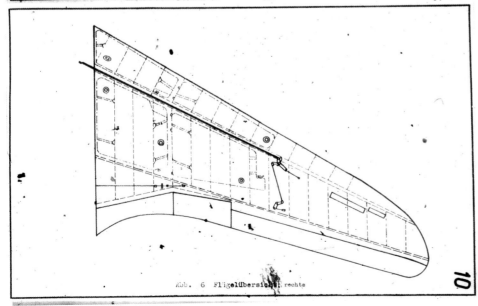

Abb. 6 Flügelübersicht, rechte

ABOVE: The internal structure of the 8-229 is illustrated in these three drawings from Gotha's November 22, 1944 report.

out about our Sonderkommando LIn 3 and they sent me a telegram, telling me to stop all the work immediately. This was about the spring of 1943. We were working with my men on all our things. When this telegram came Walter was angry."

Shortly after the arrival of the telegram, the head of the organisation in Göttingen which had leant its carpenters to Sonderkommando LIn 3 arrived at the workshop and asked for them back because he had been told that the unit was being shut down. Thinking quickly, Reimar asked the man how he had heard this information, because the work going on there was supposed to be top secret.

He sent the man away, telling him not to speak to anyone about what he had seen or heard. Reimar then remembered an order that had gone out calling for the dispersal of production facilities to protect them from bombing raids. The brothers decided to do just that. They transferred their H VI glider work to Bonn with 12 men, sent all the fully built gliders they had to the Wasserkuppe and moved their other Göttingen work to new premises in Herzfeld. Reimar told Walter to get him an order for the H IX so that work on it could continue without interruption.

Clearing out the hangar at Göttingen, Reimar said: "I found two new wings for an H III and was wondering how I might use these wings. My idea was still on high-speed flight characteristics and I decided to place them on a centre section so that they would have a sweepback of 60 . All I had to do was to make a new centre section and a few changes more and in this form was born the H XIII.

"I gave it the name of the 'XIII' because it had the wings of the H III. Also I felt too, that we must have knowledge of the highly swept-back wing, a feature we thought was very important during high-speed flight."

Shortly after the 'dispersal' of Sonderkommando LIn 3, presumably in March 1943, Walter attended a speech made to aviation industry leaders where Hermann Göring had called for an aircraft that could carry 1000kg of bombs 1000km with a maximum speed of 1000km/h. This appeared to be the opportunity that the brothers had been hoping for. If they could massage the H IX design to meet this specification, at least in part, they might have an opportunity to secure a development contract.

Reimar said later: "Walter came to Minden and he told me that 'yesterday I heard Göring speak about his desire for a 3x1000 fighter/bomber. No one in the aircraft industry has this type of aircraft'. I told Walter, let us see what we can do and we'll build a tailless plane.

"I suggested the H IX with a 16m span, with twin Junkers 004 turbojets, and the performance I calculated, we can build such a 3x1000 project in the form of the H IX. I can do it. Perhaps 950km/h is the speed we'll obtain. I said that we'll offer 950km/h speed, 700km range and 2000kg of bombs to Göring.

"I made the preliminary things and Walter came back in about two weeks and I had finished the general design proposal. It had approximately 20 pages in length.

▶

ABOVE: The 8-229 was supposed to use an ejection seat lifted from a Focke-Wulf Ta 154. This photograph shows an ejection seat fitted into an 8-229 frame for tests.

He took it to General Diesing, Göring's chief of staff. He was surprised that we had presented something. Later Göring called us and wanted us to come and meet with him."

By this time, the H IX's spec had changed to the use of BMW 003 turbojets, rather than Jumo 004s. The precise date of the Hortens' meeting with Göring is questionable. It has been given as being as late as September 28. Reimar himself however, during his interviews with Myhra, gives the date as 'August 1943' several times – presumably the very end of August – the logic being that Göring gave the brothers six months to get the H IX flying and they just about barely managed to hit a deadline of March 1, 1944, for the first unpowered flight of the H IX V1.

"I told him that he could have an aircraft with this performance," said Reimar of his meeting with Göring. "I was working with all my men to prepare the drawings etc. This was in August 1943. Göring said that he wanted this aircraft within three months. I said that it would take at least six months. Thus six months from August 1943 was February 1944, to have it flying.

"We had some good luck too, for the BMW 003 engines were not ready so we could work on the aircraft and get it ready. But I decided to fly a model of the H IX without the engine for it would be much more easy to build such an aircraft without engines, fuel tanks, wiring, pumps etc.

"We simply could not finish the powered model in six months as Göring wanted. Therefore the first H IX was the same aircraft as the powered model except without engines, fuel tanks, and so on and we made it fly in February 1944. Later on we needed more time to finish the H IX V2."

He said that even the six months to build the unpowered V1 "was only possible due to our previous preparation and work on the H IX which had taken place without any order". Walter then changed the name of Sonderkommando LIn 3 to Luftwaffenkommando

IX in honour of the project.

And then there was the money. In 1938, the Hortens had asked the RLM for 500,000RM to build the three H VII prototypes, now Göring offered them the same sum. Reimar said Erhard Milch had given Walter the order for the construction of the H IX, although it had come from Göring: "Milch drew up all the paperwork for the transfer of the 500,000RM grant from Göring. Milch asked us who should this contract be made out to? Hauptmann Horten or what? Walter paused and told Milch that he was not sure, however he would return in a day or two with the correct information. Before going back to Milch, we incorporated ourselves and called our new company the Horten Company for Aircraft Design or the Horten Flugzeugbau".

He said that he and his brother did not keep track of how much of the 500,000RM they had spent however: "I do not know how much money we had used. Walter spent several days in Dessau to arrange for funds. We never had any problems and the Ministry of Finance said that they would add up all the expenditure after the war... so for now go about and construct the aircraft which the Reich needed."

The unpowered H IX V1 was indeed ready on March 1, 1944 – albeit with a Heinkel He 177 tail wheel assembly as its nosewheel, main landing gear wheels from a Messerschmitt Bf 109G, components from a captured B-24 Liberator and other assorted bits and pieces from a damaged Me 210. Bad weather delayed its first flight however, so the brothers sent Göring a telegram anyway, telling him that the aircraft had flown, even though it had not.

Finally, on March 5, 1944, it was towed up to 3600m by a He 111 before gliding back down to the runway but on touching down the pilot found he was unable to brake effectively on the icy runway. In order to avoid collision with a hangar, he deliberately retracted the nosewheel, putting the

skidding aircraft's nose onto the ground.

More tests followed on March 23 and April 5. During the latter, the nosewheel failed and repairs led to further delays. There was still no sign of the BMW 003 becoming available for the H IX V2 – the powered version – so the Hortens reverted back to their earlier intention of using Jumo 004s and the V2's airframe was designed according to the dimensions Walter had come up with back in the winter of 1941.

These showed that each engine was effectively a tube 60cm in diameter. However, Reimar later discovered that with all the necessary accessories added to their exterior, the engines were actually closer to 80cm. This was a major problem and necessitated a redesign. Reimar said: "I resolved to make the centre section greater by one additional rib on each side – 40cm and 40cm, 80cm in total. And raise the height of the profile about 13% to 15%. With this increase in height, I could fit in the 80cm Jumo 004 turbojet. This change cost us one full month."

The original plan had called for the V2 to be flown for the first time on June 1, 1944, but work was still ongoing as this deadline passed. The RLM placed an order with Horten Flugzeugbau for a number of further prototype H IXs on June 15 with the new type designation 8-229. The '8-' simply denoting a powered aircraft.

Horten Flugzeugbau, however, did not have the facilities or the manpower to build more than the one airframe it was then working on. A subcontractor was needed.

Reimar told Myhra: "Gotha had not done any work for us before they received the order to continue production of the H IX. The name of Gotha was mentioned to us about August of 1944. Walter mentioned to me that he was thinking about using Gotha to manufacture the H IX series. I told him it did not matter to me which firm was picked to build it because I was not interested in that part of aircraft production.

"My main interest was in design and development work. Once it got to production I did not want to be involved. I had other things to do. It was now the RLM's responsibility to see our series production should take place and how. Gotha had had some practice in wood construction so they had been selected by Walter and the RLM.

"Klemm had also been selected as a builder of what was now being called the Ho 229. Klemm had had considerable experience in building light places and Walter and the RLM had selected Klemm at the same time they had picked Gotha. The thing with Gotha is that during the war they had built for DFS their 230 troop glider. They had changed the design, not aerodynamically but in structure to be built in series. With these modifications by Gotha, they had not really been wanted by the troops. For the modifications they had made in order to ease construction had been bad and several DFS 230 gliders had broken up in flight.

"So I told Walter, I want you to observe Gotha during the construction of H IX V3 through V6 that they don't make any modifications which might harm the aircraft during flight, just for the sake of quicker construction."

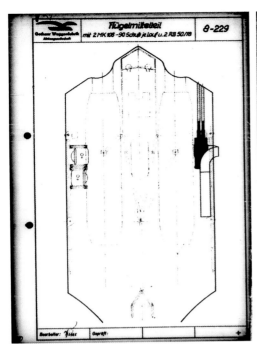 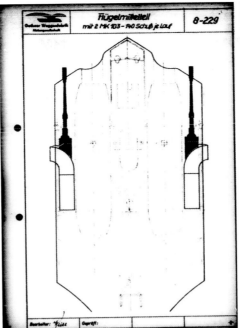 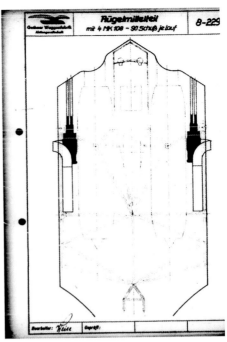

ABOVE: Three different potential armament options for the 8-229 V6 outlined in a Gotha report by Kalb and Weise dated December 15, 1944.

In fact, Gotha aerodynamics specialist Rudolf Göthert, who had worked for the firm since 1942, told his Allied interrogators in 1945 that the company had become involved with the H IX/8-229 project as early as late 1943 or early 1944. The Hortens had little faith in Göthert but nevertheless, Gotha set to work on the four airframes.

Horten Flugzeugbau was still struggling to complete the H IX V2 by November 1944. The work was briefly discussed during a meeting of the Entwicklungshauptkommission, the recently formed chief development commission for aircraft, on November 21-22: "The Ho 229 was to be developed in conjunction with Gotha, and three prototypes of the Horten VII were to be completed."

When the H IX was given its RLM designation in June, it had been the 8-229. During the normal course of a new aircraft's development, the '8-' would very quickly be replaced in reports by the lettered prefix indicating the manufacturer – so the 8-262 became the Messerschmitt Me 262 in reports and the 8-162 became the Heinkel He 162.

It would appear that, initially, this process was followed for the H IX. The earliest available Gotha report concerning the type, produced on September 7, 1944, refers to it as the Ho 229. Another report of September 23, 1944, does likewise, as does a report of October 2, 1944.

However, on October 11, 1944, a Gotha report refers to the type as the 'Ho IX'. Then a report of October 31, 1944, refers to the type as the 8-229. The 'Ho' has gone. Then 8-229, without the 'Ho', appears on reports dated November 20, 22 and 24, December 12 and 17, February 28, 1945, and March 1 and March 2, 1945. The March 1 report was written by Reimar himself and he also uses '8-229' rather than 'Ho 229'.

A report produced by Junkers on March 7, a company involved in the 8-229 project for around a year by that point, is headed "Triebwerkeinbau in Go 229 (Horten) (V3 +

V5)" and refers to the Go 229 throughout. It would seem odd for a company so familiar with the project and so heavily involved in it to suddenly begin giving it the wrong name without good reason. The report author presumably wrote "(Horten)" after Go 229 to make it clear which project they were talking about for those who were familiar with it by another name.

An inference might be drawn that the earlier 'backwards step' from Ho 229 to 8-229 indicates that something other than 'Ho' was destined to end up in the type's official designation and the most likely candidate would indeed have been the 'Go' of Gotha.

Unusually, the British report German Aircraft: New and Projected Types has two listings for the 8-229. The first is headed "Horten IX twin-jet fighter" and the second "Gotha 8-229 V6 development of Horten IX".

The description of the Gotha 8-229 V6 reads: "The Horten IX flying wing twin-jet fighter is described in another section of this report. Development of this aircraft was transferred to Gotha and it received the RLM designation 8-229.

"The V6 prototype is powered by 2 x Jumo 004 turbo-jet units and the centre section is rather different from that of the Horten IX, having been thickened by the addition of a shallow bulge on the underside. The jet unit intakes are straight instead of being upswept as on the Horten IX."

The description of the H IX states: "In shape the Ho IX is a pure wing of increased chord at the centre-section to give sufficient thickness to house the pilot and jet units. The centre-section is built up from welded steel tube and the wing tips are of metal. Wing structure comprises one main and one auxiliary wooden spar with plywood covering. All fuel tanks are housed in the wings.

"A retractable undercarriage and a castering nose wheel is fitted. Elevon controls and drag rudder are fitted, also a spoiler and landing flaps.

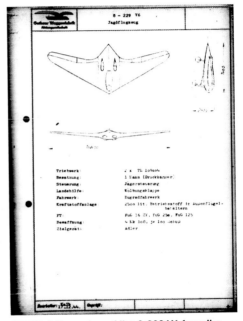

ABOVE: A three-view of the 8-229 V6 from the December 15 report. At this stage it is clear that the aircraft is to be a single seater.

"Jet intakes are spaced out in the centre section, one on either side of the cockpit, and exhaust over the upper surface. To prevent burning, metal plates are fitted aft of the exhaust and cold air is bled from the lower surface of the wing and introduced between the jet and the wing surface."

As 1944 drew to a close, the jet-propelled H IX V2 had yet to fly. Gotha was building four more examples – V3 to V6 – and the type's formal designation was in doubt. Yet more than the 8-229's name was at stake. Up until now, it appeared as though the aircraft would be a single-seat heavy fighter or fighter-bomber. But that type had traditionally been a two-seater, such as the Bf 110. Would the final production version of the 8-229 be a two-seater too?. ●

One thousand times three

While the Horten brothers were scrambling to ensure that their H IX met Hermann Göring's 1000km/h top speed, 1000kg bomb load and 1000km range, they had no idea that someone had already beaten them to the punch. In fact, it seems highly likely that the idea had originated with Alexander Lippisch in the first place…

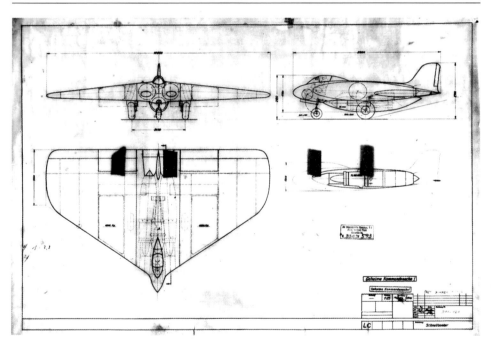

ABOVE: The earliest known post-Messerschmitt P 11 design is dated May 17, 1943. It has only a single central tailfin and is shown carrying an SC 1000 bomb in a aerodynamic centreline fairing.

When Lippisch left Messerschmitt at the end of April 1943, he went to take up a professorship at the Luftfahrtforschungsanstalt Wien (LFW) or 'Aeronautical Research Institute Vienna'.

The nature of his new position effectively put him in charge of the LFW, a subdivision of a larger parent organisation – the Luftfahrtforschungsanstalt München – with a workforce of about 100 men in factory workshops capable of housing three times that number. There was also room for design offices for about 60-70 men but even three months after Lippisch's arrival these had not yet been established.

He had taken only four men with him from the former Abteilung L – Dr Friedrich Ringleb, Handrick, Sanders and Dr Völker, none of whom had been with him at the DFS. But despite effectively gifting all the patents associated with his work at Messerschmitt to the company, he had managed to secure "free right to joint use" of them. This allowed him to take his new obsession, the twin-engine P 11, away with him and continue its development at the LFW unconstrained by the strictures of a large commercial organisation.

The loose structure of the LFW proved to be both a blessing and a curse however. Lippisch wrote in Erinnerungen: "In contrast to my team at Messerschmitt and before that at the DFS, the workforce I found in Vienna was anything but a sensible combination of engineers and factory workers.

"The institute had originally been created to develop a high-pressure gas turbine as an aircraft engine. Messerschmitt had also shown interest in this, but the liberal and individualistic Austrians could not agree on a common denominator, and thus the whole fell apart. It was attempted to create a normal research institute to deal with aerodynamic and thermodynamic issues. And I had to transform this totally disorganised group of technicians into a viable organization."

Less than a month after leaving Messerschmitt, in May 1943, Lippisch produced a 13-page report entitled Projektbaubeschreibung Versuchsflugzeug für Hochgeschwindigkeit or 'Project construction description of an experimental aircraft for high-speed'. The aircraft it outlined, powered by two Jumo 004 jet engines, was intended to fly at 1000km/h while carrying a bomb load of 1000kg for a range of 1000km – the original 1000 x 1000 x 1000 aircraft. The drawings showed the aircraft equipped with a single SC1000 bomb but other loads were possible.

Unlike the earlier P 11 designs, the single-seater May 1943 design had almost no fuselage to speak of. The pilot sat in a tiny cockpit which protruded from the leading edge of an enormous flying wing. There was a single tail fin to the rear and both turbojets were positioned close together in the central part of the wing behind the cockpit and above the huge faired-over bomb bay. Their intakes were positioned either side of the cockpit in the leading edge of the 10.6m span wing. The aircraft's length was 6.8m.

The undercarriage was a tricycle arrangement, with the nosewheel withdrawing to a position between the pilot's feet. The mainwheels went almost directly upwards into the wing. And within the wing itself were a pair of 1200kg fuel tanks, one on either side.

This was what had formerly been the Messerschmitt P 11. And given the state of the LFW when Lippisch arrived, it seems likely that he was preparing the report with Handrick, Ringleb and the others even before they left Abteilung L. This short report was presented to the RLM, probably via Hermann Göring himself, because there was no delay. Before July 22, 1943, Lippisch had been given a 500,000 RM contract to build three prototype examples – beginning with an engineless glider.

Assuming that Göring presented the 1000 x 1000 x 1000 idea at a meeting during March 1943, and given the time it would have taken to dissolve Abteilung L and move to Vienna, it seems unlikely that Lippisch only began work on a 1000x3 design after Göring's speech.

The P 11 had been a work in progress since September 1942 and designs from December 1942 show it fitted with two Jumo 004s, carrying an SC1000, and with fuel tanks capable of holding 2200kg.

Given his earlier personal contact with the Reichsmarschall concerning the P 10, it is not inconceivable that Lippisch could have given him a personal presentation on a bomber capable of meeting that impressive 1000x3 specification. Göring may well have brought up the concept during his speech because he had already been told it was possible by Lippisch.

This would seem to cast Lippisch's departure from Messerschmitt – on a full salary and on apparently good terms – in a new light. Göring had bought into his fast jet-bomber concept and encouraged him to pursue it. He must have been somewhat surprised when, months later, the Horten brothers turned up out of the blue offering an alternative flying wing concept which they also believed could meet the 1000 x 1000 x 1000 specification.

Nevertheless, Lippisch got down to business using what resources he had available. A report made up of extracts from Technical Intelligence report no. A.424, compiled for the Aeronautical Research Council on August 13, 1945, notes: "Several reports on aerodynamic and gasdynamic subjects were brought out by Lippisch and by his collaborators. The development of a high-speed experimental aircraft with two turbojet engines was started in the summer of 1943.

"It was an all-wing, tailless aircraft with 45sq m area, untwisted sweepback wing with symmetrical laminar section. It was designed for a gross weight of 8000kg."

Evidently Lippisch struggled to get hold of the necessary engines for his design, just as the Hortens had, and even by the end of 1943 he had not managed to have the glider fully built. In the meantime, the P 11 had evolved. From being a single-seat fast-bomber, at the beginning of 1944 it was revised and redesigned as a multirole fighter, heavy fighter or ground-attack aircraft with twin fins.

Lippisch wrote: "In accordance with the course of the war, it became a twin-engined fighter, which bore the designation 'Delta VI'. Then a mock-up was built and a series of quite interesting wind tunnel tests were carried out."

In the meantime, as the war entered its final full year, tailless aircraft designs came to play an increasingly prominent role in discussions about what form the next generation of Luftwaffe aircraft should take. ●

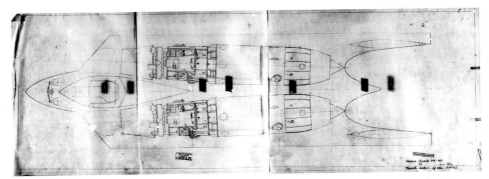

ABOVE: Soon after its initial presentation, Lippisch's P 11 became a twin-fin design. This drawing from July 26, 1943, shows how the two Jumo 004 engines would sit in the centre section.

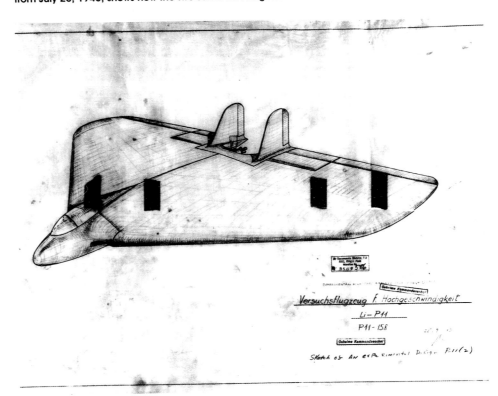

ABOVE: This perspective drawing dated September 25, 1943, appears to show the P 11 as an experimental engineless glider. It is fitted with a rocket booster to the rear for take-off.

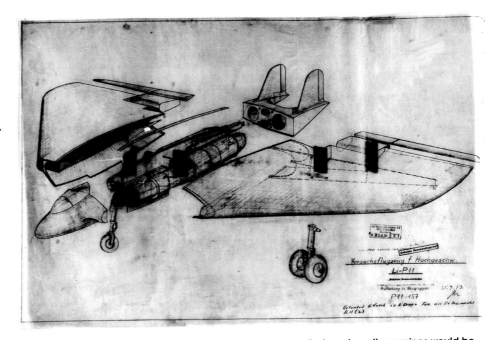

ABOVE: The internal structure of the P 11 glider with empty cylinders where the engines would be.

Challenging the flying wings

Focke-Wulf and one thousand times three

Some months after the Horten H IX and Lippisch P 11 were awarded development contracts, Focke-Wulf began to conduct preliminary work on its own designs for a twin-engine fast-bomber which could replace the Me 262 in that role. The eventual result was a direct comparison between 'normal' and tailless designs.

During October 1943, Focke-Wulf's design office began to crunch numbers on aerodynamics and performance for a fast-bomber study based on the use of two Jumo 004 Cs – with particular attention being paid to achievable speed and range.

Drag was a key factor in the calculations alongside fuel load, wing area and engine thrust. The work evidently continued at a low level of priority and without any design drawings being produced until February 1944 when the project file shows a rough sketch of a stub-nosed conventional-layout aircraft with long narrow strongly swept wings and tail planes and a podded turbojet on either side.

Unusually, rather than pointing directly forwards, the engines were toed outwards at the front. The fuselage featured a bulbous front end tapering away towards the fin and most of its interior was taken up by fuel tanks – for an overall capacity of 5630 litres. The relatively small bomb bay was squeezed in between these.

Up to this point, there had been no mention of any other company's work – simply page upon page of calculations, tables and graphs. A month later, at the beginning of March 1944, new graphs and charts appear with the Jumo 004's stats replaced by those of the Heinkel HeS 011. Also present in the file is a draft report dated March 8, 1944, entitled "Kurzbeschreibung 1000-1000-1000".

The introduction to this states: "It is to be investigated whether, with a normal jet aircraft, i.e. non-tailless design, an SB 1000 bomb can be taken over a penetration depth of 1000km, the aircraft being able to reach a top speed of 1000km/h."

The whole typed report is covered in annotations and crossings-out but it appears that the best possible performance with a pair of HeS 011s was a "best travel

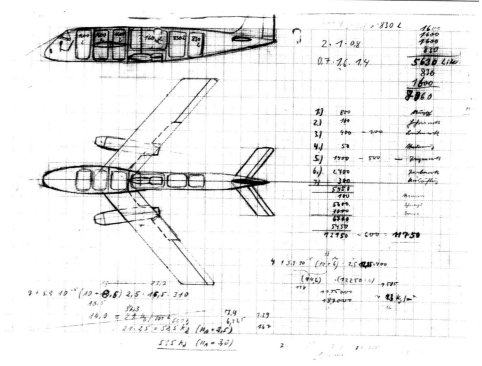

ABOVE: Focke-Wulf chief engineer Herbert Wolff's late 1943 design for a fast bomber powered by two Jumo 004 Cs. It was to be a precursor to the company's later HeS 011 bomber study.

speed" of 960km/h, a range of 2500km – 1000km there, 1000km back and sufficient fuel for manoeuvring – and a bomb load of 1000kg. However, this bomber would need to be entirely stripped of armour and defensive weaponry and the author of the report, probably Focke-Wulf chief mechanic H Wolff, does not appear convinced by the findings he is presenting.

More pages of notes follow until a complete and unmarked report dated August 14, 1944, appears entitled Vergleich zweier Strahlbomber in normaler und schwanzloser Bauart or 'Comparison of two jet bombers in normal and tailless

design'. March to August had apparently been spent studying a tailless version of the Focke-Wulf two-jet bomber so that it could be compared against the original conventional layout design.

The introduction begins: "Based on the Lippisch projects 1000/1000/1000, a test is carried out to determine whether a fast bomber with an SB 1000 bomb and penetration depth of 1000km can reach a top speed of 1000km/h. Two special engines, HeS 109-011, are selected. With respect to the high fuel consumption, the penetration depth of 1000km is equated to a range of 2500km; this condition is

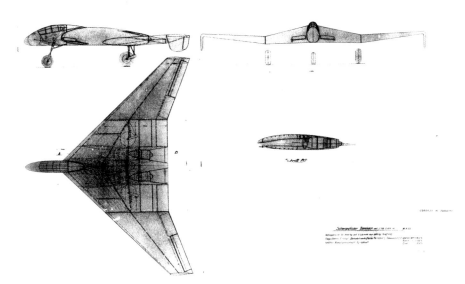

ABOVE: The first page of Focke-Wulf's August 14, 1944, report on its study comparing tailless jet bomber designs against the conventional layout alternative, begun as a result Alexander Lippisch's '1000/1000/1000 projects'.

ABOVE: The Focke-Wulf Schwanzloser Bomber mit 2 HeS 109-11, drawing number 0310 239-10, dated February 16, 1944. The company concluded time and again that conventional designs were more advantageous than tailless ones.

justified by the special use and by the low drifts resulting from the high flight speed.

"As it cannot be demonstrated by pure consideration or over-calculation, whether the intended objective can be better achieved by means of an aircraft of a normal or tailless design, two design projects have been carried out to clarify this question."

The report then goes on to examine both normal and tailless designs in detail. With regard to the normal design, it states: "Particular consideration is given to the influence of air resistance on the Mach number. It is assumed that an increase of the critical Mach number to 0.9 can be achieved by using an arrow form and low profile thicknesses, the fuselage to the wing root, etc.

"Different arrangements of the engines showed that the usual arrangement of the propeller drive units under the wing in aircraft of the normal type is probably the most favourable for jet engines. This arrangement has the following advantages over accommodation of the engines in the fuselage: the fuselage can be given the most aerodynamically favourable shape because no consideration must be given to the inlet of the combustion air and the ejection of the hot jet and the fuselage can be kept small as no room must be provided for air and air exhaust gas ducts."

Other advantages of engines positioned in under-wing nacelles included ease of maintenance and engine replacement, a short intake duct and the easier fitment of different engine types if required.

"The only disadvantage is the larger air resistance of the freely suspended engines. A faultless computational comparison of the total resistances is not possible due to the lack of sufficient documentation, but it must be assumed that the difference is small, in any case by no means so great that it can remove the mentioned advantages in favour of the arrangement.

"All other arrangements also do not have any significant advantages over the arrangement under the wing."

Less space is devoted to the tailless design. The report states: "In order to reduce the air resistance to a minimum, the bomber is executed in approximately a flying-wing form of aircraft. The small fuselage with a pressure cabin is placed in front of the wing, and the rear ends of the jet engines emerge from the wing profile.

"The wing can be made almost completely smooth in 40% of the wing depth, since only small flaps of handhole size are necessary up to the spar. The landing gear and the engines are behind the main spar and the fuel tanks are pushed through the forward main spar. As a result, the low resistance of a laminar profile can probably also be achieved in the size version over the widest range of the span."

In short, the main advantage of the tailless design is low drag.

The report concludes by citing the advantages of the normal design compared with the advantages of the tailless design. For the former, it states: "Advantages of the design in normal arrangement: the flight characteristics are to be known with greater certainty; in any case you will not receive any great surprises. The visibility is better, because the cab

structure and the fuselage bow hardly limit the field of view. The maintenance and replacement of the engines is better because of the good accessibility, the exchange against other engine patterns is hardly hindered. In addition, there are no inlet losses during the free suspension."

For the latter: "Advantages of the design in tailless arrangement: as a result of the smaller surface load, the climbing capacities and thus the starting and landing sections are better or shorter. If it is possible to obtain the laminar effect despite disturbances caused by the hull, engine inlet openings and unavoidable hand holes in the area of the fuel containers, the maximum and travel speed are greater, otherwise practically the same.

"There are no advantages compared to the others. The decision is very dependent on how much the individual points are valued. The target 1000/1000/1000 can be achieved with the tailless design with speed, but at the expense of the flying characteristics, especially at the high Mach numbers."

Focke-Wulf appears to have abandoned its twin-jet bomber project at this point after some 10 months of work and no further competitor for the H IX and P 11 emerged.. ●

ABOVE: The Focke-Wulf Bomber mit 2 HeS 109-11, drawing number 0310 239-01, dated February 19, 1944. It was concluded that this design would be slower than the tailless version but overcame this disadvantage by virtue of being easier to operate.

ABOVE: Focke-Wulf tailless bomber. Art by Daniel Uhr

On giants' shoulders

Gotha P-60

The Hortens had been forced to choose a subcontractor to handle production of the V3 to V6 prototypes of their 8-229 and the company picked was Gothaer Waggonfabrik. But working on the jet-powered flying wing highlighted problems which the firm felt could best be fixed with a new type of its own – the P-60.

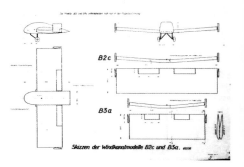

ABOVE: P-60 designer Dr Rudolf Göthert previously worked at the DVL, during which time he assessed a number of tailless designs. This drawing shows two DFS models, designated B2c and B3a, that he tested during June 1941. The following year he joined Gotha as chief aerodynamicist.

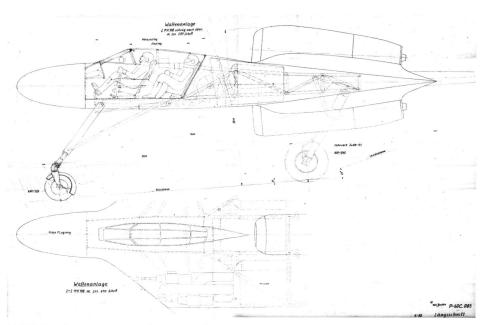

ABOVE: The first version of the Gotha P-60 C night fighter with the crew seated in tandem.

When he was interviewed during the 1980s Reimar Horten stated that Gothaer Waggonfabrik (GWF), commonly known as Gotha, had been chosen to produce further examples of the 8-229 during August 1944.

But the company's own chief aerodynamicist, Dr Rudolf Göthert, interrogated by the Americans on June 5, June 30 and July 5, 1945, less than a year after the fact, had a different recollection. According to Technical Intelligence Report I-68, he told his captors that "the Horten brothers did not have sufficient production facilities to produce the 229 and the RLM

had ordered the Gothaer Waggonfabrik to produce the 229 in late 1943 or early 1944".

It is believed that a second company, Klemm Technik, based at Stuttgart-Böblingen, was also hired to build 8-229s but was unable to fulfil the contract, leaving Gotha as the sole subcontractor.

Some 80% of the Gothaer factory at Gotha in Thuringia, central Germany, was destroyed during an air raid on July 20, 1944, which set production back considerably but nevertheless the firm pressed ahead with the 8-229 prototypes. The further this progressed, however, the less satisfied Göthert was with the Hortens' design.

Having worked at the Luftfahrtforschungsanstalt (LFA) aeronautical research institute for seven years before joining Gotha in 1942, Göthert was dismayed by what he saw as the 8-229's failings – particularly with regard to centre of gravity. During his interrogation he told the Americans that "the GWF were reluctant to continue production of the 229, however, because they believed they could design a superior flying wing".

He set to work on designing this superior flying wing, designated P 60 by the company, during the autumn of 1944 and his efforts were summarised in a report issued on March 11, 1945, entitled Go P-60 Hochgeschwindigkeitflugzeug or 'High-speed aircraft'.

The foreword begins: "In the following pages, the Gotha-based Waggonfabrik submits the results of its design work for a high-speed flying wing craft. The intended uses are: heavy fighter, fighter-bomber, reconnaissance, night fighter. In the course of the development, three different designs were produced by the Gothaer Waggonfabrik with the following designations:

"P-60 A. This project is the result of the experience gained during the development work on model 229. At the request of the OKL, these should be taken into account in a new draft and the other requirements are drawn up: 2 man crew, pressure-tight altitude chamber, nose gear in standard design, range increase, possibility of installation for stronger engines.

"The state of high-speed research, which has been more advanced since

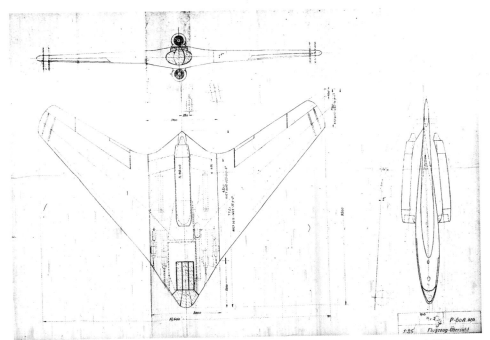

ABOVE: The basic Gotha P-60 A which was designed as a direct response to the Horten 8-229. The long BMW 003 engines stretch along its upper and lower sides.

the design of the 229, has been largely taken into account. The latest findings in the field of new construction methods and the experience gained with the jet engines have also been utilized.

"P-60 B. In the basic design, this project is closely related to the initial project P-60 A. It has arisen from the additional requirements of the OKL regarding: further increase in range and flight endurance, preferably use of TL engines of performance class 109-011, creation of more plentiful space for more extensive equipment than for P-60 A.

"P-60 C. With the exception of the wing centre section, P-60 C corresponds to the project P-60 B. P-60 C was designed especially for night fighter use. The prescribed FuG 240 made it necessary to provide a fuselage on the wing centre section. This measure also led to the seated arrangement of the two crew members and also necessitated the use of normal vertical stabilisers."

The direct competitor for the 8-229 was the P-60 A – although all three P-60s had two crewmen compared to the single-seat 8-229. The P-60 B incorporated the HeS 011 jet engine, which was seen as the successor to the Jumo 004, and the P-60 C was intended to compete against a host of new night fighter designs being prepared by most of the major manufacturers towards the end of 1944.

The report continues: "Flight deck – P-60

A and P-60 B. The pilot's compartment was placed completely within the space defined by a normal profile of 12% thickness. This was made possible by the arrangement of the crew. Pilots and radio operators lie side by side in the longitudinal and vertical direction. This gives the operator an excellent view, while the operator is ensured the necessary freedom of movement for the operation of his equipment.

"The pilot's compartment is designed for a pressure of 7000m. The air which is at the same time used for the heating of the crew compartment is removed from the two turbojets. Control valves and chokes, as well as a fresh air timer ensure correct pressure and temperature maintenance. While the pressure chamber itself is single-skinned, the viewing windows are of double-walled design and are air-heated in order to reliably prevent impaired visibility by fogging the windows.

"The protection of the crew is by a 100mm thick armoured disc with adjoining sides against fire from the front, by lined couches with high led side walls against bombardment from below and from the side. Since these measures assure protection against the bombardment from the main directions, it was possible to dispense with an even more extensive armouring, as the two engines and the fuselage fuel tanks are a very effective protection

against bombardment from the rear.

"The couch of the pilot is air-cushioned and can at any time be adapted by the pilot himself during the flight to his comfort requirements. Emergency exit is carried out by dropping the entire crew cab floor. The device for this purpose is designed in such a way that the discharge is so effectively supported that a special catapult device could be dispensed with.

"A floor flap designed as a staircase is used for normal entry and exit. Joysticks and pedals are arranged hanging in the crew cabin and enable unimpeded entry and exit of the aircraft. The entire crew cab is constructed in such a way that it can be removed and installed as a whole by loosening a few screw connections."

For the P-60 C, the pilot and radio operator were seated upright one behind the other in a pressurised cabin, which was to work the same way as that proposed for the P-60 A and B.

"The protection of the crew against bombardment is provided by all-round armouring of the entire trough-shaped crew space. The front cover is made of armoured glass. The normal entry and exit is through the movable Plexiglas hood. When emergency exit is necessary, the entire upper section of the canopy, including the visor, is thrown off and the crew are thrown out by activating catapult seats."

The central part of the P-60 wing was to be a plywood-lined steel tube construct containing or mounting the crew cabin, undercarriage, engines and fuel tank system, weapons and ammo, and most other equipment. The outer wings were made of wood and housed the main fuel tanks along with "internally balanced rudders for the combined vertical and horizontal control of the aircraft". A smaller outer surface was directly controlled by the pilot via the control linkage but the main inner surfaces were

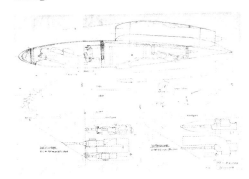

ABOVE: Side view of the P-60 A showing the prone crew positions, short undercarriage main legs and weapons loadout.

ABOVE: Gotha P-60 A. Art by Daniel Uhr

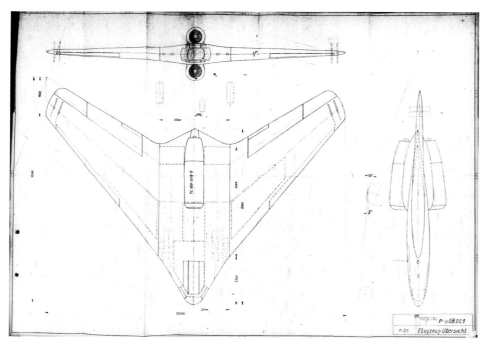

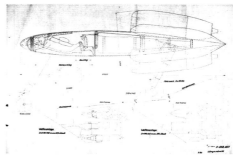

ABOVE: A view of the P-60 B from the side.

ABOVE: The HeS 011 was a much shorter engine than the BMW 003 and the difference is evident in this drawing of the P-60 B. The design also features different cockpit glazing.

actuated by servo tabs; "this arrangement relieves the pilot from the otherwise very large control forces, but nevertheless gives him a real sense of control (the principle of this arrangement has already been applied successfully to model BV 222)."

There were additional control surfaces on the P-60 A and B which extended downwards towards the wingtips to act as fins. The P-60 C had a small fin of normal design on either wing; "they were necessary in order to bring lateral stability, which was reduced by the design necessary for the FuG 240, to the necessary degree".

The tricycle undercarriage of all three P-60s was the same – with a castering nosewheel and mainwheels lifted from a Junkers Ju 88 A-4 or A-7.

Regarding the engines: "Two TL engines are provided, which should be installed in such a way that one engine is symmetrical to each other above and below the central wing. Favourable intake ratios are to be expected at the start, thus maximum starting power as well as favourable drag ratios at high altitudes.

"Simple design and easy maintenance of the engines are further advantages of this installation. In a variant, a twin arrangement, in which the engine units are arranged below the central wing, recessed next to one another, is possible. Current wind tunnel tests will prove whether this type of installation is also suitable.

"P-60 A uses two 109-003 (the optional installation of similar or stronger engines is possible). The P-60 B and P-60 C use two 109-011 (or other TL of the same performance class). The installation of an additional rocket-unit (thrust-2000kg) for take-off and climb is provided in the tail of the wing centre part between the TL.

"The fuel supply is arranged in three tanks, two of which are located in the outer wings, one in the middle wing. The fuel supply is switched in such a way

that, in normal cases, the two outer tanks feed into the central tank from which the engines are fed. Immediate removal from the outside containers is possible by switching over. In the case of the use of rocket units, their fuel tank arrangement is installed instead of the central tank."

Weapons options were four MK 108s or MK 213s, two on either side of the cockpit in the centre wing section. An upgrade could be installed of two additional MK 108s or MK 213s for firing upwards at an oblique angle. Bomb racks and arming equipment could also be added as an upgrade. Ammunition was limited to 670 rounds but "an increase in the number of shots is easily possible".

The reconnaissance version of the P-60 could be fitted with two

RB 50/18s and one RB 30/18 "in the immediate vicinity of the crew room".

The Gotha report on the P-60 actually lists six potential versions of the design – P-60 A mit BMW 003, P-60 A mit HeS 011, P-60 B mit HeS 011, P-60 B mit HeS 011 und R-Gerät, P-60 C mit HeS 011, and P-60 C mit HeS 011 und R-Gerät. There is no mention of a version of the P-60 A with 'R-Gerät' – rocket propulsion.

Göthert's interrogation, three to four months after this report was written, sheds a little more light on the development process: "The engines for all three models were mounted externally at the rear of the centre section, one above and one below in the plane of symmetry. An alternate design with the engines partially buried side by side in the undersurface of the centre section was proposed for the P-60 A, but only to obtain wind tunnel data for application to possible future designs of larger flying wings.

"In addition, a Walter-type rocket engine of 2000kg thrust could be added to any of the models for use in take-off and climb. Dr Göthert stated that this engine would not be used for high speed because the speed increase would not be large. All three models were equipped with pressure cabins.

"The P-60 C was entered in the night fighter competition which was opened by the RLM in December 1944. Seven aircraft including two other tailless aircraft were

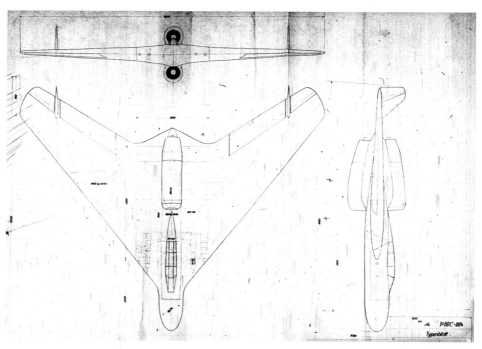

ABOVE: A three-view drawing of the original Gotha P-60 C.

entered by the following firms: Arado, Blohm & Voss, Dornier, Focke-Wulf and Gotha. At the conference on night fighters, held in March of 1945, the P-60 C was shown to have the best performance of these aircraft, and Dr Göthert believed it would have won had not the war disrupted the competition.

"The P-60 B was not entered into the day fighter competition because the requirements for the day fighter included that it have only one turbojet engine. However, a comparison of the performance of the P-60 B with the 229 showed it to be the superior aircraft. The P-60 A has slightly less drag than the Ho 229, but the BMW 003 engine has slightly less thrust than the Jumo 004 and consequently the high-speed at sea level is approximately the same. At higher altitudes the high speed of the P-60 A is considerably higher because the critical Mach number of the P-60 A is higher.

"The wind tunnel programme for the P-60 series had been started. Tests on the location of the engine nacelle had been run at Göttingen. Dr Göthert had received some of this data. There was no provision in the models tested to simulate the thrust of the engine, but the inlet velocity ratio was varied from zero to almost one by varying the nose plug and/or the tail plug. Models for the remainder of the wind tunnel programme were under construction."

The programme included a complete model being tested in the 2m high-speed DVL tunnel in Berlin, wing profile and control surface tests at the 8m LFA wind tunnel at Braunschweig, damping characteristics in yaw and pitch in the 2.5m LFA wind tunnel, and a continuation of engine installation tests at Göttingen.

The interrogation report continued: "The Gotha firm had also planned to make flight tests on the 229 to obtain data for use on the P-60. These tests would include: the determination of neutral points, the effect of sweepback on lateral stability, tests on various types of rudders such as drag rudders. Some of these tests may have been run on the Horten VII. Tests of landing flaps etc."

For their part, the Horten brothers did not think very highly of Göthert, almost to the point of derision – although they

seem to have known little about him.

Reimar Horten told Myhra: "At Gotha there was a man named Dr Göthert who had joined Gotha in 1944 coming from DVL. He had considerable experience with wind tunnels there. He was no pilot but only had experience with wind tunnel scale model airplanes.

"He had received support from the RLM in the past to investigate the aerodynamics of swept-back wings and control surfaces. His real speciality was control surfaces such as ailerons, flaps, rudders, and elevators. He had taken a swept-back aircraft scale model and had placed it in the wind tunnel at DVL and had measured the aerodynamics of the model.

"This could not be. For the moments were different during the angle of attack and Walter and I learned of his testing and then saw the results of his investigation... we both laughed. He was completely wrong. He later joined Gotha, by the way, and claimed our tailless H IX would experience directional stability problems."

Reimar's attitude to Göthert is hardly surprising, given their very different approaches – where Reimar would always build practical models or aircraft and flight test them, Göthert relied on calculations and lab testing. The latter approach, however, was the industry standard in Germany for much of the war.

Reimar went on, saying: "We did not take him or his work seriously" and "So Göthert was testing a swept-back wing but he had no practical application so his tests were without use to anyone. It was about the summer of 1944. When all this test result information came from DVL, Walter and I felt that it was a great pity that we cannot speak with this man Göthert and tell him what errors he had made.

"However, DVL as well as Dr Göthert, felt that they were in such a position, that they wouldn't accept any criticism, especially from people like us who had no formal training. Most of Göthert's work was completely out of date, his methods, concepts of placing scale models in highly turbulent wind streams etc. had been shown to give false readings.

"I saw different test results with wind tunnel tests run on Lippisch's designs.

These wind tunnel tests, like those of Göthert, were false too. Whenever we read the results of this work our only response was laughter. It was a big joke because all these men who ran the wind tunnels had no practical experience like Lippisch and we did. The stuff which Göthert ran in his wind tunnel which did show good results were practically worthless if we tried to apply them on a practical basis. So the money and the time they spent at DVL and other places was a waste. After Walter and I read the summary of Göthert's work we simply put it aside and never went back to it again."

Asked if he had ever spoken to Göthert, Reimar replied: "No. I had seen him from time to time at different functions and conferences which we both attended, but we never sat down and talked about aircraft design and production. Göthert did not appear to be interested in how the Horten brothers had designed and built the H IX and I too was not about to teach him. We had come from different backgrounds.

"However, if a man such as Göthert would have come and asked me, how did you come to design these things, then I would welcome him and discuss my design ideas with him. But if the person showed complete disinterest like Göthert did, then I would not bother with him. Also, I do not believe that Göthert could design the so-called Gotha Go P-60 because he had no design experience.

"What we see in the Go P-60 is a picture of a proposed aircraft only. Any schoolboy can draw a picture of an aircraft. But to build it he needed a staff to make it as it should be. All this he had to learn. If it had been built, it would have performed about the same as the H IX. Since he had copied the profile of the H IX, the Go P-60's performance would have also depended on the thrust of the two turbojets."

Yet whatever the Hortens thought about Dr Göthert, he was sufficiently well respected for his P-60 C to be accepted as a serious contender for the Schlechtwetter und Nachtjäger competition he mentioned during his interrogation. As the competition progressed however, the P-60 C underwent a significant change from its March 11, 1945 configuration as will be detailed in the chapter on that contest.. ●

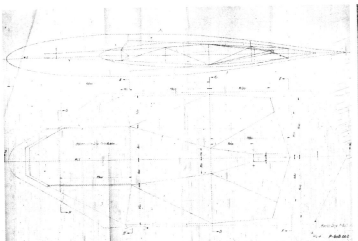
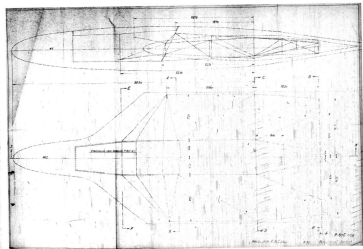

ABOVE: Internal structure details of the Gotha P-60 B and P-60 C.

Turning to tailless

A contest intended to produce a single-jet replacement for the expensive Me 262 began with three conventional competitors but would go on to spawn some of the most radical tailless designs ever seen.

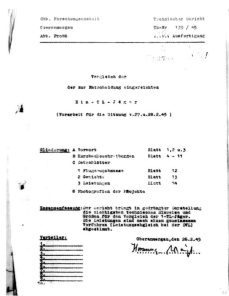

ABOVE: The title page of the pre-conference report on what was intended to be the final round of the Ein-TL-Jäger competition.

Messerschmitt may have worked on single-jet fighter designs since before the beginning of the Second World War but it was not until the advent of the Heinkel HeS 011 turbojet as a viable proposition in late 1943 that a high-performance fighter with just one jet engine became a realistic prospect.

On July 15, 1944, a requirement was issued for a new day-fighter to be powered by one HeS 011. The successful design would need to have a top speed of 1000kph (621mph), an endurance of one hour at 7000m (23,000ft), armour protection for the pilot, and standard fighter equipment such as gunsight and radio.

At first only three companies were invited to submit designs – Messerschmitt, Focke-Wulf and Heinkel – with Blohm & Voss joining later in the year. Messerschmitt started a new project to meet the specification – P 1101. Focke-Wulf began updating its Baubeschreibung Nr. 272 aircraft (later given the company nickname 'Flitzer'), which had first been devised in January 1944, and Heinkel created a single-engine version of its P 1073, a twin-jet project which had commenced at the beginning of July 1944.

While the P 1101 and P 1073 featured swept wings and V-tails they were still relatively conventional in layout. The 'Flitzer' had a twin-boom tail design that the company had already exploited with its Fw 189.

Each company produced performance figures for its design but these varied wildly even though the designs themselves were not that dissimilar – it was clear that each firm was using quite different calculations. Therefore, a conference was scheduled

for September 8-10, 1944, at Messerschmitt's Oberammergau facility where, according to the post-conference summary, "the task was to create comparable fundamentals for the performance calculation and, as far as possible, to carry out a comparison of the present jet aircraft designs".

A brief description of each firm's design was then given – it being noted that Blohm & Voss's Hans Amtmann had attended but opted not to present a design.

The Focke-Wulf design was presented in three slightly different forms – outwardly identical but with differing quantities of fuel for the supplementary rocket engine depending on mission. It was armed with two MK 103s in the fuselage and one MG 151 in each wing. Wing area was 17sqm, span was 8m and length was 10.5m. A pressure cabin was an option.

The P 1073 was a "pure jet" with two MG 213s in the fuselage, or two MK 108s or one MK 103 and one "20mm weapon". It had a wingspan of 14sqm, wingspan of 8m, wing sweepback of 35 and length of 9.3m. It also offered a pressure cabin as an option.

And the P 1101 was offered in three forms as a seemingly modular concept similar to the company's piston-engined P 1090, dating from February 1943. The summary notes: "Mtt AG. 1) Smallest jet single-seater with maximum flight performance. 2) Jet and rocket fighter with rocket fuel for fast climbing or as a combat aid. Extending possibility by inserting a fuselage intersection. 3) Possibility of expansion to two men by inserting a fuselage intermediate section, whereby the space for second man can also be used for additional weapons, additional fuel or additional drive."

In order to compare the weights of the different designs, a basic armament of two MK 108s each with 60 rounds and a fuel load of 830kg was assumed – no matter what the firms had put in their brochures. Then the companies' stats were played around with to try and find some common ground. The Heinkel and Messerschmitt designs were found to be heavier than the figures given, while the Focke-Wulf was deemed to be 70kg lighter – the difference corresponding to swapping steel components for ones made of duraluminium.

In terms of performance, Heinkel and Messerschmitt claimed similar top speeds but it was considered that the Heinkel design would suffer a loss of thrust because of the design of its jet inlet and unfortunately for Focke-Wulf, "the FW design should be less than 50-100km/h slower compared to the designs of Heinkel and Messerschmitt".

There was disagreement from the outset

over the calculations used to determine top speed: "In the opinion of Heinkel and Focke-Wulf, the determined speed level is too high, whereas Messerschmitt, on the basis of the experience with the Me 262 and the Do 335, is in the opposite opinion and hopes to achieve even higher speeds with further improvements. For the calculation performed by Messerschmitt, the flight measurements of the Me 262, which has a relatively poor series state, are used as the basis."

At the end of the conference "a broad exchange of experience has been agreed upon in order to clarify these questions with a view to forthcoming designs. It is urgently necessary that, by the disposal of the RLM, all the development companies and the experimental stations are asked to provide flight results, together with the necessary documentation, for the evaluation".

It was the first attempt to come up with a standard basis on which the new single-jet designs could be compared. However, on the last day of the meeting, September 10, a new requirement was issued for a single-jet fighter or 1-TL-Jäger with reduced performance compared to the designs just discussed, to be powered by a single BMW 003 engine. This is what would become known as the Volksjäger competition and prospective participants had just five days to prepare their entries.

This temporarily stalled the primary 1-TL-Jäger competition, with the next conference for comparison of designs being delayed until December 19-21. Heinkel retained its P 1073, now referred to as 'He 162 development'. Blohm & Voss entered both the forward-swept wing version of its P 209 and the tailless P 212, while Junkers entered the tailless EF 128. Messerschmitt put forward the radical P 1106 – the P 1101 having now been dropped. Focke-Wulf swapped its twin boom design for its Baubeschreibung Nr. 279 aircraft (given the company nickname 'Huckebein' – a number of contemporary documents are known to exist which use this name).

At a third meeting, on January 12-15, 1945, the DVL put forward a new mathematical formula by which the expected performance of all designs could be calculated and this was agreed. Now Heinkel's P 1073, presumably thanks to the experience gained while building a downgraded version as the He 162, had been replaced with a new tailless design, the P 1078. However, the DVL assessors commented in their report afterwards that Heinkel had "brought a tailless project, which was still so little worked through, that the comparison was not used with it".

Messerschmitt retained the P 1106 as 'Messerschmitt I' and offered a new layout design – the P 1110 – as 'Messerschmitt II'. Focke-Wulf put forward its Nr. 279 aircraft again, now as 'Focke-Wulf I' plus a new but similar design, described in Kurzbaubeschreibung Nr. 30, as 'Focke-Wulf II'. Blohm & Voss put forward an updated version of P 212, having withdrawn the P 209, and Junkers retained and refined the EF 128.

A date was then set for a fourth and, it was hoped, final round of comparison and assessment of the 1-TL-Jäger design submissions – February 27-28, 1945.

The pre-conference report was prepared by Messerschmitt on February 26 and detailed the eight designs due to be discussed. These were an updated Blohm & Voss P 212, the same Focke-Wulf 'I' and Focke-Wulf 'II' as before, the Heinkel P 1078, the Junkers EF 128, a revived Messerschmitt P 1101, a revised Messerschmitt P 1100, and a radical new tailless Messerschmitt design, the P 1111. The Messerschmitt designs were now referred to by their project numbers, presumably because the Messerschmitt offering had changed so much since the January conference.

The February report states: "At the request of the Entwicklungs Hauptkommission and the head of the Technische Luft Rustung, designs for single-jet fighters were tendered by the following firms: Blohm & Voss, Focke-Wulf, Ernst Heinkel, Junkers, Messerschmitt. At the meeting of the Entwicklungs Hauptkommission on February 27-28, 1945, a decision concerning the completion of these designs is to be made.

"The purpose of this report, after careful work on the material in question, is to present a comparison between the designs tendered and, thus, to serve the EHK as the basis for decision.

"A considerable interruption of the work necessary for this report was brought about by war conditions. On account of the bad traffic and communication facilities, it was not possible to obtain in written form the report of the DVL on general performance and criticism of the characteristics of the aircraft.

"For the same reasons it was not possible to compare in the general discussion with DVL the additional designs tendered (design from Heinkel and designs P 1101 and P 1111 from Messerschmitt)."

In order to ensure the fairest possible comparison, reference was made to the performance and weights of all the designs submitted with regard to equipment and armament.

"The aircraft weights were determined against each other at the beginning of the performance comparison. The bullet-proofing was not assumed to be of equal weight for the individual designs, but the bullet-proofing for each plane was set out so that an equal extent of protection was obtained wherever possible.

"Exceptions can be made for designs P 1101 and P 1111 from Messerschmitt, as these have to be considered with a view to their stronger armament (3 x MK 108 and 4 x MK 108 respectively, instead of 2 x MK 108). This happened on account of the fact that the arrangement of the supplementary armament at the extreme front of the aircraft presented great difficulties on both models in regard to

the centre of gravity, and thus the firm provided additional armament as a fundamental.

"The design of EHF (Heinkel) was not included in the comparison of performance and weight, as it was not ready at the time. The comparison was finished, but the result has not yet been submitted at this time to Special Commission for Day Fighters. The estimated performances are thus the firm's specifications.

"The estimated performance for the designs P 1110, P 1101 and P 1111 from Messerschmitt do not correspond entirely to the values which were ascertained at the comparison of performance. For the design of P 1110, an increase of wing and fuselage surface is contemplated and considered according to the fundamental process of calculating the performance comparison.

"The designs P 1101 and P 1111 which were not submitted for the performance comparison by Messerschmitt, were calculated by the firm according to an agreed process and were submitted for decision in place of the project P 1106.

"The estimated performances are comparative figures, which will serve as the deciding factor for the value of the designs submitted. They are not to be considered as absolute estimates of the velocities.

"The report consists of a short description, in concise form, of the separate projects, with the most important technical points such as the main dimension weights and important performances in comprehensive tables. These served the Special Commission for Day Fighters on January 12, 1945, as a basis. In the meantime, alterations proposed by the firms have not been considered."

From a competition that had begun with just three conventional-layout entries from three companies, in the space of five months the contest had expanded to eight entries from five companies – and fully half of them were tailless, the Blohm & Voss P 212, the Heinkel P 1078, the Junkers EF 128 and Messerschmitt's P 1111.

DVL director Günther Bock noted on March 12, 1945, that at a meeting of the Entwicklungshauptkommission on March 1, 1945, "the direction of the development work was discussed. In this case, the following picture emerged according to the intended use of the aircraft types: a) Day fighter. Development work for day fighters with the HeS 109.011 A jet engine, the companies Focke-Wulf and Messerschmitt are expected to have one development contract each. Whether the companies Junkers or Blohm & Voss are also activated for development is still undetermined".

It would appear that Focke-Wulf was expecting a development contract for the Nr. 279 aircraft, what was designated the Ta 183, and Messerschmitt was expecting a development contract for either the P 1110 or the P 1111. It is unlikely to have been the P 1101, since the company seems to have largely abandoned work on the prototype of this model that it had already built.

The EF 128 and P 212 had not been ruled out either – meaning that of the eight designs, either three tailless and one conventional design remained, or two tailless and two conventional. Either way, the Entwicklungshauptkommission (EHK) had chosen to eschew convention in favour of increasingly radical projects in the search for greater performance gains.

1-TL-JÄGER COMPETITORS

AS OF SEPTEMBER 8-10, 1944
- Heinkel P 1073
- Messerschmitt P 1101
- Focke-Wulf Nr. 280 ('Flitzer')
- Blohm & Voss (no proposal)

AS OF DECEMBER 19-21, 1944
- Heinkel P 1073 ('He 162 development')
- Messerschmitt P 1106
- Focke-Wulf Nr. 279 ('Huckebein')
- Blohm & Voss P 209.02
- Blohm & Voss P 212.02
- Junkers EF 128

AS OF JANUARY 12-16, 1945
- Heinkel P 1078
- Messerschmitt I (P 1106)
- Messerschmitt II (P 1110)
- Focke-Wulf I (Nr. 279)
- Focke-Wulf II (Nr. 30)
- Blohm & Voss P 212.03
- Junkers EF 128

AS OF FEBRUARY 27-28, 1945
- Heinkel P 1078
- Messerschmitt P 1101
- Messerschmitt P 1110
- Messerschmitt P 1111
- Focke-Wulf I (Nr. 279)
- Focke-Wulf II (Nr. 30)
- Blohm & Voss P 212.03
- Junkers EF 128

ABOVE: The 12th page of the Ein-TL-Jäger pre-conference report, a table of the eight projects' various dimensions, shows them evenly divided between schwanzlose flugzeuge 'tailless aircraft' and normalflugzeuge 'normal aircraft'. However, four out of the five companies involved are offering tailless designs.

A further meeting of the EHK took place on March 20-24 at Focke-Wulf's Bad Eilsen facility, two days of which, the 22nd and 23rd, were devoted to a fifth comparison of the 1-TL-Jäger designs. It is unknown whether the companies chose to revise their entries or whether they remained the same. A brief summary of the meeting is given in the war diary of the chief of the TLR: "No final decision on the proposals, since the chairman of the Special Commission for Fighter Aircraft – Prof. Messerschmitt – was absent. Fl-E-Chef has, with the approval of the plenipotentiary for jet aircraft, SS-Obergruppenführer Kammler, commissioned the Junkers firm with the development of design EF 128."

It would appear as though, with Germany on the very brink of collapse, the tailless Junkers EF 128 was approved for development. With Germany now being invaded on both eastern and western fronts and defensive positions being hastily prepared around Berlin in anticipation of the imminent arrival of Soviet forces, it seems unlikely that this development got very far.

However, it is worth examining each of the four tailless designs presented at the February 27-28 conference in detail to trace their development histories and see just why the 1-TL-Jäger competition came to feature so many tailless types. ●

Super Volksjäger

Ein-TL-Jäger – Heinkel P 1078

The main strand of Heinkel's advanced single jet fighter development, P 1073, was interrupted when it was stripped back to become the basis for the basic single-jet He 162. When P 1073 continued, experience from building the tiny Volksjäger led Heinkel to adopt a radical change of direction…

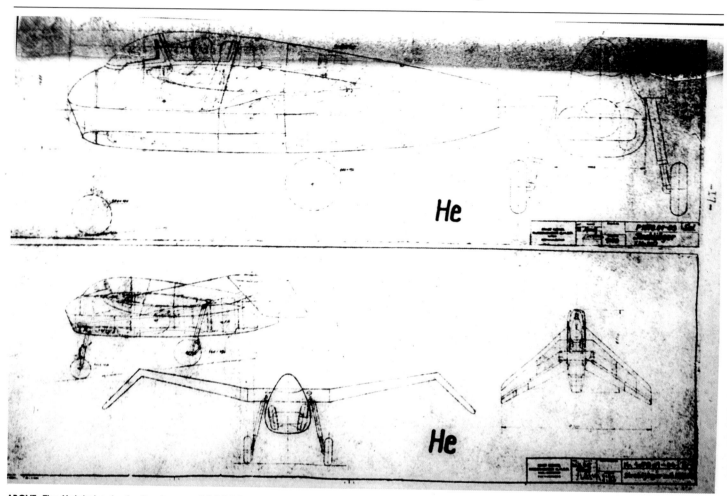

ABOVE: The Heinkel entry for the January 12-16 1-TL-Jäger comparison meeting was this tailless design, marked P 1078.01.

Heinkel was one of the first three firms involved in the 1-TL-Jäger competition and its submission for the conference on September 8-10, 1944, was a version of the P 1073 with a conventional layout with a V-tail, wings swept back 35 and the HeS 011 engine mounted on its back.

However, also on September 8, away from the conference venue at Oberammergau, Heinkel's designers were putting together a report on a smaller, simpler, less capable, BMW 003-powered version of their P 1073 single-jet design in the confident expectation that a new specification was soon to be issued. The P 1073 project as a whole had been ongoing since July 1944, originally as a twin-jet design, and the new downgraded version

of September 8 was the 15th of the series.

The HeS 011-powered 1-TL-Jäger entry itself – the peak performance version – had a relatively compact wing area of 14sqm, a wingspan of 8m and was 9.3m long, whereas the simplified P 1073 design, outlined on a sheet headed 'Jagdeinsitzer P 1073 (II)', was even smaller with a wing area of just 11sqm, a wingspan of 7.2m and a length of 8.65m.

It retained many of its sibling's distinctive visual features, particularly the dorsally-mounted engine and nose cockpit, but the elegant swept gullwings were swapped for stubby straight ones and the V-tail became a near-horizontal tailplane with endplates acting as rudders. The long slender fuselage was cut down by more than half a metre too.

While the advanced P 1073 came away from the September 8 competition looking somewhat less impressive than Messerschmitt's design, though far more impressive than Focke-Wulf's effort, the smaller, simpler version was a triumph in the Volksjäger competition and went on to enter full production as the He 162. This may have been because of the fact Heinkel appears to have had advance warning that the Volksjäger requirement was about to be issued – whereas Messerschmitt, Focke-Wulf and the other companies asked to submit designs at less than a week's notice were caught off-guard.

It would appear that Heinkel stuck with its advanced P 1073 design until the end of 1944 while concentrating most

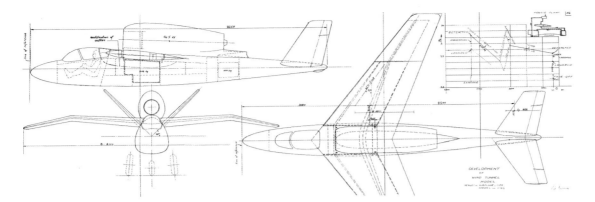

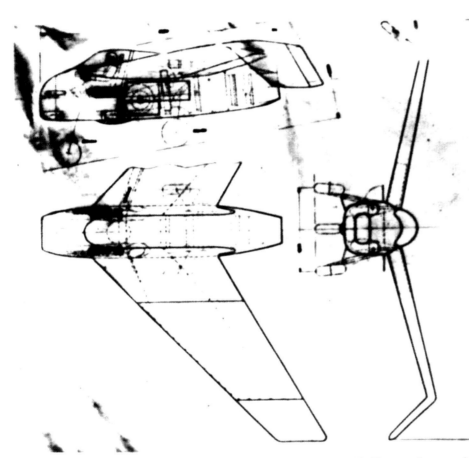

ABOVE: The drawing of the Heinkel P 1078 handed to delegates at the 1-TL-Jäger conference of February 27-28, 1945. It represents a significant refinement of the January design.

ABOVE: The precise appearance of the earliest Heinkel 1-TL-Jäger is unknown but its dimensions correspond almost exactly with those of this design, included in a postwar report as representing a development of the He 162.

of its efforts on developing the closely-related He 162 but then fielded a new design in January 1945 – the P 1078.

Surviving drawings of this design show a tiny fighter with a very short fuselage that was egg-shaped in cross section. A short flat section of wing protruded on either side before rising and then falling into a gullwing form. The undercarriage mainwheels were attached to the flat section but folded up into the sides of the crowded fuselage.

The cockpit was positioned as far forwards as Heinkel's designers might feasibly have been able to put it, with the rectangular nose intake almost under the pilot's feet. The canopy blended smoothly into the fuselage to the rear which appears to have housed the generator and starter for the engine. The only known drawing – marked P 1078.01 – is too degraded for dimensions to be made out but the design is clearly very different from what had been offered up previously. The date of the drawing appears to be January 10, 1945 – two days before the design comparison conference.

It was refined considerably for the final 1-TL-Jäger meeting of February 27-28 and the report prepared in advance of this meeting, 'Comparison of Designs for 1-TL-Jäger', indicates that Heinkel's submission is new or a substantial redesign when it notes: "The design of EHF (Heinkel) was not

ABOVE: Heinkel P 1078.01. Art by Daniel Uhr

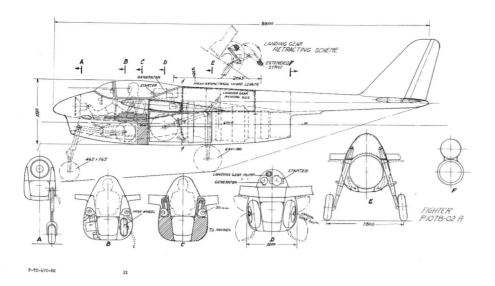

ABOVE: Drawing of the Heinkel He 1078 A from a report produced for the Americans.

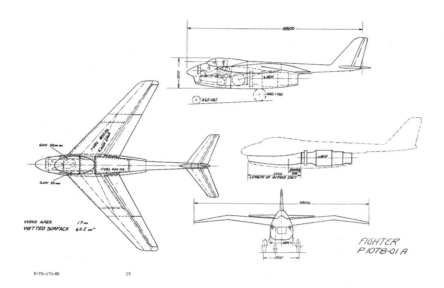

ABOVE: The He 1078 A appears to combine elements of the P 1078.01 with aspects of the He 162.

it has a new location for the generator and starter. Air is carried from the point of the fuselage through a flat curved inlet pipe."

Armament was to be a pair of MK 108 30mm cannon, one on either side of the pilot. Fuel load was 1450 litres and bullet-proofing was "in hand".

The radical tailless P 1078 was not looked upon favourably at the February 27-28 meeting and appears to have gone no further as part of 1-TL-Jäger, but Heinkel's chief designer Siegfried Günter appears not to have given up on it entirely. When the war ended, Günter and a number of his men wound up at Penzing airfield at a technical office set up for them by the Americans – who wanted them to make fresh reports on Heinkel's end-of-war projects. These included developments of the He 162, the P 1076, P 1077 Julia, P 1078, P 1079 and P 1080.

The report on the P 1078 by Eichner and Hohbach outlines two different designs, curiously neither of which was the one presented at the January 12-16 meeting nor the one on February 27-28.

It states: "This report contains two projects of single place fighters with one HeS-11; one project with tail, with turbojet in the lower part of the fuselage, the other is that of a tailless aeroplane, as far as possible designed as an all-wing aeroplane.

"The project with tail has a considerably smaller ratio of wetted area/wing area than the He 162. The idea for this new project was conceived before the construction of the 162 and it was also known that this design would give somewhat better performances.

"But, the questioned production engineers of those firms which were engaged for the production of the 162 declared that the preparation for the series production of the He 162 would be considerably more rapid. Because of the situation at that time, this was the deciding factor."

This suggests that what is presented as the 'P 1078 A', a design with a conventional tail, internal engine and nose intake, was conceived after work on designing the He 162 had commenced but before actual

included in the comparison of performance and weight, as it was not ready at the time."

The data that was to hand, including drawings, showed a "tailless mid-wing plane with swept back wings and controls at the end of the wings. Wings contain the total fuel supply. Nothing further known. Fuselage: In the point of the fuselage above the flattened out, curved and elongated inlet pipe, the pilot's cabin is situated, the same applies to both the MK 108s, and under it is the nose wheel housing.

"The main undercarriage is under the wings and the equipment above it. This is completed by the engine. The function of the controls (elevators, lateral controls and ailerons) is performed by the downward sloping wing tips."

The part of the report focusing on the P 1078's engine appears to acknowledge differences from the P 1078.01 designs previously submitted for the type: "The engine built into the fuselage is different from those previously supplied in copies, as

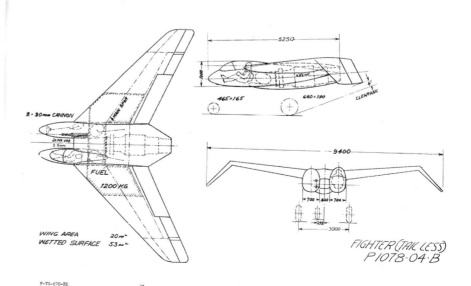

ABOVE: The radical P 1078 B – which may or may not have been an entirely postwar creation. The available evidence suggests that it was not, but it was never an entry for 1-TL-Jäger.

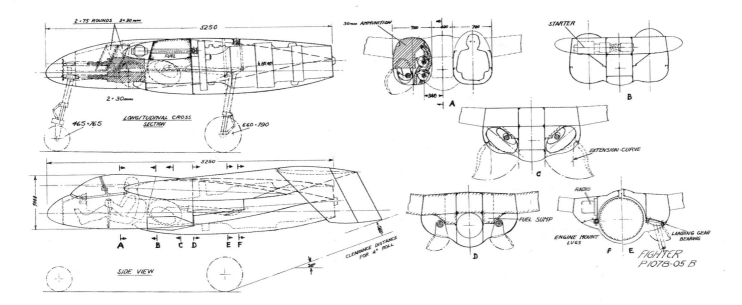

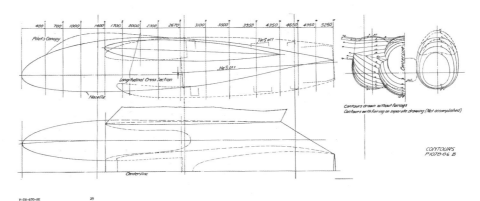

ABOVE: A sectional view shows the compact interior of the He 1078 B.

construction work had taken place – which would suggest that it dates from after the original September 8 design but before the gullwing design of January 1945. This would seem to make it the earliest P 1078, as the 'A' would obviously suggest, but it was never put forward for 1-TL-Jäger.

Regarding the P 1078 A, the report says: "The static structure has only a small fuselage cross-section above the turbojet, and in the forward part of the fuselage loads are transmitted to a construction of flat side walls in the interior of the fuselage about the air intake duct.

"The retracted wheels lie beside the air intake duct. This construction is particularly suitable for the HeS-11 because the diameter of this turbojet is considerably larger than the diameter of the air intake cross-section.

"The structural walls just described stop the retracting wheels so that only between wheel and door is a clearance margin necessary, thus the landing gear well is not wide. The bearing of the shock absorber strut is in the upper part of the fuselage and the extended strut is locked in this bearing so that the retracting mechanism is not subjected to landing loads.

"The armament, ammunition, radio and the nose wheel lie beside the air intake duct in front of the main wheels. The utilisation of the total space for these parts necessitates changed armament and carefully considered construction, and limits the possibilities.

"A considerable increase of the armament weight would also cause an inadmissible loss of performance for an aeroplane with only one HeS-11. There is space in the fuselage nose for the radar aiming mirror. Most fuselage skin panels are detachable. Only the area next to the nose-wheel strut bearing is constructed integrally for strengthening."

It concludes: "Electric deicing is used. The use of fuel in wooden wing compartments was sufficiently proven by the last He 162 aeroplanes. In case of fire, the pilot is

ABOVE: Contour drawing shows how the two 'noses' of the He 1078 B gently curved inwards towards the aircraft's centreline.

able to escape by a catapult seat."

And regarding the bizarre-looking twin-fuselage tailless P 1078 B, the report says: "It was tried to construct this project as far as possible as an all-wing aeroplane, that is to make the ratio of wetted area/wing area as small as possible."

The design's highly unusual double nose layout apparently did no harm, aerodynamically: "The relatively slender two noses of the fuselage when taken singly have a considerable higher critical speed than the wing, DVL wing tunnel tests giving nearly M = 0.9. The noses are bent slightly together to decrease their reciprocal disturbance.

"The critical speed for the double nose is probably still better than for the wing with 40 degree sweepback. This can only be proved by wind tunnel tests. The air intake duct for the turbojet is particularly favourable."

The two designers then seek to justify their decision to have a vision-restricting second nose without putting the jet engine into it: "When considering the arrangement, thought must be given to the problem if it would not be possible to build to advantage an asymmetrical type, that is, fuselage beside turbojet. However, without regard to the complication of the landing gear, a one-sided moment would have to be trimmed.

"It is almost impossible to achieve this

trimming independent of the dynamic pressure and flight path incidence. This distribution would be unpleasant for a tailless aeroplane because the thrust/weight ratio is very great.

"The reduced vision to the front on the right seems to us the lesser 'evil' of the two particularly because an attack from this direction is not to be expected. Because of the very high speeds (1000kph) and the corresponding radii of turns, attack will probably come from behind and above."

The two nose sections were detachable and the armament was placed on the "inside wall" of the second nose "so as to keep the moment about the normal axis due to firing recoil as small as possible."

The document seems intended to give an insight into the P 1078 project during the war, although it has been suggested that the P 1078 A and P 1078 B outlines were simply new designs drawn up for Americans.

The P 1078 design submitted to the February 27-28 meeting is labelled the 'P 1078 C' in the British report German Aircraft: New and Projected Types of January 1946. While there remains no conclusive evidence as to whether the February 27-28 design came before or after the P 1078 A and B, Eichner and Hohbach's report seems to suggest they are earlier – even though the only surviving drawings of them were produced later. ●

Bats from Hamburg

Ein-TL-Jäger – Blohm & Voss P 212

Backed up by its parent company's hugely successful U-boat and surface vessel business, Blohm & Voss Flugzeugbau could afford to invest in research and offer the most radical design solutions without worrying too much about whether bulk orders would be forthcoming. The company was a latecomer to 1-TL-Jäger but its designs were worth waiting for…

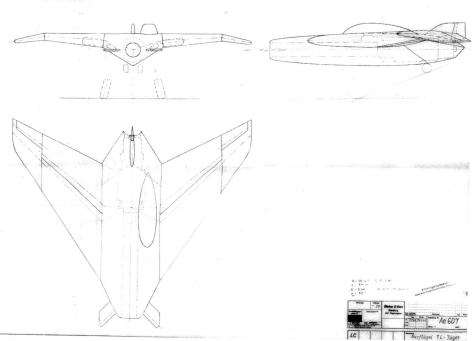

ABOVE: The Blohm & Voss Nurflügel-TL-Jäger of drawing number Ae 607 by Thieme, dated February 5, 1945.

Blohm & Voss came late to single-seat fighter design. Naturally most of its early work had focused on seaplanes, flying boats and maritime patrol although the company had also branched out into ground-attack by the beginning of the Second World War.

All that changed when it took over Messerschmitt's stalled Me 155 high-altitude fighter project in August 1943. Blohm & Voss complained that the project it had received seemed sketchy and barely started but Messerschmitt was unable or unwilling to explain itself. Therefore, a Blohm & Voss team set about completely redesigning it.

Rapid progress was made, and by the time the company was invited to tender for the 1-TL-Jäger competition, the first prototype of what had now been redesignated BV 155 was close to completion.

Meanwhile, beginning in late 1943 or 1944, Blohm & Voss seems to have become associated with the AVA's Göttinger Programm run by Dietrich Küchemann and Hans Drescher. As a result of this, its design team under Richard Vogt began to experiment with different arrangements of jet engines and their intakes, and piston engines and their radiators.

Access to the wide range of different aerodynamic forms being studied by Küchemann and Drescher resulted in Blohm & Voss producing ever more unusual aircraft designs. In particular, the firm's designers became increasingly convinced by two layouts – an internal jet engine with a nose intake, or a piston engine driving a pusher propeller. Each allowed for a relatively compact and efficient form, minimising the use of precious resources in construction, and each seemed to offer improved performance if a tailless layout could be adopted. The usual functions of the rudder and tailplanes would be transferred to the wings themselves, either through their shape or by fitting them with wingtip booms.

This form was first adopted with the P 208, apparently designed as an alternative to the conventional layout P 207 drafted to meet a requirement for a Hochleistungsjäger mit Jumo 222 E/F or 'High-performance fighter with Jumo E/F engine' issued on July 21, 1944. This tailless piston-engined pusher propeller fighter had the virtues of being lightweight, cheap to build, fast and agile – at least on paper. Its control

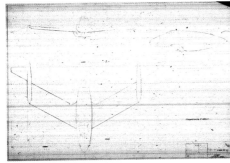

ABOVE: The P 208.01-01 was designed as an alternative to the conventional layout pusher prop P 207 for a high-performance fighter competition begun in July 1944.

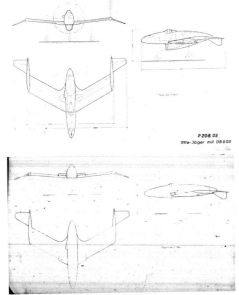

ABOVE: For its third iteration, the P 208 was designed with a DB 603 L engine. The P 208.03-01 featured a circular radiator intake, whereas the -02 featured wing root intakes instead.

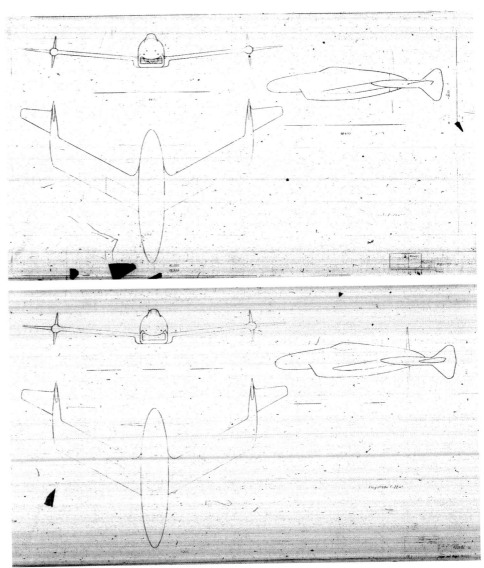

ABOVE: The P 208.02-01 and -02 were similar in appearance but where the former was powered by a Jumo 222 E, the latter was fitted with an Argus As 413.

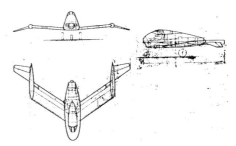

ABOVE: The only known version of the tailless P 209.01, the .01-03. This was a work in progress when the first 1-TL-Jäger design comparison meeting was held and was therefore not offered for consideration.

surfaces took the form of downturned wingtips mounted on booms attached to the ends of the main wings. These served simultaneously as elevators and rudders.

First came the P 208.01-01, which had a simple elliptical fuselage and naturally was powered by a Jumo 222 E with a pusher prop. The engine's large radiator, mounted centrally beneath the fuselage, was wider than the fuselage itself.

The P 208.02-01 retained the Jumo 222 E but was otherwise a substantial redesign, with the flattened cockpit moved to a more central position. The radiator intake was narrowed, lengthened and more integrated into the forward section of fuselage. Rather than simply mounting one control surface apiece, each wingtip boom had small upper and lower fins as well. The P 208.02-02 was powered by an Argus As 413 engine but was otherwise similar to the -01.

A third engine was introduced with the P 208.03-01 – the Daimler-Benz DB 603 L. This design featured a smaller cockpit canopy and a large circular radiator intake underneath the fuselage. Its wingtip booms were longer, more slender and finless. The final P 208 appears to have been the P 208.03-02. This kept the DB 603 L but lost the circular belly intake.

Instead, it had a pair of narrow radiators mounted on top of its wing roots, allowing the aircraft a completely flat underside.

In order to create a competitor for 1-TL-Jäger, Vogt's team reworked the P 208 layout around a Heinkel HeS 011 powerplant as the P 209.01. This was the design that simply wasn't ready in time for the initial comparison of designs on September 8-10 and in the end it was never circulated.

When the Volksjäger requirement was issued on September 10, Blohm & Voss swiftly devised a pair of fighter designs based on their work up to this point – the P 210 and P 211. The former was a straightforward simplification of the P 209 to take a BMW 003 engine, with the aircraft also being made less complex for ease of production. The latter was a conventional tailed design with the P 211.01-01 having swept wings and the P 211.01-02 having straight wings. Initially offered alongside the P 211.01-01, the P 210 appears to have been quickly set aside. The P 211 was evidently better received but ultimately rejected in both forms.

With the P 210 and P 211 defeated, Blohm & Voss went back to the P 209 and subjected it to a dramatic revision in light

of the Volksjäger failure. The P 209.02 had almost nothing in common with the P 209.01 – its nose intake retained the same slant but the cockpit shape was switched to that of the P 211.01-02, while its tail and rear fuselage became that of the P 211.01-01. Most incredibly of all, its swept back wings were swapped for a pair of strongly forward-swept wings.

At the same time the jet intake shape, wings and tailless layout of the original P 209 were transferred to a new project – the P 212 ▶

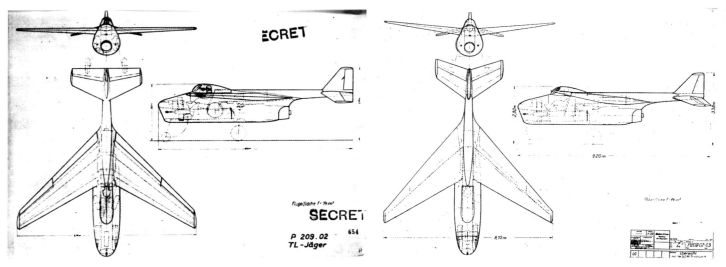

ECRET

SECRET

P 209.02
TL-Jäger

654

ABOVE: The P 209.02 featured sharply forward-swept wings. While the first of these drawings, simply labelled 'P 209.02', shows only a slight upwards wing angle and unswept tail, the P 209.02-03 featured a stronger wing dihedral and a swept tail.

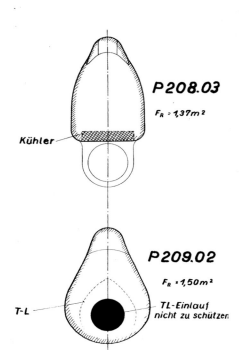

P 208.03

$F_R = 1,37 m^2$

Kühler

P 209.02

$F_R = 1,50 m^2$

T-L

TL-Einlauf
nicht zu schützen

ABOVE: Illustration from a Blohm & Voss report comparing the merits of 'Otto' or piston engine designs with those of aircraft powered by turbojets.

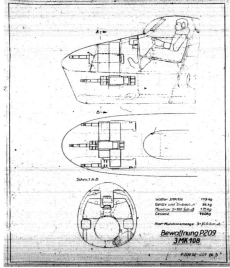

ABOVE: Weaponry for the P 209 – a trio of MK 108 30mm cannon.

– along with the cockpit form that had first appeared on the P 211.01-02. Blohm & Voss was mixing and matching design features.

On November 8, 1944, the company responded to a memo it had received from the EHK under the heading 'Why produce the Otto fighter?', in other words, what did the firm perceive to be the advantages and disadvantages of continuing to design and build new piston-engined aircraft, rather than jets, at this stage in the war?

The response compared four aircraft projects the Blohm & Voss said it was working on simultaneously – the conventional layout BV 155 C "the extreme high-level fighter", the tailless P 208.03 "Otto fighter with DB 603, pusher airscrew and outer tail unit", forward-swept P 209.02 "TL fighter with HeS 011, with central inlet pipe connection and built-in engine" and the basic "midget fighter" P 211.01

"TL fighter with BMW 003, detailed projects for it having been worked out".

It stated: "Our own people having during the past months been very busy on plans for high-speed fighters on both lines of development – Otto as well as TL lines – and the projects having therefore reached an equal state of maturity, it seemed appropriate to answer the above question by simply comparing the operational efficiency of both types."

In the comparison of speed: "At low altitudes the Otto fighter is inferior to both types of TL machines, midget as well as high-speed fighter. At its full pressure height level the Otto fighter is steadier than the midget fighter whose range hardly enables it to reach that altitude.

"At absolute maximum speed the midget fighter gains slightly while remaining somewhat below the full pressure height level of the Otto fighter. The extreme high-speed fighter with HeS 011 engine is much more efficient at all altitudes. The extreme high-level fighter built on Otto lines lacks speed when performing at altitudes which however as yet, it alone is able to attain."

Comparisons of climbing power,

range and endurance, fuel efficiency, weapon carrying capability, acceleration and ease of production follow. While an overall conclusion is lacking, the report ends with: "However indispensable the Otto fighter in its further stages of development may prove to be, it is nevertheless advisable to reduce its production while simultaneously switching over to the production of TL fighters."

Between the submission of this report and the publication of the first P 212 brochure, the type's design underwent two substantial revisions. The first of these was the P 212.02, which shifted the P 212's wings to sit much lower and further forward on the fuselage while adding a large dorsal 'spine' which extended rearwards to a point beyond the jet engine's exhaust. It also featured a new flat rectangular intake in place of the slanted circular one.

Next came the P 212.02-01, which saw the wings shifted back to the higher position and the nose intake reshaped again. This design was the one chosen to appear in the first P 212 brochure, dated November 28, 1944, and bearing the title "Fastest fighter with HeS 011 – P 212" and the subtitle "tailless with edge control surfaces".

The first line of the first page gets straight to the point: "Compared to the P 209 project, the design described here shows a free outflow of engine gases that does not influence the stabiliser. This was achieved by the complete removal of the tail from the wing downwash."

On the tailed forward-swept P.209.02, the tail surfaces were angled downwards – towards the jet exhaust outflow – thereby conceivably posing problems in the event of manoeuvring causing jet wash to effect the rudder/elevators. In addition, judging from what is stated later on, it seems that concerns had been raised about the potential for the aircraft setting its own tail on fire.

The high-wing P 212 design prevented both problems by placing the control surfaces well away from any interference from jet wash.

The brochure continues: "Incidentally, we had tried the same fuselage arrangement as that of the P 209 project. However, the

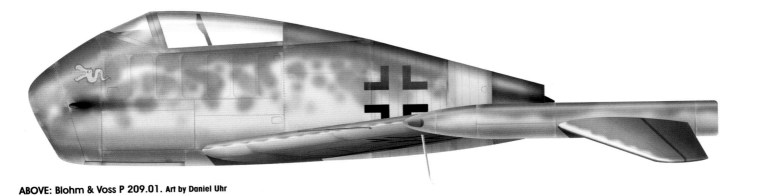

ABOVE: Blohm & Voss P 209.01. Art by Daniel Uhr

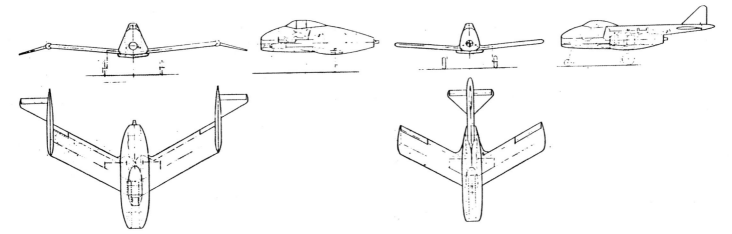

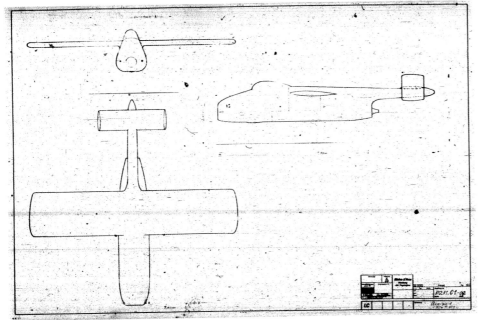

ABOVE & LEFT: Blohm & Voss's trio of Volksjäger designs. The tailless P 210 was offered alongside the swept wing P 211.01-01. These were both then abandoned in favour of the even simpler straight-wing P 211.01-02.

performance of the new design resulted in such a considerable gain in speed – namely 35km on the ground and 45km in 6000m altitude – that it was necessary to increase the sweep of the wing to 45 degrees."

Presumably the "35km" and "45km" refers to the speed increase in km/h over the figures given for the P 209. The brochure goes on: "This high sweep pushed the wing joint on the fuselage so far forward that a rearrangement of the cockpit and armament was required. The high sweep brings an increase in the flight weight but on the other hand it means that the tail booms can be reduced to insignificant stumps without affecting the effectiveness of the control surfaces.

"With regard to the production expense, everything that was said in the brief description of the P 209 project remains true. It is therefore advisable to consult them simultaneously. In summary it can be said that the technical benefits of the P 212 project against P 209 are both in the operational and performance areas.

"Operational – in order to avoid the consequences of an outlet-fire – an unobstructed gaseous effluent is always desirable. Performance-wise, the big speed gain is considered particularly important. With a 1030km maximum speed the new project should be placed at the top of any comparison of projects with the same engine."

By January 1945, Blohm & Voss had developed the P 212 to what would be its final form – the P 212.03. It is briefly described in the notes prepared in advance of the EHK's end of February meeting. A pressure cabin is a new feature and standard armament has been reduced to just two MK 108s but with a variety of options to increase it: "General: Tailless mid-wing plane with swept back wings and controls at the end of the wings. Wings: Steel skin wings in the Blohm and Voss type of construction can be constructed whole or in parts. Part of the inside of the wings built to hold fuel. Very deep landing flaps at the trailing edge, and nose flaps which slide into the wing leading edge.

"Fuselage: The curved steel TL duct is the inside support of the fuselage. Just in front of the TL inlet the support pipe broadens out to attach to a longitudinal beam, each side of which is attached to the wing in front and the TL behind. The guns are placed in front of the pressure proof pilot's cabin, which is situated above the inlet pipe. The engine is in the stern.

"Stabilisers: At the end of each wing are two surfaces, of which, one slanting downward fulfils the function of the elevator ▶

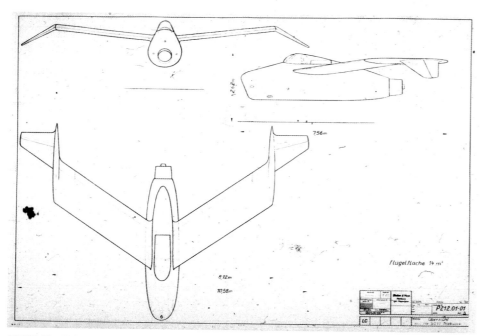

ABOVE: The first design in the P 212 sequence was this – the P 212.01-01 – which featured wings similar to those of the P 209.01 and a cockpit similar to that of the P 209.02.

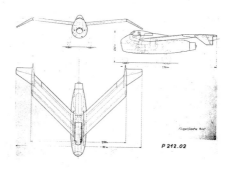

ABOVE: The first P 212 to become a firm entry for the 1-TL-Jäger competition was the P 212.02-01. It had wings similar to those of the P 212.01 but with the revised wingtips of the P 212.02. The fuselage was revised again to form a gently curving rear fuselage rather than a spine and the cockpit was brought forward.

and partly the functions of the vertical stabiliser and ailerons. The second fin is an additional small vertical stabiliser. In addition there is a small normal aileron.

"Undercarriage: Main undercarriage rests on the fuselage beams and moves forward into the fuselage. The nose wheel likewise moves forward. Main 710mm x 185mm, nose wheel 465mm x 165mm.

"Engine: The HeS 011 engine is fixed to the fuselage. Air is introduced through bent inlet pipe in the tip of the fuselage. Fuel installations: 820 litre unprotected and 150 litre protected in the wings behind the pilot, and in front of the turbo a well-constructed protected tank of 480 litres. Additional tank in wings to make a total of 1370 litres. Equipment: Standard equipment for fighter aircraft.

"Armament: 2 x MK 108 with 100 rounds each next to the air duct in the fuselage nose. An additional MK 108 possible above the duct. Further additional 2 x MK 108 with 60 rounds each provided behind the pilot in the under part of the fuselage. Possible armament variation with MG 103 and MK 112. Possible to build a place in the fuselage for 500kg bomb. Bullet-proofing: The pilot is protected from shots back and front by armour."

But having completed sufficient design work on the P 212.03 for the proposal by mid-January, and having continued worked on the P 208.03 into the P 208.03-03, powered by a DB 603 N, Blohm & Voss was able to undertake further work in connection with the AVA's Göttinger Programm and on January 23, 1945, produced drawing Ae 605 showing an aircraft similar to

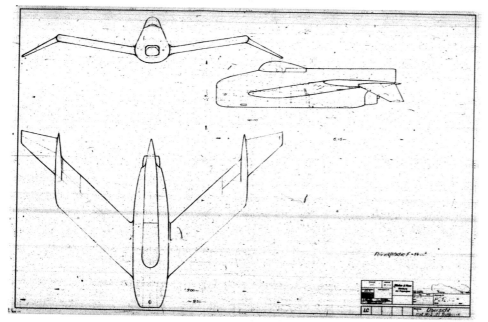

ABOVE: The P 212.02, dating from late October 1944, featured a prominent spine – presumably to house extra fuel – a revised nose intake form, revised wingtip surfaces, a shorter fuselage and a shorter wingspan.

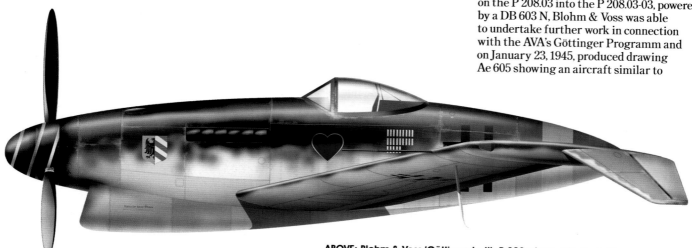

ABOVE: Blohm & Voss 'Göttinger' with P 208 wings. Art by Daniel Uhr

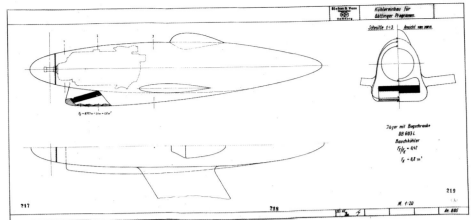

ABOVE: While work was ongoing on the P 209 and P 212, Blohm & Voss also carried out work for the Göttinger aerodynamics programme – such as this design in drawing Ae 605, showing a tractor prop tailless design.

when deciding on a layout for fighters. The offset cockpit allowed a 'flat' profile, the canards could help an aircraft with strong sweepback land more slowly and the uneven undercarriage prevented dirt and dust from rough makeshift airfields from entering the engine intake by tilting the front of the aircraft up away from the ground.

The authenticity of the Nurflügel-TL-Jäger has been questioned for years but, oddly enough, it has proven to be an entirely genuine wartime design.

The P 212 lined up against its competitors on February 27-28 and was not rejected outright, effectively coming joint third with the EF 128, but in the final analysis it failed to attract a development contract. It would, however, provide the basis for one final Blohm & Voss project – the P 215. ●

the P 208 but with a tractor propeller, rather than a pusher; the key feature being a chin-mounted radiator inlet.

Just under two weeks later, on February 5, 1945, Blohm & Voss designer Thieme produced drawing number Ae 607, depicting an entirely bizarre-looking aircraft and labelled it "Nurflügel-TL-Jäger" or 'all-wing jet fighter'. This had a unique combination of features besides its 45 sweepback: an offset cockpit allowed a very narrow wing profile while at the same time retaining a completely straight flow of air from the circular intake at the tip of the wing to the HeS 011 engine mounted internally at the rear. Small forward-swept canards at the front of the aircraft would have presumably lowered the permissible landing speed, while a four-wheel undercarriage, two large wheels at the front, and two small wheels to the rear, would have kept the engine intake well away from any surface debris.

The Blohm & Voss Nurflügel-TL-Jäger never received a 'P' number and was probably only intended to showcase ideas for solving particular problems facing designers

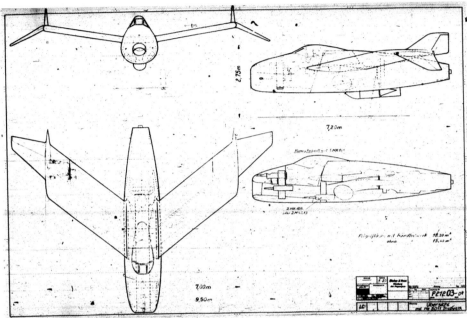

ABOVE: The final evolution of the P 212 – the P 212.03-01. This features a nose and wings similar to those of the P 212.02 married to the curved rear section of the P 212.02-01. This design failed to attract a development contract at the February 27-28 1-TL-Jäger conference.

ABOVE: Blohm & Voss Nurflügel-TL-Jäger. Art by Daniel Uhr

ABOVE: Blohm & Voss 'Göttinger' with P 212 wings. Art by Daniel Uhr

Going back to tailless

In the wake of Lippisch's departure and the dissolution of Abteilung L, Messerschmitt's project office largely abandoned tailless and flying wing designs. Yet during 1944, it came increasingly to reconsider their potential...

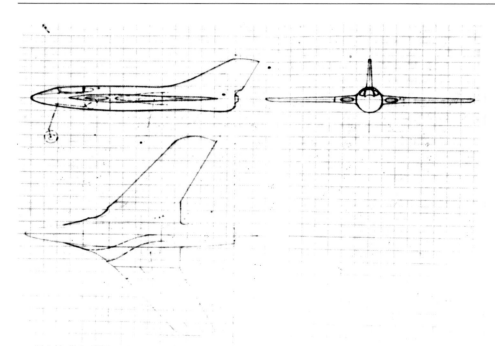

ABOVE: Previously unknown version of the Messerschmitt P 1112 drawn on graph paper and appended to a sheaf of notes dated April 18, 1945, with '1 TL-Jäger / allgemein' or 'single-jet fighter / general' written on the cover.

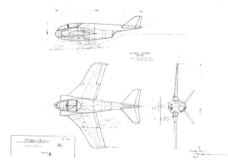

ABOVE: The earliest known single-jet P 1101 design of July 24, 1944. Messerschmitt had been studying two- three- and four-jet designs under P 1101 since May and scaled down some of their features to create a '1-TL-Jäger'.

Messerschmitt had a wealth of experience in designing single-jet fighters by the time the 1-TL-Jäger requirement was issued in July 1944.

In the wake of Abteilung L, the department's only surviving project beside the Me 163, the P 20, was compared against the main project office's single jet P 1092 in three different variations and the Me 262.

A Messerschmitt report published on July 3, 1943, assessing each type based on all of them being fitted with the Jumo 004 C found that the P 20 was too slow and incapable of carrying heavy loads. The P 1092 was significantly cheaper than the Me 262 but also lacking in capability and the more expensive Me 262 offered superior performance to the others in all areas.

In October 1943, the project office came up with a way of making a more attractive single-jet fighter, P 1095, by utilising components from both the Me 262 and Me 209 in its construction. In an undated 'preliminary note' on the project the company states: "Tests carried out so far show that the superior jet engines (up to approx. 1000 kg thrust) cannot achieve a performance superiority (apart from manoeuvrability and landing) of the single jet aircraft against the two jet aircraft, but on the other hand only about half the fuel is needed.

"A complete new development of the single jet fighter with the current jet engines is probably hardly worthwhile but on the other hand it is urgent, in the current air-war and fuel procurement situation, to have the great superiority of the single jet fighter over the enemy airplanes with piston engines. A suitable compromise solution should be the following suggestion.

"From the starting series of the Me 262 and Me 209, as many parts as possible are weighted and accepted without or with minor modifications for the single jet aircraft project P 1095 to be produced therefrom. The development and updating expenses are then reduced to a minimum.

"In the enclosed short description, the parts which can be transferred from the series are listed for the single jet fighter and their share is estimated as part of the total production. It is unimportant whether the metal version or the later wood version of the Me 262 is used."

The P 1095 detailed was to use an underslung Jumo 004 B-2 fitted to an Me 262 fuselage, Me 209 tail, and undercarriage and systems from bits of both Me 262 and Me 209. Evidently the

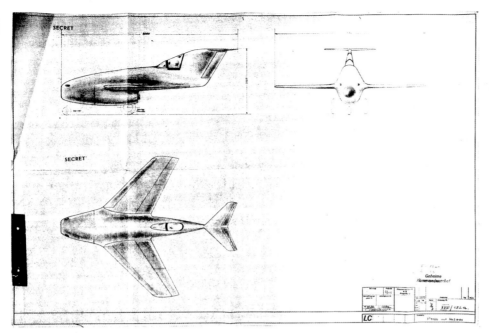

ABOVE: For the second 1-TL-Jäger comparison meeting in December 1944 the P 1101 was dropped and replaced with this – the P 1106. This drawing, XVIII/152a, dated December 12, 1944, is by Hans Hornung.

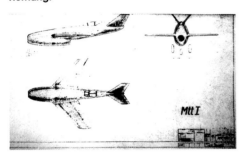

ABOVE: The form of the Messerschmitt P 1106 had changed significantly by the time of the January 1-TL-Jäger conference, where it was presented as 'Mtt I'.

ABOVE: The P 1110 was Messerschmitt's January 1945 design, presented as 'Mtt II'. It featured an unusual annular intake for its single HeS 011 jet engine plus a boundary layer suction system.

wings were to be the only new part.

Neither the P 1092 nor the P 1095 went any further and by March 1944 Messerschmitt was concentrating instead on creating new twin-engine aircraft based on the Me 262 – the P 1099 heavy fighter and P 1100 bomber. These were essentially all-new 'fat' fuselages with Me 262 wings and tail surfaces.

The P 1101 project began during spring 1944 as a continuation of P 1099/1100, comparing the Me 262 against new HeS 011-powered two-jet, three-jet and four-jet designs. A single turbojet design does not appear to have been considered at this stage.

It was only in July 1944 when the company began to look again at single-jet designs and created the first one by simply scaling down the aerodynamic features of its earlier P 1101 studies.

The first drawing, of July 24, 1944, showed a stubby aircraft with swept wings, a V-tail, low slung built-in turbojet and intakes which flared on either side of the cockpit. In profile, it resembles the tailless P 01-112 drawn up more than four years earlier but in truth it was much more closely related to the P 1101 studies which immediately preceded it, such as the P 1101-104 – featuring similar cockpit, wing and tail arrangements.

This design was evidently revised on August 22, with the cockpit being brought

further back away from the nose and the turbojet, while still internal, being raised up to exhaust over the V-tail rather than under it. On August 30, another version was drawn up which returned to the low turbojet layout but added a longer nose and slightly longer tail – and it is believed that this was the P 1101, first presented during the meeting on September 8-10.

After the September meeting, however, the P 1101 was revised again and simplified. A nose intake was adopted and the V-tail was replaced with a conventional fin.

Before the next meeting to discuss the 1-TL-Jäger however, on December 19-21, Messerschmitt decided to drop the P 1101 and submit another design in its place – the P 1106. This took ideas from both the P 1092 and P 1101 and the result was decidedly odd. It had a nose intake and fuselage-mounted engine but instead of having the cockpit at the front of the fuselage (P 1101) or in the centre (P 1092), it was positioned far to the rear. This unusual shape apparently gave the best aerodynamic performance but hampered the pilot's visibility forward and down.

By the next assessment and comparison meeting on January 12-15, the P 1106 was joined by another new tailed design, the P 1110. This appeared to be a development of the earlier solid-nose designs but significantly refined.

The P 1106's design drawbacks, and

perhaps the successful completion of a flyable experimental P 1101, not to mention its apparently above-average performance, meant that for the February 27-28 conference the P 1101 made a comeback, the P 1106 was dropped and alongside it were the P 1110 and yet another new design, the tailless P 1111.

Undoubtedly building upon the aerodynamic research carried out by Alexander Lippisch during his years at Messerschmitt, the P 1111 had entirely new wings – unlike the P 1101, P 1106 and P 1110 which had generally had similar or the same set of swept wings with only the fuselage arrangement being altered.

The P 1111's large wings contained unprotected fuel tanks with an overall capacity of 1500 litres. Its fuselage was all-metal but housed only two MK 108s in its nose – with an option to fit a further two in the wing roots just outboard of the uncomplicated engine intakes. There was a pressurised cockpit but no ejection seat.

Unlike the other Messerschmitt designs for 1-TL-Jäger, only one version of the P 1111 is known and from only one drawing. This has led to the general impression that the P 1111 was something of an irrelevant afterthought, yet a company report dated February 26, 1945 – the day before the 'final' conference – suggests that Messerschmitt rated its performance highly, particularly against Junkers' EF 128.

The report exists as an appendix to the outline brief prepared by Messerschmitt for the other conference delegates, although as might be expected it only appeared in copies given to members of the Messerschmitt team. It is headed "Beurteilung" or 'Evaluation' and begins: "There is no doubt in the totality of performance. Put the Messerschmitt P 1111 project at the top. In the top speed, this design is the fastest except for the P 1110 (and there is little difference, 5km/h), while it is at the top in all other calculated performances: climb rate is 23.7m/s versus 23.2 of Focke-Wulf II and 21.5m/s of the P 1110. Landing speed is 155km/h compared to 164km/h for Focke-Wulf I and 178km/h for P 1110. Landing distance is 450m compared to 490m for Focke-Wulf II and 610m for P 1110. The take-off distance is 600m compared to 650m for Focke-Wulf II and 790m for the P 1110.

"The design of Junkers is roughly equivalent to the P 1110 from Messerschmitt: in the top speed, it is 10km/h slower (it is in third position in relation to the top speed), in the start and climb performances it is somewhat better, in landing performance slightly worse than P 1110. The P 1101, in terms of the top speed, is 20km/h behind the P 1110 (assuming that the latter is capable of 4% thrust loss in intake) with top speed of 980km/h. The starting and climbing performance of this design is higher than that of the P 1110 and very close to those of the Junkers design, landing performance is better than that of P 1110 and EF 128.

"The other designs are so far behind the above-mentioned speeds that they are able to be dismissed from the selection. Experience so far has shown that a performance disadvantage of around 30-50km/h would be an intolerable tactical lag behind the fastest possible fighter aircraft. The differences between the best top-speed designs and, for example, the Focke-Wulf II design with regard to take-off, climb and landing services, ▶

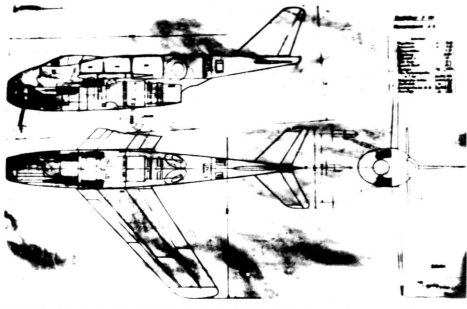

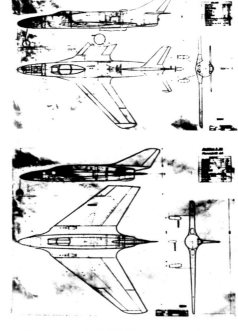

ABOVE: The three Messerschmitt designs presented at the final design conference on February 27-28, 1945 – P 1101, P 1110 and the tailless P 1111.

do not justify the speed difference."

Messerschmitt had effectively written off both the Blohm & Voss and Heinkel entries and regarded the Focke-Wulf entries as inferior due to their lower top speed compared to the Messerschmitt trio and the Junkers EF 128.

Next the Messerschmitt evaluation posed the question of "whether the calculated performances are linked to considerable uncertainties in any of the above-mentioned models". Jet intake design, particularly combined with boundary layer removal by suction, was seemingly the biggest cause for concern: "The greatest uncertainty in the power calculation of all the designs lies in the estimate of the loss of thrust at the engine inlets of the Junkers and Messerschmitt P 1110 designs. In both models, the engine inlets are located laterally and quite far behind the fuselage and lead the air with considerable curvatures towards the engine.

"In both designs, the influence of the boundary layer occurring before the engine inlet is to be eliminated by sucking off this boundary layer. Junkers wants to perform the suction by the contraction under pressure at a suitable location of the fuselage and by means of a special suction blower. The arrangement chosen by Messerschmitt is more complex, but appears more reliable and probably associated with lower power losses.

"The magnitude of the performance uncertainty due to the boundary layer suction is quite considerable, especially since wind tunnel tests cannot give binding results at low speeds; It is quite conceivable that, at high Mach numbers, a boundary layer thickening or detachment due to a pressure surge occurs before the engine inlet, and that the conditions are decisively influenced thereby. The power loss caused by the intake is calculated as 4% thrust.

"The P 1110 design can experience a loss of 14%, EF 128 9.5%, until the speed has fallen to that of the slowest four draft designs. This number, however, applies only to high-speed flying (Mach influence) and only on the assumption that the Mach influence actually has the magnitude

assumed in the comparative calculation, and that the flight speed is sufficient to reach the steep resistance range to come!"

The next point concerns "deviations of the fuselage from the theoretical spindle shape" – a reference to what is known as area rule. The report notes that the P 1101 was likely to suffer problems in this regard: "The fuselage of the P 1101, which was calculated in the case of power adjustment on the basis of measurements on spindle bodies and circular cross-sections, is in fact substantially different from this form. It is, on the one hand, in the side view, because of the arrangement of the engine; on the other hand, its cross-section is not ideal for its high frame shape; It is to be assumed that these facts will have an adverse effect on performance."

The report then mentions the lack of leading edge slats on the EF 128's wings: "With the large arrow shape of 45 , there is a considerable likelihood that the Junkers EF 128 design will be retrofitted with a slat, which would result in a top speed reduction of about 10km/h."

In terms of flight characteristics, both the P 1110 and P 1101 were described as being superior to the EF 128 and P 1111. In addition, "the designs P 1101 and P 1110 should most likely be on the safe side. They have the smallest sweep, a medium taper, thick profiles in the outside tail, and a slat which is exceptionally deep in the outer wing, to achieve the greatest possible safety against local tearing".

In summing up, the Messerschmitt pre-meeting report states: "The three designs P 1110, P 1111 and EF 128, which are truly satisfactory in the top speed, are subject to risks (engine run-in) or disadvantages (unprotected tanks) which do not allow a decision in their favour now.

"All further designs are so much inferior to the top speed that a final decision in their favour seems to be impossible, as they would justify the use of the aircraft as an obstacle to the technically achievable (also the opponent!).

"The performance results of the P 1111 design seem to indicate that it is possible to achieve a combination of maximum speed and take-off, climbing or landing

performance, which is higher compared to the standard aircraft and the tailless design with a relatively large fuselage, by developing towards the flying wing aircraft."

Messerschmitt was set to suggest a four-part decision to the other delegates at the conference:

"1. An order with the immediate goal of serial production cannot yet be given.

2. The P 1101 study aircraft under construction is to be completed and tested as soon as possible; The same may be true of changes to study aircraft that may be located in Pau.

"3. New designs shall be drawn up for the single jet fighter aircraft to be purchased in series, in which the achievements are as unambiguous as possible and without any decisive risks or disadvantages. A preliminary note for the technical requirements is available.

4. On the basis of the drafts submitted so far, only three companies are given the project contract: this restriction is intended to avoid a fragmentation of the design capacity by parallel work of some companies on too many tasks as well as a concentration of the German development on the one task of the 1-TL-Jäger to the detriment of other militarily equally important tasks."

P 1112

While Bock's note on the Entwicklungshauptkommission meeting held on March 1, 1945, shows that Messerschmitt and Focke-Wulf were each to receive a development contract with no firm decision on Junkers and Blohm & Voss, it seems that Messerschmitt went ahead with its own proposal anyway and began working on the new designs it had suggested.

This work was given the designation P 1112 and it was to be Messerschmitt's final project of the war. The British summary of the project in German Aircraft: New and Projected Types reads: "The P 1112 was designed to correct some of the faults which became apparent after study of the P 1111.

"The wing area was reduced to 236.5sq ft since it was felt that the wing loading could be increased. The pilot's cockpit is situated

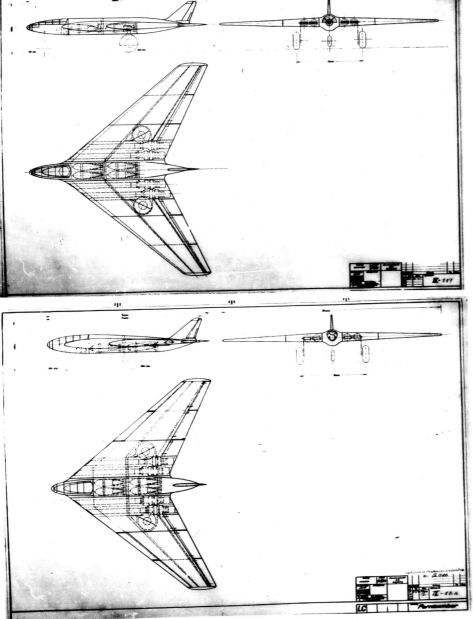

ABOVE: Two designs for Messerschmitt's tailless P 1108 bomber. The flying wing project grew out of studies for the conventional layout P 1107 and was eventually halted while still incomplete and handed over to Junkers.

at the extreme nose of the aircraft and 2 x MK 108 guns are fitted in the wing.

"The remainder of the design closely resembles the P 1111. Performance calculations were not completed."

Interviewed on September 7, 1945, by the British, the head of Messerschmitt's project office, Woldemar Voigt, said: "P 1101, P 1106, P 1110, P 1111, P 1112. A project investigation of the single engined jet fighter was being carried out. The project drawings are known here, I assume.

"A final conclusion had not been drawn until the end of the war; the results secured by that time were: a speed of 1000kph (620mph) is obtainable and had been guaranteed to the government.

"The tailless designs P 1111 and P 1112 showed the best performance out of the hitherto completed project series. They had the special advantage of combining best max speed with best landing speed. They seem to

be dangerous at high Mach numbers (pitching moments). It seems to be possible to reach the same performance with more conventional designs (or even to exceed it) with less risk."

P 1108

Beginning in November 1944, shortly after the P 1106 was conceived, a four-jet bomber was developed in parallel with Messerschmitt's advanced single-jet fighter designs: the P 1107. Like the other Messerschmitt products of the time, this had a conventional tailed layout.

P 1107 project leader Ludwig Bölkow was interviewed for Allied intelligence by de Havilland Mosquito designer Richard Clarkson, who wrote: "In November 1944, Professor Messerschmitt suggested to the German government that it might be possible to carry 8800lb of bombs for 4350 miles range at 500mph with jets. The Government were interested in the possibilities of the project for convoy

raiding and strategic bombing of Russia.

"An analysis of a conventional layout with tail showed that with four Heinkel 011 engines of 2860lb thrust each it might be possible to do 3100 miles range with 8800lb of bombs, but that a tailless layout had better promise of realising the desired figures.

"A number of tailless layouts were examined between November 1944 and February 1945 and these were all available at the plant."

Messerschmitt's proposal resulted in a new competition – known as Langstreckenbomber – initially with only one other contender, the Ju 287. In January it was decided that a third contender should be added, the Horten brothers' H XVIII. But even as Messerschmitt's P 1107 was being compared against its rivals, the company was studying a range of different flying-wing configurations under the designation P 1108.

While the P 1107 foundered because of the long development period that would be required if it was to be built, the P 1108 seems to have found some support from the committee members charged with judging the H XVIII. However, when the four-day Langstreckenbomber conference concluded on February 23 and the Ju 287 was given a production contract, it was decided that Messerschmitt did not have the manpower available to continue developing the the P 1108. Therefore, the project was passed on to another firm.

Clarkson noted: "The Government decided that Messerschmitt's had no available design and production capacity for tackling the job and gave it to Junkers and the Horten brothers. The latest of the Messerschmitt general arrangement drawings therefore does not represent the final solution.

"Herr Bölkow stated that the figures given corresponded to a range of 3100 miles and that the subsequent proposal was to load the aeroplane up to about 77,000lb to get the 4350 miles range.

"Take-off would be by rockets or catapult on a trolley, the aeroplane to be cruised throughout at its operational ceiling which would be about 18,500ft initially and 29,500-33,000ft finally, the undercarriage only being used for landing."

He said that one of the key issues that had occupied the Messerschmitt team had been where to put the engine intakes and what shape they should take.

"The best location of entry ducts was under discussion and undecided, i.e. whether above, below or in the leading edge of the wing. Considerable wind tunnelling would be needed. It was noted that as with the P 1101-1111 fighters the question of entry duct position and losses played a very important part in the settling of the layout."

Clarkson concluded: "As mentioned earlier in these notes the final general arrangement and the above notes do not represent Messerschmitt's considered and final thoughts on the project, the design was still fluid and the size and number of engines were undecided."

The Horten brothers found themselves in a similar situation as their own H XVIII and the P 1108 were both given to Junkers, which rolled them up into its own flying-wing development – the EF 130, the story of which continues on page 96. ●

The latecomer

Ein-TL-Jäger – Junkers EF 128

While the EF 128 tailless fighter might seem to have appeared fully formed from a company that specialised in aircraft with two or more piston engines, Junkers had in fact spent years working on the aerodynamics underpinning its design before the 1-TL-Jäger competition began…

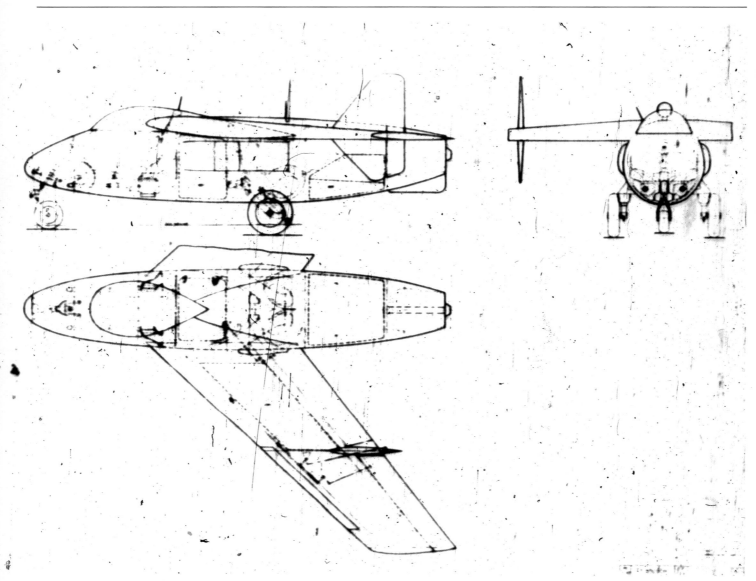

ABOVE: The Junkers EF 128 as it was presented at the 1-TL-Jäger comparison conference of December 19-21, 1944. It was developed in parallel with the Ju 248 rocket fighter.

Messerschmitt's reluctance to pursue any further work on tailless manned aircraft designs following the departure of Lippisch meant further development of the Me 163 beyond the Me 163 B was stalled. The company had decided on July 27, 1943, to conduct further work on his extended-fuselage Me 163 C with a second rocket engine for cruising at altitude, but this made little progress.

Similarly, full series production of the Me 163 B was slow to get going. Hanns Klemm Flugzeugbau had been chosen to build the Me 163 B but the company had no equipment for building the type's metal fuselage and its largely semi-skilled and unskilled workforce required extensive retraining. Therefore, Junkers took over responsibility for the Me 163 on September 1, 1944. In doing so, it

implemented its own design changes to make production quicker and easier.

This work continued and on October 11, 1944, Junkers produced a description of its own design, the Ju 248, which it compared against the last version of the Me 163 C, drafted by Messerschmitt. It had a long slimmed-down fuselage that would be constructed in three main sections to speed up production – a pressure cabin

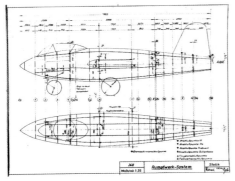

ABOVE: Fuselage dimensions of the Junkers Ju 248, dated December 1, 1944.

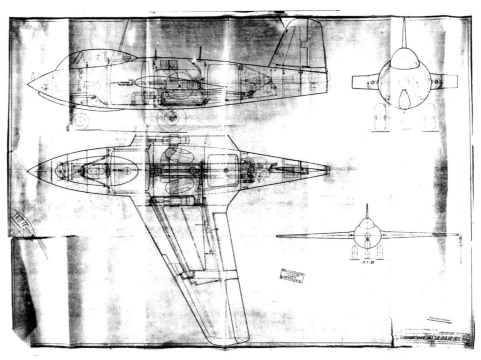

ABOVE: A detailed plan of the Ju 248, dated December 30, 1944. The number '263' now appears in the info panel.

with a bubble canopy which would be riveted onto the main fuselage section, and finally a detachable tail section for easy access to its two rocket engines.

The main fuselage incorporated a fully retractable tricycle undercarriage, while the fin, rudder and wings were almost entirely standard Me 163 components. In all only 60-70% of the aircraft was new.

Just 10 days later Junkers was awarded a contract to develop the Ju 248, though not for series production. The firm began by creating two development aircraft, dubbed Me 163 D, out of Me 163 Bs – the V13 and V18. These were given new fuselage sections in front of and behind the wing plus a fixed tricycle undercarriage that could be shifted to different positions on the airframe to determine which worked best.

By mid-November, Messerschmitt had

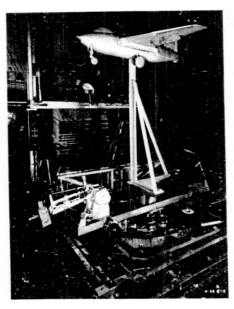

ABOVE: Wind tunnel models of the Ju 248 with undercarriage in the retracted and lowered positions.

ABOVE: A mockup of the Ju 248 showing the cockpit and a view over the 'shoulder' looking towards the tail end.

evidently protested about a derivative of its Me 163 receiving a Junkers 'Ju' prefix and a unique RLM code. The Ju 248 was therefore the second design to receive the designation Me 263, though Junkers seems to have persisted in calling it the Ju 248 or 8-248 in its internal documents.

At this point, the design was in competition for a full production contract against several others as a 'target defence aircraft'. According to the British report German Aircraft: New and Projected Types, discussing minutes of an EHK meeting on November 21-22, 1944, under the heading 'target defence aircraft': "The importance of target defence was emphasised and consideration was narrowed down to the 8-248 (8-263), a development of the Me 163 B; the Heinkel 'Julia'; Bachem

'Natter'; and the Me 262 interceptor with supplementary rocket propulsion.

"It was decided that since these developments were in an advanced state it was not expedient to abandon any of them. A proposal by the Special Commission for Jet Aircraft and Special Aircraft to defer or reject the 8-263 in favour of the He 162 was opposed on the ground that further development and series production of the 263 could be based on the work already undertaken in connection with the 163.

"The four types of target defence aircraft already enumerated were to be developed in the following priority: 1. Me 262 with supplementary rocket propulsion. 2. Heinkel 'Julia'. 3. 8-248. 4. Bachem 'Natter'.

"The development of the BMW rocket 109.708, using nitric acid, was to proceed on ▶

ABOVE: The earliest EF 128 model tested by Junkers – a simple fuselage and swept wing combination.

EF 128 used a system based on boundary layer suction methods investigated by Junkers back in April 1943. The performance of the wings and the aircraft as a whole was to be improved through a redirection of air at high speeds.

Most of the aircraft entered for the contest had a fuel capacity of 1250 litres – as per the required specification – but the EF 128 could hold a substantial 1030 litres in two armoured tanks in the fuselage and another 540 litres unprotected in the wings for a total of 1570 litres. This would have potentially have given it the range and endurance to outlast all of its competitors except the Focke-Wulf II design.

The capacious nose also offered the possibility of expanding armament from two to four MK 108s with 100 rounds each and there was bulletproofing with "the pilot protected against 12.7mm ammunition from the front and 20mm from behind".

The EF 128 entry in German Aircraft:

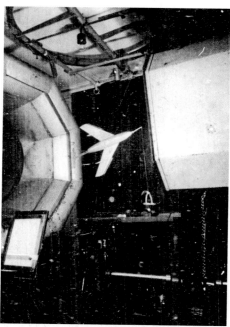

New and Projected Types offers a couple of titbits of additional information about Junkers' plans for further development of the type: "Good results were obtained in the wind tunnel with the first completed model. A mock-up fuselage with a HeS 011 was built. This was to be mounted above the fuselage of a Ju 88 for testing... a variation of the EF 128 was planned as a two-seat night fighter. It was to have a lengthened fuselage."

While the Ju 248/Me 263 and the EF 128 had significant differences, most obviously that the former had a rocket engine rather than a jet, the basic internal layout of the two aircraft was similar, with a large fuel tank directly behind the pilot, and the tricycle undercarriage retracting into the fuselage.

Where the two designs differed most greatly was the wings – those of the EF 128 were all-new while those of the Ju 248 were taken from the Me 163 B – and the central/

a high priority as this unit was intended for the three last-named developments."

While the Ju 248/Me 263 was undergoing rapid development, Junkers was also working in parallel on a tailless single-turbojet fighter design of roughly similar proportions – the EF 128. This was first presented as a competitor for the 1-TL-Jäger requirement during the conference on December 19-21. The design tested by the DVL in January 1945 was a tailless high-wing aircraft with 45 swept back wings made entirely of wood. The inner part of these was designed to hold fuel. There was a small upper and lower fin about halfway along each wing.

According to CIOS report XXXI-3 German High Speed Airplanes and Design Development: "Junkers had still another approach in the use of sweptback wings. On their EF 128, proposed tailless fighter, they had two vertical tails each centred on the aft portion of the wing at a point half the semi-span outboard of the fuselage. This procedure was said to stop the spanwise boundary layer flow along the wing and transfer the stall point from the tip to a point just inboard of the fin."

The fuselage was all metal with a blunt nose which had "room for nose wheel and additional special equipment," according to the report prepared in advance of the February 27-28 meeting on the 1-TL-Jäger designs. There was a pressure cabin and ejection seat for the pilot and behind that an air duct. Regarding the engine, it had its single "HeS 109-011 enclosed in rear of fuselage. Accessible through removable parts of the outer shell of the fuselage. Intake openings for the air suction on the side walls of the fuselage under the wings. Boundary layer split provided. Suction of boundary layer air outlet duct at the end of the pilot's cabin dome".

The only other entry to the 1-TL-Jäger competition to have a feature like this was the Messerschmitt P 1110. The

ABOVE: Wind tunnel tests on a model of the December 1944 version of the Junkers EF 128.

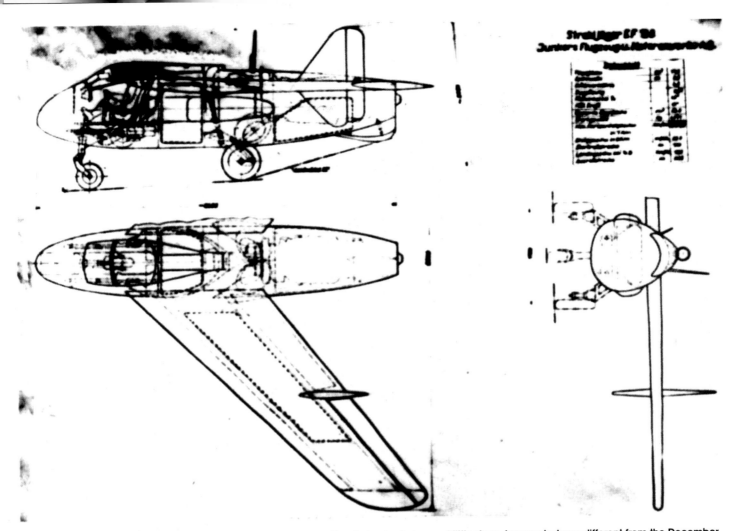

ABOVE: The EF 128 as it appeared at the February 27-28 meeting. The design had changed little since January but was different from the December version in having a reprofiled nose, longer wings and a different tail skid.

rear fuselage where the latter had no need for a single vertical fin but did require intakes for its innovative air suction system.

Although Junkers came away from the February 27-28 meeting empty handed, at the end of March, as previously noted, the company received a development contract for the EF 128. Unfortunately, by this time it was far too late for Junkers to get beyond even the most preliminary of designs.

Meanwhile, the Ju 248/Me 263 had been approved for full production in January 1945 and the first full prototype made a total of 13 test flights between February 8 and February 19. The airframe had its rocket engine installed on March 23, 1945, but this needed to be modified by engineers from Walter Werke on March 29. All testing had come to an end by the time Junkers' airfield at Dessau was captured by the Americans on April 24, 1945.. ●

ABOVE: A static display model of the EF 128 in its final form.

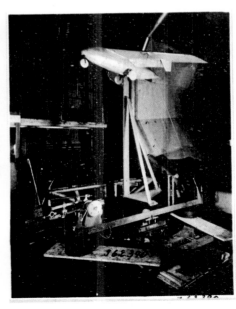

ABOVE: Wind tunnel tests on the late-version EF 128.

Dark destroyers

With radar allowing Allied bombers to carry out increasingly accurate raids on targets in Germany whatever the weather and during the night, the Luftwaffe began to sorely feel the lack of a high-performance night fighter. A requirement was issued and among the resulting designs were some of the most spectacular tailless project aircraft of the war.

When the RAF introduced ground-scanning radar at the end of 1942 and bombing accuracy began to steadily increase, the need for an effective night-fighter force became ever more pressing. Early on, this involved the use of converted Bf 110s, Ju 88s and Do 217s with new dedicated night-fighter designs such as the Heinkel He 219 and Focke-Wulf Ta 154 being hastily prepared to take over from them.

However, both of these advanced piston engine types suffered development setbacks and the Luftwaffe was forced to carry on with its relatively small fleet of converted zerstörers ('destroyers' or heavy fighters) and medium bombers.

During the summer of 1944 it was decided that a new effort should be made to create high-performance night fighters through two parallel development efforts. The first called for the interim conversion of advanced 'day' designs, while the second was intended to produce the most technologically advanced dedicated night fighter possible.

The requirement for the latter was issued on August 31, 1944, and began: "Subject: Project new destroyer. The development of a new destroyer to combat enemy combat aircraft in bad weather conditions by day and by night is urgently required.

"1) Usage: Day-to-night bad weather destroyer with complete blind flight capability incl. start and landing with the greatest possible flight time including combat. 2) Engine: a) Jumo 222 E/F. b) As 413 c) DB 603 L d) DB 613. The number and arrangement is set aside to ensure the high flight performance. Combination piston engine-jet must be looked at."

Weaponry was to be four MK 108s and two MK 213s fixed forward firing with space also allowed for Lichtenstein radar equipment and the Bremen airborne warning device. Oblique weaponry was to be two MK 108s angled at 70. The aircraft was also to be capable of carrying two 500kg bombs. A pressure cabin was to be fitted, along with armour for the crew, and top speed needed to be 800km/h at an altitude of 11km, with a flight time of four and a half hours without drop tanks.

Copies of this requirement were sent to Blohm & Voss, Focke-Wulf, Heinkel, Messerschmitt and Dornier. Arado and Gotha, which would both later submit designs, were not included at this stage.

Meanwhile, for the first development strand, Messerschmitt put forward the Me 262 B-1a/U1 in late August or early September. It was a relatively straightforward radar-equipped conversion of the two-seater Me 262 B-1 trainer. Arado put forward the Ar 234 B-2/N on September 12, 1944, which was a conversion from the Ar 234 B-2 bomber. A cramped compartment would be built into the type's tail where the radar operator could sit with a small window above his head.

Finally, Dornier put forward the Do 335 A-6, another two-seater conversion of a single-seat fighter. Like the Arado conversion, the radar man only had a small glazed panel above him but at least he was directly behind the pilot.

All three of these underwent rapid development and evolved through a number

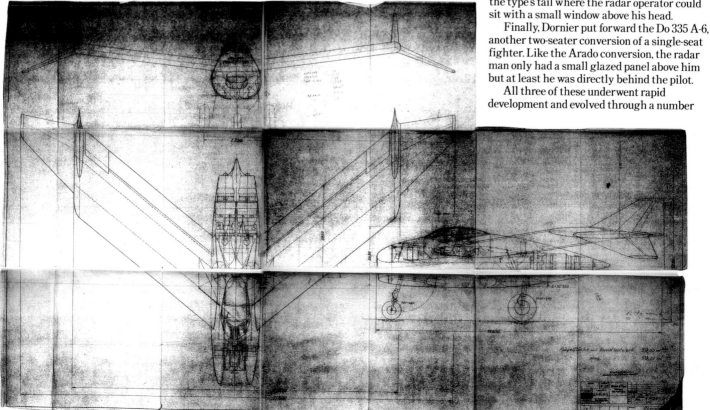

ABOVE: The only known drawing of the Blohm & Voss P 215.01, pieced together from surviving fragments. The P 215.01 was the most radical night-fighter design presented during the February 26 conference.

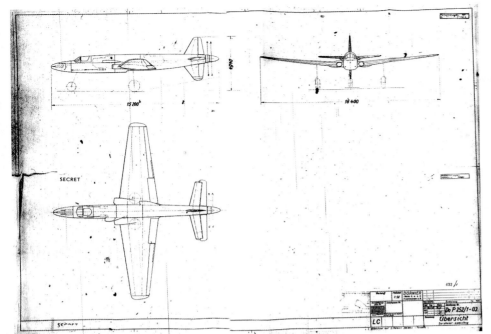

ABOVE: With straight wings and a tail fin, Dornier's P 252/1 contrasted sharply with Blohm & Voss's P 215.

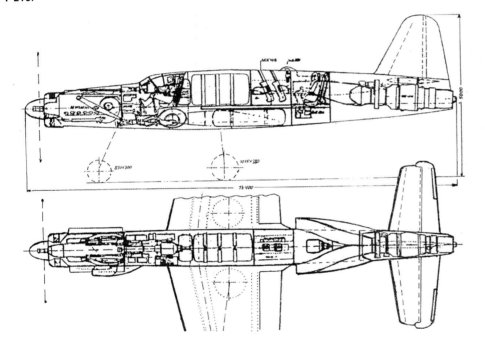

ABOVE: The second Dornier design in competition with the B&V P 215 – the P 254/1.

of different versions. Arado switched the basis for its night fighter from the Ar 234 B-2 to the Ar 234 C-7, which then became the solid-nose heavily-armed Ar 234 P in January 1945. Dornier's Do 335 A-6 became the B-6 in late November 1944, with the back-seater getting a glass bulb canopy.

The competition to meet the high-performance requirement seems to have been delayed by first the 1-TL-Jäger conference on September 8-10, 1944, then the Volksjäger requirement of September 10, which demanded the immediate attention of the competing firms. The requirement was slightly altered on January 27, 1945, calling specifically for a two-seater machine that could achieve 900km/h at 9000m and fly on full throttle for four hours.

There may have been designs presented and assessed between September and February 1945

but the first confirmed comparison meeting for what was dubbed 'Schlechtwetter und Nachtjäger' took place on February 26, 1945.

Only three firms offered designs – Blohm & Voss put forward its radical tailless twin-jet P 215.01, Messerschmitt offered its Me 262 in either two- or three-seater configuration and Dornier put forward two conventional layout projects – the P 252/1 and P 254/1.

All four designs were at the cutting edge of what was technically possible for early 1945. In two-seater form, the Me 262 B-2 or 'B2' as it appears in the project description document of January 18, 1945, featured a fuselage lengthened by 1.5m to provide room for a radar operator and equipment without compromising fuel load

The canopy over the men's heads was tall to accommodate the bulky FuG 350 Naxos Zc homing device scanner and the radar operator

was even to be given blackout curtains so the screen could be read more easily. Radar aerials would be fitted to the aircraft's nose.

The second option was an even longer fuselage to allow room for a navigator. In addition, the engines would be installed in the aircraft's wingroots, rather than underwing pods. The wings themselves would also have a 45 degree sweepback, compared to the standard Me 262's sweep of just 18.5 degrees.

Dornier's P 252/1, drafted on January 20, 1945, was perhaps the simplest of the four. It had unswept wings and a pair of DB 603 LA piston engines mounted in tandem within its fuselage, with two Jumo 213 Js offered as an alternative option. The two crew sat side-by-side with the pilot slightly further forward on the left. Armament was given as two MK 108s fixed forward with another two at an oblique angle. However, the separate project description of February 9, 1945, showed three fixed MK 108s in the nose and two MG 213s set into the fuselage to the side of and below the forwardmost engine.

Set against the twin-jet Me 262, twin-jet P 215 and twin-piston engine P 252/1, the Dornier P 254/1 was unusual in being the only mixed propulsion design put forward. In design, the forward section and wings were similar to those of the Do 335 A series except for the installation of a DB 603 LA piston engine in place of the DB 603 A.

However, the space where the second pusher, DB 603 A, would have been, aft of the main fuel tank, were a pair of oblique-firing MK 108s. To the rear of them was the radar operator's position. On either side of him was a wide intake for the HeS 011 jet engine positioned in the extreme rear of the fuselage, exhausting beneath the fin. Also unlike the Do 335, there was no lower tail fin – just the familiar horizontal tailplanes and fin arrangement.

Neither Dornier design came with a pressure cabin.

Finally, there was the Blohm & Voss P 215.01, the design apparently drawn up in a hurry on February 21, 1945 – just five days before the conference. By this point the P 215.01 probably looked slightly less bizarre than it might otherwise have done, since Blohm & Voss had been pitching similar tailless types with wingtip booms for several months. Those adjudicating the 'Schlechtwetter und Nachtjäger' competition would already have been familiar with the similar P 212 from the 1-TL-Jäger conferences of December 19-21 and January 12-15, and the P 215.01 was essentially an up-scaled version.

It featured a crew of three seated within a pressure cabin – two facing forwards and one to the rear. Armament was four MK 108s but these could evidently be fitted in a number of different arrangements since the side-view design drawing shows eight MK 108s – four in the upper nose, firing forward, two lower down on the sides of the nose air intake, angled slightly upwards, and a further two positioned towards the rear of the aircraft, firing upwards at an angle of 70. There was no defensive armament.

THE SECOND ROUND

Apparently none of these designs was entirely suitable, since the day after the conference, February 27, 1945, a new set of specifications was issued which emphasised ▶

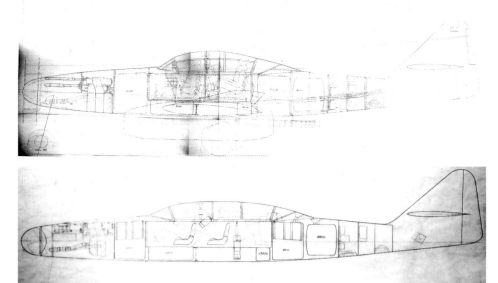

ABOVE: Messerschmitt offered both two- and three-seater versions of its Me 262 B-2 night fighter.

heavier armament, the ability to carry more equipment and the inclusion of a third crewman to manage all the additional kit if one wasn't present already.

At this point Messerschmitt seems to have dropped out of contention, offering no designs for the new specification. Neither of Dornier's previous proposals were able to meet the revised specification and both were dropped. Only the Blohm & Voss P 215 remained of the original competitors. However, it was now set to face even an even stiffer challenge. A new date was set for the discussion of Schlechtwetter und Nachtjäger designs – the next EHK meeting at Bad Eilsen on March 20-24.

There would now be seven designs in contention – three tailless and four conventional: Blohm & Voss's slightly revised tailless P 215.02,

Dornier's new P 256/1, one tailless and one tailed design from Arado simply labelled 'Arado I' and 'Arado II', Gotha's tailless P-60 C and two designs from Focke-Wulf labelled 'Focke-Wulf II' and 'Focke-Wulf III' – designations which this time corresponded with the company's own internal numbering, rather than being simplifications for the contest.

BLOHM & VOSS P 215

The Blohm & Voss P 215.02 appears almost identical to the P 215.01 at first glance but in fact it is a larger aircraft in almost every respect. The wingspan, including control surfaces, is 18.8m, compared to 17.6m; wing area is 63sq m compared to 59sq m and fuselage width is 2.2m compared to under 2m. The only dimension which remains the same is overall length at 11.6m.

According to the introduction to the P 215.02 brochure, dated March 1945: "The 215 project grew out of the P 212 design, a day fighter with only one turbojet." Comparing the P 215.02's dimensions to those of the P 212.03 reveals a startling difference in size however. The wingspan of the P 212.03 was only 9.5 – nearly half that of the P 215.02. Wing area was less than a quarter of the P 215.02's at just 14sq m, and overall length was 4.2m shorter at a relatively diminutive 7.4m.

The brochure quickly acknowledges the P 215.02's sheer size as it continues: "With a three-man crew, with reinforced armament, with increased flight time and with two turbojets the dimensions of the aircraft are correspondingly large. However, the entire arrangement is largely similar to that of the day-fighters.

"The two turbojets are built into the rear fuselage and get fed from a front fuselage nose intake via a common channel. The armament is gathered in a weapons section, which is directly behind the antenna devices and in front of the crew cabin. Nose and main landing gear are both hinged to the fuselage. The aircraft is therefore transportable after removing the wings. This brings advantages in the final assembly, because

the transport scaffolding can be omitted.

"The hull itself is easy to assemble because the principal components are reattached to the TL-inlet pipe. The swept wing is particularly characterized by its tail edge."

Regarding the wings, the brochure states: "In order to get not too large aircraft dimensions, the wing size of 50 square metres was left unchanged (without border control surfaces)."

This might have been true of the main wing, but including the control surfaces, overall size was substantially increased. The aspect ratio had also been increased, to provide more fuel-efficient flight at an altitude of 32,800ft. The brochure continues: "If no consideration is given to this, the required fuel weight increases significantly. The wing component is divided into a body portion and the left and right wings, each with a flange separation point on the hull.

"The fuselage wing piece is mounted on the fuselage pylon, with a pair of main terminals on the rear spar and one each right and left. The actual support system is a broad wing box, made of welded steel plate. All these boxes can also be used as fuel tanks.

"The wing leading edge, made of either duraluminium or steel and is firmly attached to the load bearing structure. The outer ends in the aileron area are fed warm air from the engine for de-icing."

The landing gear consisted of a He 219 nosewheel, according to the brochure, and large mainwheels which tucked up neatly inside the fuselage.

Then came the weapons. The normal 'attack' armament (option A) was to be five MK 108 cannon with 200 shots each. This could be exchanged for (option B) five MK 108s with 150 shots each that could be tilted upwards at an angle of between 0 and 15 degrees.

Option C was four MG 213/30s with 200 shots each. Option D involved the installation of two massive MK 112 cannon with 50 shots each. Finally, option E allowed for no fewer than 56 R4M unguided rockets to be installed in the P 215's nose – alongside either four MK 108s, four MG 213/30s or two MK 212/214s.

Like the P 215.01, the P 215.02 could also be fitted with a pair of MK 108s aimed to fire upwards. There was also an option to carry a pair of 500kg bombs semi-recessed within the fuselage. Where the P 215.02 again differed significantly from its predecessor was the inclusion of a rear-facing FHL 151 remote-controlled turret armed with a single MG 151/20 20mm cannon. This was to be aimed and fired by the navigator.

Dornier's P 256/1 illustrates the difficulties the company faced in trying to design a night fighter based loosely on the Do 335 but powered by two turbojets. With no room left in the fuselage thanks to the armament, fuel and crew requirements, the firm was forced to position the jets in simple under-wing pods. Armament was four MK 108s firing forward and two more firing upwards.

ARADO I AND II

Arado appears only to have started work on its designs on March 7, with its 1. Entwurf zum Nacht- und Schlechtwetterjäger – a tailless design with no vertical control surfaces and the distinctive kinked wing that the company had developed during its E 560 project. This had an armament of six forward-firing MK 108s, two

ABOVE: A page from the February 26 night and bad-weather, fighter-comparison conference, showing the four competitors.

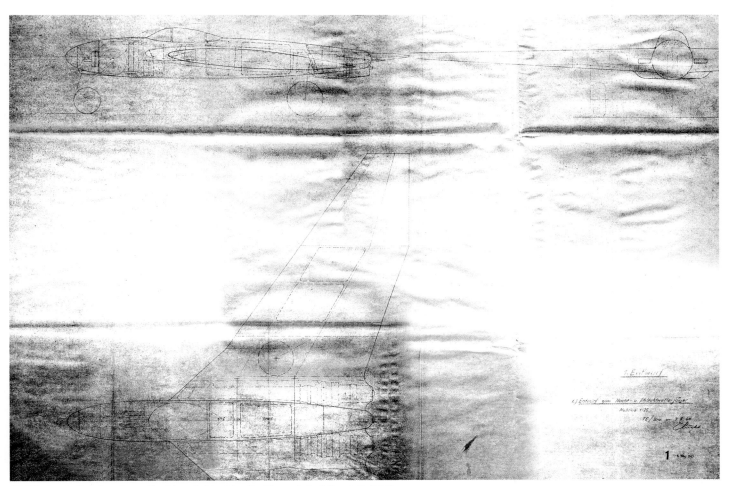

ABOVE: Arado 1. Entwurf zum Nacht- u. Schlechtwetterjäger, dated March 7, 1945.

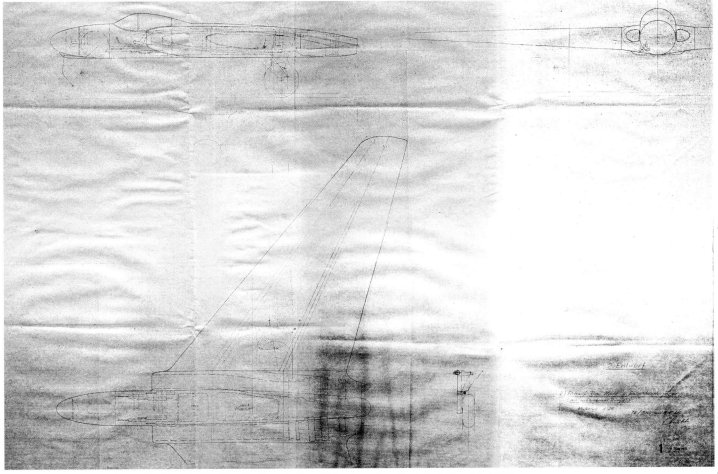

ABOVE: Arado 2. Entwurf zum Nacht- u. Schlechtwetterjäger (mit verkleinertem Rumpf), dated March 8, 1945.

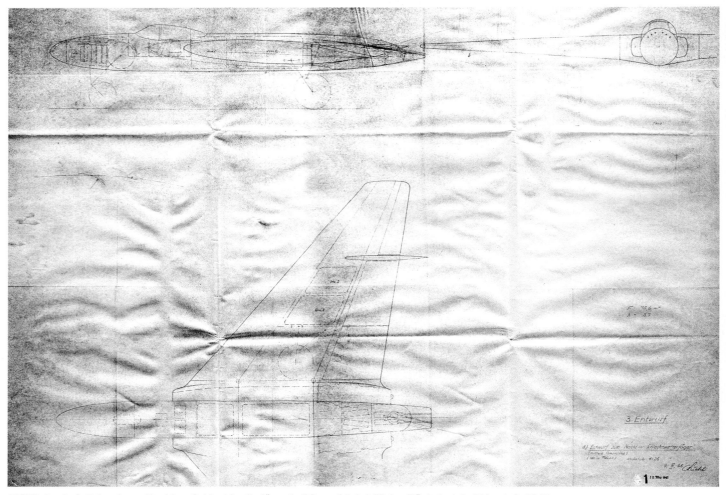

ABOVE: Arado 3. Entwurf zum Nacht- u. Schlechtwetterjäger (mit Rumpfdicke) (Kleine Fläche), dated March 9, 1945.

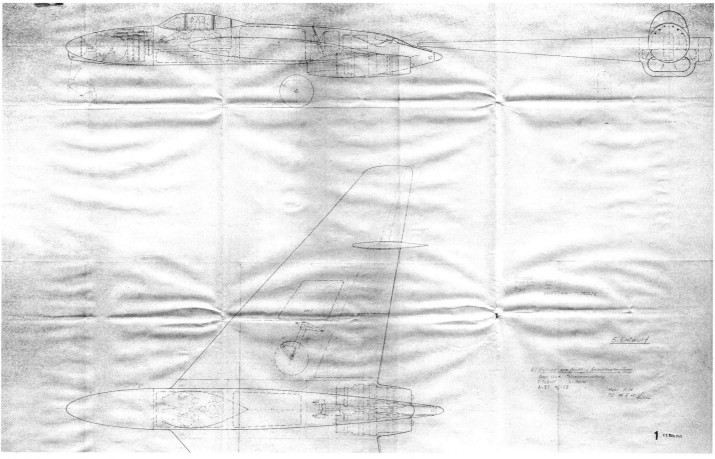

ABOVE: Arado 5. Entwurf zum Nacht- u. Schlechtwetterjäger, dated March 13, 1945.

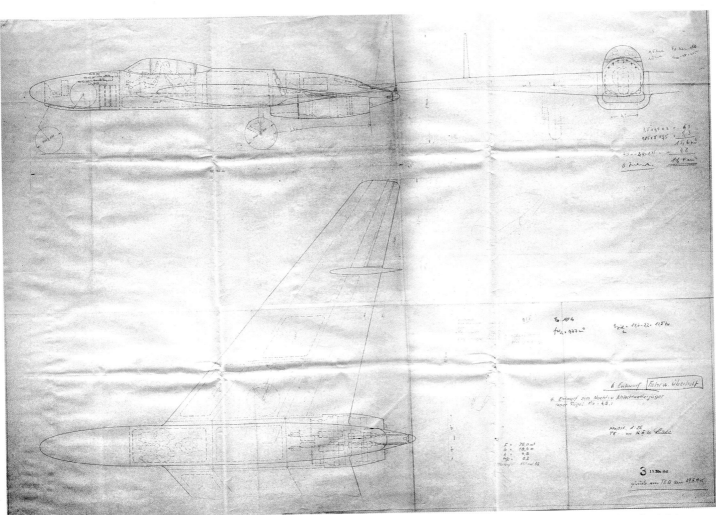

ABOVE: Arado 6. Entwurf zum Nacht- u. Schlechtwetterjäger, dated March 14, 1945. The note 'Fahrw. überholt' means 'undercarriage obsolete'. The 6. Entwurf was chosen to go forward as Arado's 'Arado I' design for the night-fighter competition, with a slightly different undercarriage retraction arrangement.

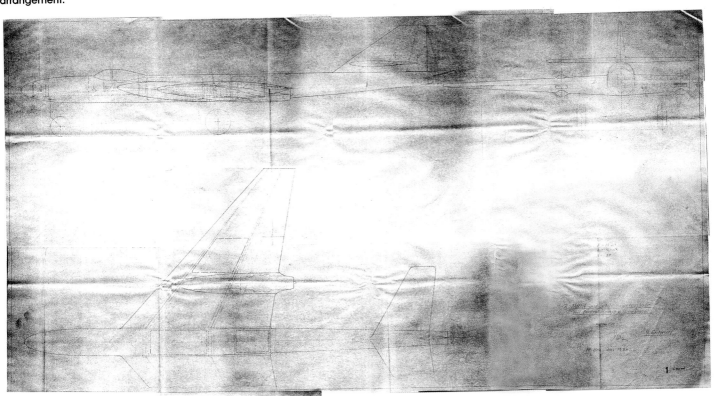

ABOVE: Arado 7. Entwurf zum Nacht- u. Schlechtwetterjäger mit Zentral Rumpf u. TL im Flügel, dated March 13, 1945. Presumably the seventh design, the first to feature a conventional tailed layout, was drafted at the same time as the fifth but only numbered after that design had become the 6. Entwurf.

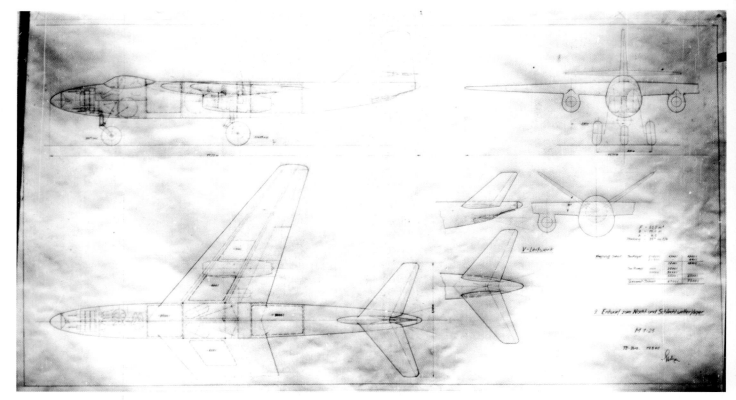

ABOVE: Arado 9. Entwurf zum Nacht- u. Schlechtwetterjäger, dated March 17, 1945. This would become the second Arado design presented at the March 20-24 comparison meeting, as 'Arado II'.

BELOW: Arado 7. Entwurf zum Nacht- u. Schlechtwetterjäger. Art by Daniel Uhr

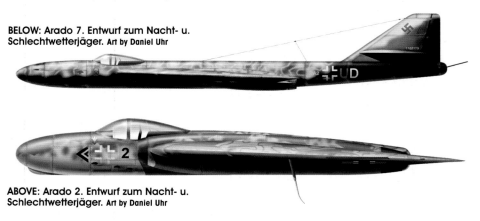

ABOVE: Arado 2. Entwurf zum Nacht- u. Schlechtwetterjäger. Art by Daniel Uhr

ABOVE: Page from a report on the March 20-24 night- and bad-weather fighter-comparsion meeting, showing the seven competing designs.

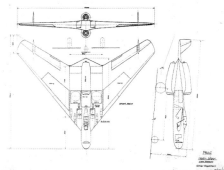

ABOVE: The final form of the Gotha P-60 C, with three seats – two of them in the wings beneath large Perspex fairings.

more firing upwards and a small rear turret set between its turbojet exhausts mounting two unspecified remote-control weapons.

The 2. Entwurf zum Nacht- und Schlechtwetterjäger (mit verkleinertem Rumpf) dated March 8, 1945, was another tailless design which had, as the name suggests, a shortened fuselage. Against it had six forward-firing MK 108s but no rear turret, and its swept wings had a dead straight leading edge. 3. Entwurf zum Nacht- und Schlechtwetterjäger dated March 9 was again tailless but moved back to the longer fuselage. Now, however, it also featured a vertical fin towards the end of each wing. The forward-firing weaponry stayed the same but a rear turret mounted what appeared to be a pair of MK 103s on a pivot allowing them to track left and right.

The fourth design is lost but the 5. Entwurf zum Nacht- und Schlechtwetterjäger, dated March 13, marked a substantial refinement on its predecessors. Forward armament was the same but now two oblique MK 108s made an appearance and the MK 103 rear turret could track up and down rather than left and right. The 6. Entwurf zum Nacht- und Schlechtwetterjäger was very similar to the fifth design but refined still further in the detail of its wings and fuselage.

Curiously, the 6. Entwurf is dated March 14, whereas the 7. Entwurf is dated March 13. This design is the first in the sequence to feature a conventional layout – albeit with an extremely long fuselage, huge swept tailfin and engine nacelles integrated into its wings. There is no forward armament depicted – only oblique-firing cannon and a tail turret. There are no dimensions either, suggesting that this design was more of an idea than a likely candidate for further development.

The 8. Entwurf is again missing and the 9. Entwurf zum Nacht- und Schlechtwetterjäger, dated March 17, 1945 – just three days before the conference – is another conventional layout design. Shorter than the 7. Entwurf, everything about it seems designed to be straightforward. The wings are swept but not dramatically so, the engines are fitted into underwing pods making them easy to access for maintenance, the three crew sit together under a blister canopy offering good visibility over the not-overlong nose, and the tricycle undercarriage appears not dissimilar to the tried and tested undercarriage of the Ar 234 B-2. A V-tail was presented as an option.

From these nine designs, Arado chose the 6. Entwurf to offer as its 'Arado I', albeit with a slightly modified undercarriage retraction arrangement, and the 9. Entwurf to offer unaltered as 'Arado II'.

FOCKE-WULF II AND III

Focke-Wulf had spent months working on a huge variety of night-fighter designs between September 1944 and March 1945. On July 21, 1944, a requirement was issued for a Hochleistungsjäger mit Jumo 222 E/F or 'high-performance fighter with Jumo 222 E/F', prompting Focke-Wulf to begin working on a series of pusher-prop fighters.

When the night-fighter requirement was issued at the end of August, these became pusher-prop night-fighter with supplementary jet engines. And on November 23, 1944, the firm dispensed with the piston engines all together with a design called Zweimotoriges TL-Jagdflugzeug mit HeS 109-011, outlined in Kurzbeschreibung Nr. 23.

This was followed on January 27, 1945, with Nachtjäger mit 2 x HeS 011, outlined in Kurzbeschreibung Nr. 26. Further work was carried out throughout February and into early March, resulting in four further twin- or triple- jet night fighter designs, outlined in a Focke-Wulf report entitled simply Nachtjäger mit HeS 011 Entwurf II-V on March 19, 1945.

From these, designs II and III were chosen for presentation during the design conference.

Focke-Wulf II had a conventional tail with swept-back, single-spar wings. The fuselage nose was bulbous and housed the

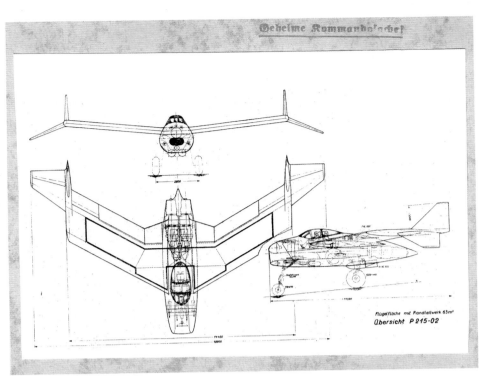

ABOVE: The Blohm & Voss P 215.02, slightly enlarged from the .01 and now with a rear-facing FHL 151 barbette mounting an MG 151 cannon.

ABOVE: Blohm & Voss P 215.01. Art by Daniel Uhr

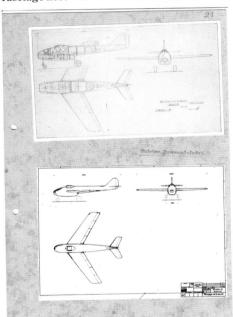

ABOVE: Focke-Wulf's two entries for the night-fighter competition, taken from a series of five.

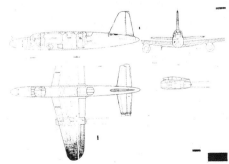

ABOVE: Dornier's P 256/1 was intended to be a relatively simple and easy-to-produce design – an approach which resulted in it being roundly rejected.

two HeS 011 turbojets positioned side by side but slightly angled within the fuselage. This created a space between them for the nosewheel of the tricycle undercarriage.

The pressurised cockpit housed three crew sitting on ejection seats and behind this were two self-sealing fuel tanks. Armament was four fixed forward-firing MK 108s and two more firing upwards. Wingspan was 16m. Focke-Wulf III was the same but with larger main undercarriage wheels and a wingspan of 14.1m.

GOTHA P-60 C

Just nine days before the conference, Gotha P-60 C had been a two-seater with the crew sitting in tandem. However, in order to meet the latest design criteria, a three-seater was needed. Therefore, Gotha came up with a novel solution: leave the pilot where he was but put a seat on either side of and slightly behind him within the aircraft's wings themselves. There is no mention of it in the documentation but the drawing appears to show these two positions covered by a large curving sheet of Perspex – giving their occupants a reasonable degree of visibility. Armament remained the same: four fixed-forward MK 108s plus two more angled upwards.

AND THE WINNER IS…

According to a report on his interrogation, the P-60 C's designer Dr Rudolf Göthert believed that his design "was shown to have the best performance of these aircraft, and Dr Göthert believed it would have won had not the war disrupted the competition".

However, Göthert appears to have been ill-informed. None of the designs, tailless or conventional, came out on top in the end. According to the war diary of the TLR: "Meeting EHK in Bad Eilsen from March 20-24 clearly showed that the requirement cannot be achieved, particularly with regard to flight duration and defence. Requirements of the weapon side rest on today's state of the night fighters and take no regard for device development. The decisive factor for the use of high-quality jet fighter aircraft is the development of new armament methods.

"Joint processing by company representatives revealed that the original TLR requirement of January 27, 1945, is to be realised. The TLR revised requirements will be published and distributed on April 2. EHK, in contrast to TLR, also requires an optimal piston-engine fighter."

But by now it was too late for a revised requirement. Focke-Wulf's design offices at Bad Eilsen would fall to the British on April 8, 1945.. ●

Night fighter in captivity

Heinkel P 1079

Heinkel's designers had worked around the clock on the He 162 yet still kept turning out plans for cutting edge aircraft. The P 1079 night fighter was originally a conventional layout design – but would its performance be improved by making it tailless?

Undoubtedly one of the most impressive German tailless designs of the 1940s was a version of Heinkel's P 1079 night fighter.

Despite apparently being conceived as the company's entry for the Schlechtwetter und Nachtjäger competition, the P 1079 was evidently put together too late even for the final round. Although evidence suggests that some work was done on it before the end of the war, the only known full report on the project was drafted by Heinkel designers Hohbach and Eichner while they were being held at Landsberg-Lech air base, formerly known as Flugplatz Penzing, then under US occupation, and is dated August 11, 1945.

A translation of this report, F-TS-675-RE, was finally issued by American intelligence in October 1946, with copies being forwarded on to the British.

It was entitled simply 'Night Fighter and Destroyer Fitted With Two HeS-011 Power Plants P 1079' and offers no real context or preamble before commencing a straightforward technical description. It begins: "The subject of the following report is a night-fighter airplane fitted with two HeS 011 turbojet engines (static thrust = 2 x 1300kg). By variation of weights and dimensions the determination of the best compromise with regard to characteristics of take-off, climb, range and speed will be facilitated."

In other words, several different shapes and sizes of aircraft had been looked at in trying to determine which combination of features was likely to offer the best performance.

Some details were common to all, however. The report goes on: "The

basic fixed data used for all designs are: powerplant – 2 x HeS 011; armament – 4 guns type MK 108 (30mm) forward firing, 2 guns type MG 151 (20mm) rearward firing; armour plate – 220kg, radio equipment – set for long wave and short wave bands, direction finding set, blind landing equipment, set for distance measurement and aiming (with parabola registering mirror) provided fore and aft; crew – 2."

Next came a summary of the four different layouts to be assessed: three with 35 degree swept-back wings and a V-tail, but with wing areas of 30m sq, 35m sq, and 45m sq, and a 30m sq area design with a sharper 45 degree sweepback.

It states: "High flight Mach numbers require the use of swept-back wings. In order to reduce the wetted surface of the airplane and to avoid interference effects to obtain a minimum drag, the

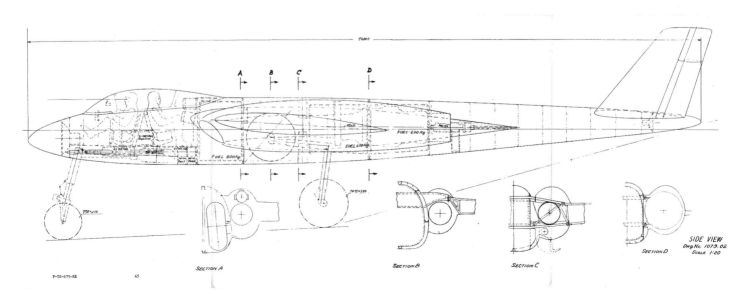

The conventional layout version of the Heinkel P 1079 night fighter.

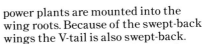

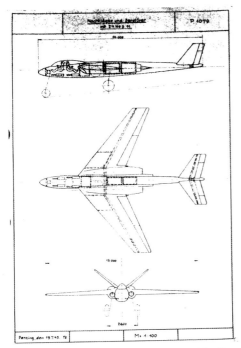

Before detailed reports were prepared for the Americans, Heinkel's engineers created a single document which offered sketches of all the company's late-war projects. This is the page on the P 1079, the forward view showing its V-tail to advantage.

A page from a report on the late-war night- and bad-weather fighter competition from Focke-Wulf's design office, demonstrating that Heinkel did at least have P 1079 under way before the war came to an end.

power plants are mounted into the wing roots. Because of the swept-back wings the V-tail is also swept-back.

"The maximum speed of the three layouts with a 35 degree sweepback having respective wing areas of 30, 35 and 42sq m, lies between 960km/h (30sq m) and 915km/h (45sq m). Calculations based on a 45 degree sweepback for the 30m sq layout gave an increase of speed from 960km/h to 980km/h."

After a table of weights, a structural description outlines how the P 1079 was to be made: "The middle part of the wing is of metal construction. The outboard parts of wood. The main spar of the swept-wing is sloped aft as much as possible through the fuselage in order to keep torsional stresses small by transmission of the normal forces acting on the spar.

"A dihedral of the wing would produce too great rolling moments (moment for condition of constant angle of yaw) due to the sweepback of wing and V-tail. If fuel tanks are located in the wing structure to a greater extent than illustrated in the drawings, fuel drainage towards the fuselage could be improved by a dihedral extending to the ailerons. Rolling moments due to the dihedral could be compensated by cathedral tips.

"The V-tail area amounts to 25% of the wing area. The rolling moment (and stresses imparted to the fuselage) of the V-tail is reduced by split counter acting control surfaces, the tip portions counteracting the main inboard surfaces.

"Two seats, one behind the other, area provided for the crew. Besides the usual equipment of four 30mm forward firing cannon, there is fitted an electric device for distance measurement and sighting both in the nose and the rear of the fuselage (parabola shaped reflector). Rearward defence is accomplished by two fixed 20mm cannon mounted between the fuselage and engine nacelles.

"The main landing gear (wheel base ▶

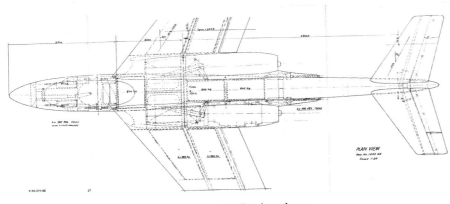

Plan view of the P 1079 from the report prepared for the Americans.

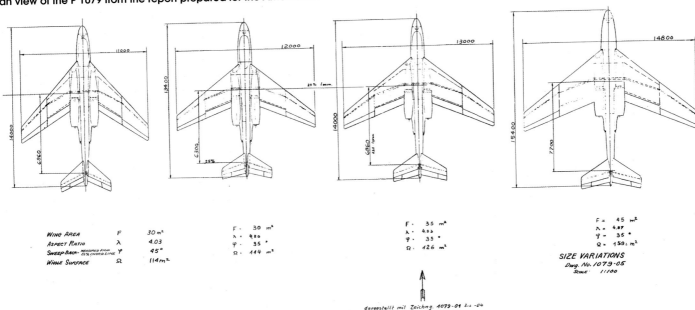

Heinkel was adept at altering its designs to suit requirements and in this case roughly the same layout for the P 1079 was assessed in different sizes to determine which offered the best performance.

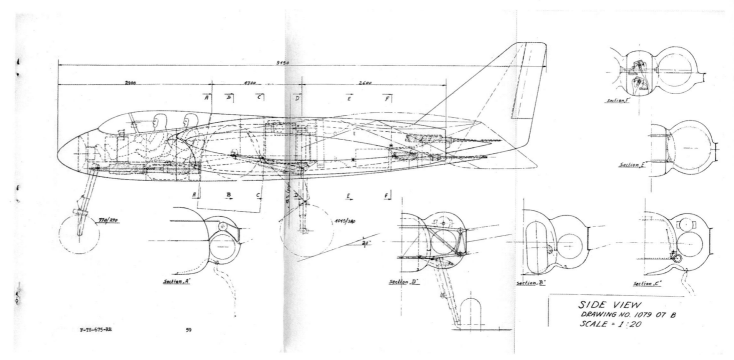

F-TS-675-RE

SIDE VIEW
DRAWING NO. 1079 07 B
SCALE = 1:20

The tailless version of the P 1079 would, according to Heinkel chief designer Siegfried Günter, outperform its conventional counterpart. Whether it was originally designed during the war or only afterwards is debatable.

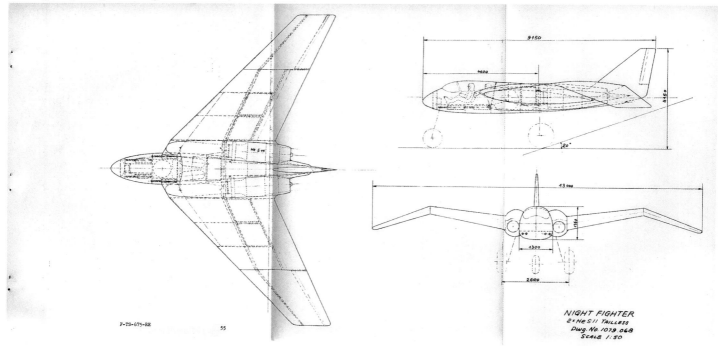

NIGHT FIGHTER
2 × HeS11 TAILLESS
Dwg. No. 1079.06B
SCALE 1:50

A head-on view of the tailless P 1079 illustrates its gullwing design, while the plan view shows a layout not entirely dissimilar to some of those tried by Lippisch for his P 11 some three years earlier.

nearly 2.6m) is retracted into the fuselage and is so designed that a small fuselage has been obtained, the breadth of which is determined by the space needed for the two wheels lying side by side. When retracted the struts are turned 180 degrees by means of guide arms.

"The construction of this type of landing gear was completed for incorporation into the He 343 jet-propelled bomber. Flat location of the retracted nose-wheel in the floor of the cockpit is provided. Special spar design is required for mounting the two HeS 011 power plants in the wing root next to the fuselage as the intake ducts pass through the spar.

To keep the weight of this portion of the spar small, lateral stresses are transmitted by means of a streamlined brace.

"The power plant blower section begins close behind the spar. The intake duct is 1.8m longer than usually furnished, thus causing a mean thrust loss of about 3% which was taken into account when calculating performances. Fuel is carried in bulletproof fuel tanks located in the fuselage and in the wing structure where bag-form bulletproof tanks are provided. In the case of overload take-off, additional fuel can be carried in unprotected sealed portions of the wing."

A lengthy section then follows where

the authors explain how their performance calculations for the four designs were made using formulae provided by the DVL, and concludes: "Performances for the wing area of 35sq m. Performances attained with this wing represent a favourable compromise concerning take-off, climb, maximum speed, range and landing speed."

Tables compare the likely performance of this design alternatively powered by two BMW 003 As, two BMW 003 Ds, two Jumo 004 Bs or two Jumo 004 Ds, and it is shown that the HeS 011 provides markedly better performance in every area except 'weight of power plant' and fuel consumption.

But what of the tailless P 1079? All

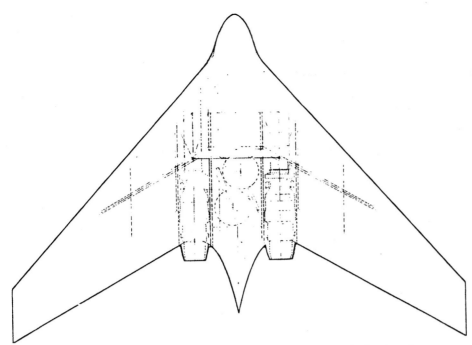

While only one tailless version of the P 1079 was included in the report for the Americans, it would appear that a second was also prepared. The only known drawing of it is this faded off image from British report German Aircraft: New and Projected Types.

designs assessed by the report are of conventional layout. In its 'contents' section at the beginning, the original August 11, 1945, report lists five appended drawings – numbers P 1079-01 to P 1079-05. Yet the October 1946 translation comes with three more, numbered P 1079-06B, P 1079-07B and P 1079-08B.

These are appended to a section at the back signed by Siegfried Günter himself, entitled Supplement to P 1079. It states: "The project P 1078 B is a tailless airplane with one HeS 011. Because it is projected with two fuselages, this project cannot be a normal case of a tailless airplane. Therefore, as a comparison with the P 1079 (this is an airplane with two HeS 011s) we have also designed a tailless airplane. To have comparable projects, the landing speeds should be as equal as possible.

"The wing area is 41.5m sq while the airplane with tail had an area of 35m sq. Because the maximum lift for sweepback wings is not well known, it would be advisable to make wind tunnel tests.

"The project has a wetted surface of 106m sq against 126m sq of the fuselage airplane. But this comparison is not quite correct; for the airplane with fuselage will attain a better damping about the normal and lateral axis. The damping of the tailless airplane might be sufficient for flying; for the attack flight and aiming the best possibility is to improve the damping by a gyro control (DVL fighter control).

"In addition, the airplane with fuselage has better fuel spaces and it is possible to protect all the fuel; it is also possible and easier to enlarge the fuel tanks. The difference of speed is given by the critical speeds (steep increasing of drag). With the same sweepback angle and the same relative profile thickness a difference of the critical speeds can only be found by wind tunnel tests."

A brief chart then shows the tailless design beating the 'with tail' design in every area – a top speed of 1015km/h at sea level and 910km/h at 11km altitude, compared to 950km/h and 880km/h; a range of 850km and 2160km compared to 750km and 1900km and a fuel load of 3450kg compared to 3150kg.

Finally, "while the tailless airplane P 1078 B had the centre of gravity at 80% of the half span, this point was shifted to the start of the aileron for the new project.

"The reduced directional stability was compensated by a small fin. The stability lever arm of this fin is somewhat larger than the lever arm of wing twin vertical fins. With regard to oscillation and because of a probable loss of sweepback effect by wing twin vertical fins, the central fin is to be preferred. For the P 1078 B the construction of a central fin would be more difficult."

It is difficult to say whether a tailless version of the P 1079 was contemplated during wartime or whether this was solely a postwar development. Most of Heinkel's project documents appear to have been captured by the Russians or destroyed, making this even harder to verify.

In his autobiography Ein Stürmisches Leben, concerning the war's aftermath, Ernst Heinkel wrote: "My Marienehe factory had been seized by the Russians and quickly dismantled. The Bleicherstrasse works in Rostock were blown up and the other factory in the same town had been taken over by the Russians. Oranienburg had been completely dismantled and taken piecemeal to Russia, as had the Waltersdorf branch of Zuffenhausen.

"The fate of the decentralised works during the last months of the war – those tunnels, mines and caves in Achensee, Stassfurt and Kochendorf, where we had

worked to protect ourselves from bombing attacks, I knew only much later. They had all been destroyed, damaged or plundered.

"The repair shops which had been set up during the war behind the fronts in Poland, Denmark, France and even in Como, and which had been built and managed by Heinkel specialists, had been scattered to the four winds in the general collapse.

"The Jenbach factory was seized by the French occupation troops. Most of the machines were carried away and the rest of them handed over to the new Austrian government in trust in November 1948. Only the Zuffenhausen factory near Stuttgart remained in its damaged state on West German soil. But the American military authorities had laid hands on this, too, and given it over to one of those 'trustees' who like spotless blooms emerged in surprising numbers from the slime of defeat. I no longer dared to cross the threshold.

"As soon as I returned home on August 4, 1945, I wanted to see the position in Jenbach with my own eyes, and went to Lindau to try and get a pass from the French military government to visit their Austrian zone. It was a fruitless effort.

"I stopped in Landsberg and searched for Siegfried Günter who had withdrawn there in the middle of April 1945, and had still managed to carry on a primitive office with 35 other employees of my design office. I found him – the most important expert on aircraft structures and aerodynamics in Europe at that time – living with his wife in a small room. He was working with 10 more of my people, including Töpfer, in a technical office which the Americans had established on Penzing airfield. Töpfer had tried in vain to draw the attention of the American military authorities to the presence and importance of Günter.

"Günter was as usual too ignorant of the ways of the world to push himself forward. Only when an American officer had been sent to Penzing from headquarters had he been able to go on working as a scientist.

His work embraced everything that we had planned for the future in the way of fresh developments in jet propulsion, since the rejection of the He 280, and independently of the He 162. He was particularly engrossed, too, with new 'flying wing' types. I hoped on this visit to Landsberg that Günter would find a permanent outlet for his activities, either there or in America."

In the end, Heinkel's chief designer appears to have appreciated the value of tailless designs and was willing to demonstrate what he saw as their advantages. The P 1079 was not quite the last Heinkel project either – that would be the tailless P 1080 fighter.

Günter remained in Landsberg until the spring of 1946 when he used the last of his money to travel to Berlin, where his father-in-law had a garage. He hoped that the Americans would recruit him but the call never came. Instead, he went to work for the Russians. ●

The arrow form

Arado E 555

Arado came to flying wings early and later studied them from the middle of the war almost to the end without ever building one. The result was some of the most outrageous, tantalising and puzzling German project aircraft designs.

During late 1941 and early 1942, Arado chief design engineer Walter Blume compiled a wide-ranging report on his company's work regarding defensive armament on aircraft, beginning in 1925.

It was entitled Arbeiten und Gedanken über die bewegliche Bewaffnung der Flugzeuge or 'Working and thinking about the mobile armament of aircraft' and was concerned primarily with the placement and function of gun turrets with a view to achieving the best possible fields of fire.

A wide variety of positions and armaments were looked at up to 1935 when, Blume writes, "the following ideas emerged: the best form for low air resistance would ideally be a flying-wing aircraft, in which only parts of the barrels, the protrusion for the head of the shooter and the lenses of the gun sight would be distinguished from the surface of the wing profile.

"When considering the accommodation option of two turrets in a wing profile, it was self-evident that they would be placed in the area of the greatest profile thickness in order to achieve the ideal small air drag. In contrast to the previous bow and stern positions, an upper turret and a lower turret were used, and thus the new division of the ball turret into an upper and lower half.

"This arrangement has the very great advantage that each turret can shoot forward and backward, and in addition, in the main firing fields, the combat power of the other can be doubled by overlapping the sectors."

A flying-wing design with upper and lower turrets housing the smallest possible 20mm guns and taking advantage of unimpeded lines of sight seemed like the best defence solution, albeit with one problem: "In spite of the small arms, there were wing depths which caused a wing surface of about 165sqm. And at an unheard-of flight weight of at least 22 tons.

"So that version was not to be expected. In order to obtain a smaller aircraft, adapted to the views of the time, and without giving up any of the knowledge gained, a solution was seen in the way that, in a small wing, a thickened and prolonged middle section in the form of a gondola for the housing of crew and bombs, as well as the two turrets, was provided.

"It seemed to be of the utmost importance to unite the four men as closely as possible and to place them together at the top of the gondola. A project of this kind now involved the problem of finishing a large tailless aircraft in a short time with benign flying characteristics."

The result, arising from the too-heavy flying-wing idea, was the radical Arado E 500 twin-boom bomber project. This twin boom approach persisted beyond the E 500 with the E 340, Arado's competitor in the Bomber

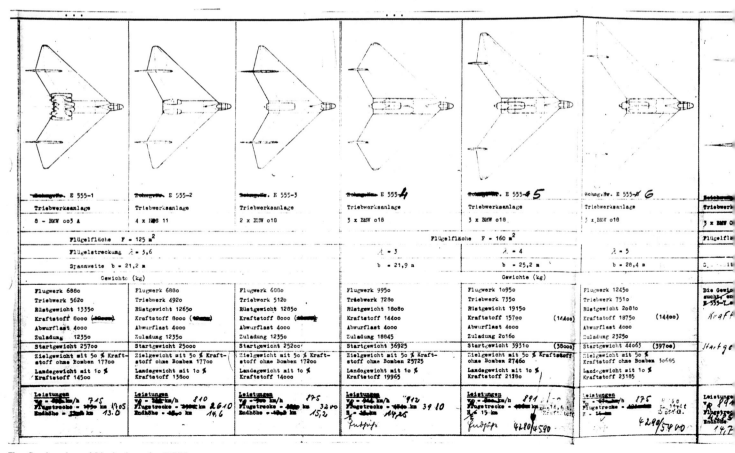

The final series of 11 designs for E 555.

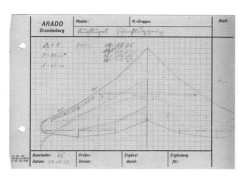
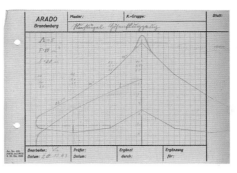
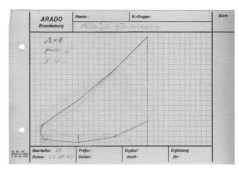

Arado carried out a great deal of work on determining the best shape for its flying wings.

B competition to find a replacement for the Dornier Do 17, Heinkel He 111 and Ju 88.

The E 340 had been first presented in 1940 and was discontinued in mid 1941. Two years later in mid 1943, around eight years after it had initially dismissed flying wings as unworkable, Arado was apparently ready to revisit the concept.

The company's chief aerodynamicist, Rüdiger Kosin, produced a report on June 15, 1943, entitled Nurflügelflugzeuge für grosse Reichweiten und grosse Geschwindigkeiten or 'All-wing aircraft for long ranges and high speeds'. There was little preamble – Kosin began with: "The results of a wide-ranging survey are provided, which is based on all-wing aircraft with jet engines."

The report looked carefully at how much fuel might reasonably be carried by a flying-wing aircraft in order to achieve the maximum possible range. In doing so, it briefly examined the fuel-carrying capacity of previous long-range aircraft including the Atlantic-crossing Junkers W 33 Bremen, the De Havilland

Comet, the Bellanca 28-70, the Ryan NYP (Spirit of St Louis) and the company's own Ar 79 long-range record attempt aircraft.

It then examined how much fuel might be carried in a flying-wing against the anticipated high fuel consumption of jet engines.

Kosin concluded: "A range of 6000 to 7000km with a speed of 800km/h can be achieved with a swept flying wing aircraft with jet engines if the payload ratio of fuel/take-off weight = 1: 2. From a certain aircraft size, this amount can be accommodated without difficulty in the wing. In this case, the smallest absolute fuel quantities are required for a machine with low surface load, which must fly at a high altitude."

The company had already commenced studying kinked and straight swept wing shapes under the project designation E 560 in November 1942 and now it launched a second strand of aerodynamic research to run in parallel – E 555 – to examine the all-wing form.

The earliest known document which

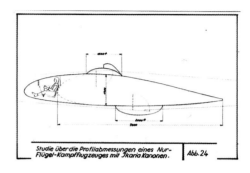

Studie über die Profilabmessungen eines Nur-Flügel-Kampfflugzeuges mit Ikaria Kanonen. Abb. 24

actually bears the label E 555 is dated July 14, 1943, and comprises a chart showing the horizontal top speeds of configurations E 555-6, -7, -8 and 10, each of which was to have been fitted with a trio of BMW 018 engines.

Activity on the project seems to have peaked between September 1943 and February 1944 but on October 18, 1944, Arado issued a report entitled Bomber für Höhe Geschwindigkeit und Grosse Reichweite or 'A high-speed long-range

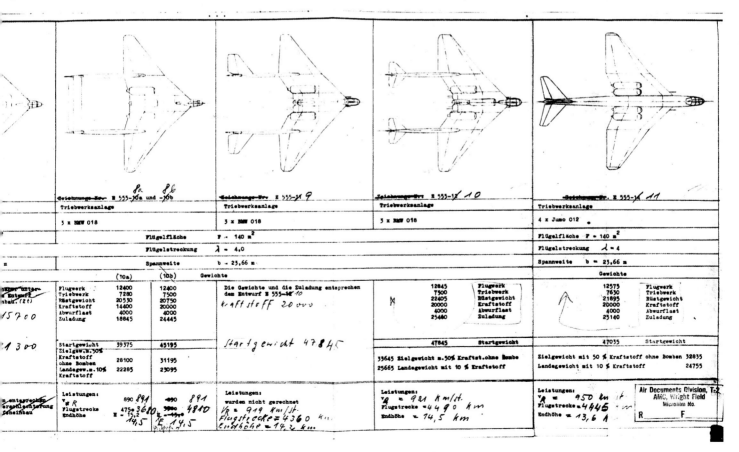

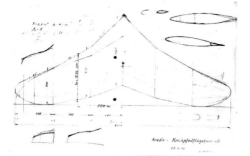

This twin-turret flying-wing design was studied by Arado in 1935 as part of the firm's twin-boom E 500 bomber project.

Finished front and side views of the E 555 designs have never been found, but these front-view sketches offer some idea of how the aircraft might have looked.

bomber' which offered up the E 555 flying wing designs that had existed in one form or another since the summer of 1943 configured as a selection of bombers.

The original notes used by the report's author, Dr Wolfgang Laute, suggest that there were originally at least 15 different configurations examined, numbered E 555-1 to -9, 10a and 10b, and -11 to -14. However, before a final version of the report was compiled, the original E 555-4, E 555-5 and E 555-13 were removed and now appear to be lost.

The remainder were renumbered to provide an uninterrupted sequence of 11 designs. E 555-1, -2 and -3 remained the same as they had been, but E 555-6 to E 555-12 each dropped two numbers to give a sequence up to E 555-10. So -6 became -4, -7 became -5 and so on. Finally, E 555-14 dropped three numbers to become E 555-11, making up for the fact that design -13 had also been removed.

The completed version of Laute's report begins: "It was the task to design a bomber for high speed and long range. There were four tons of bombs and 4000km of flight. These conditions seemed to be

A comparison chart from the Bomber für Höhe Geschwindigkeit und Grosse Reichweite report by Dr Wolfgang Laute, showing E 555 designs compared against other contemporary bombers.

most likely to be fulfilled by a flying-wing aircraft, which can be used to implement an arrow shape and sharp, thin profiles.

"These two features are, however, extremely important for the attainment of high velocities, which thus succeeds in pushing out the known air resistance increase to even higher Mach numbers. When using swept wings, it is also at the same time to forego the truncated fuselage and to build tailless.

"As a result of the required structural height for the crew space, landing gear and bomb space, a very deep wing results with a percentage of thin profiles, the stretching ratio of which is small. Nevertheless, the area will be about twice as large as usual.

"The large wing area compensates for the sharp laminar profiles in its effect on lift and the landing speed. Thus, the landing flaps can be kept small, which is very desirable, because the moment which is produced by them is hardly supportable. The relatively low surface loading also results in better vibration damping, which is particularly important in the case of a tailless design.

"It can be seen that the application of the arrow form entails a whole realm of further structural features, which usually complement one another happily. Thus the designs E 555-1 to -3 were created with a wing area of 125sqm, a profile of 3.6 and a weight of 25 tons.

"In all three designs, the same wing is swept by 45. The thickness corresponds to the height of the undercarriage with double main wheels, which are pivoted forward and retracted. The nose wheel is housed in the wing centre piece behind the pressure-tight bow cockpit. As crew two men are envisaged. The bombs lie inside the wing."

A table then shows that the E 555-1, -2 and -3 each weighed 25 tons with an eight-ton fuel load but each had different engines, a different top speed and a different range. The E 555-1 was powered by eight BMW 003 As for a top speed of 715km/h and a range of just 1705km. The E 555-2 had four HeS 011s, a top speed of 810km/h and 2610km range, while the E 555-3 had two BMW 018s for a top speed of 875km/h and a range of 3200km.

Laute comments: "The total thrusts are approximately equal. It is, however, evident that the velocities and flight distances which are very large with a few large engines are obtained by comparison with many small engines."

The next three designs in the sequence

each had three BMW 018s and a larger wing area at 160sqm, allowing each a fuel load of 14.4 tons. They were evidently intended to show what happened to weight, speed and range when the wing form was made progressively wider and narrower.

The E 555-4 had a weight of 36.9 tons, a speed of 912km/h and a range of 3980km, the E 555-5 weighed 38 tons with 891km/h speed and 4280km range (or 4590km with a fuel load increased to 15.7 tons). And the E 555-6 weighed 39.7 tons with 875km/h speed and 4290km range (5400km if fuel load was increased to 18.8 tons).

Laute then discusses the advantages and disadvantages of making ever larger wings to accommodate more fuel for better range – particularly the necessary increase in the size of undercarriage needed to support the weight on the ground and the effect this would have on the thickness of the wing necessary to house it. Speed would decrease in proportion to wing size increase.

He also discusses the positioning of the engines in the E 555-4, -5 and -6: "Two of the engines were placed under the wing, one on the wing top. All three engines are located close together on the wing part. Different factors are decisive for the engine distribution, which partly contradict each other."

These factors included the possibility of engine fouling by nosewheel, landing gear height, rearward view, the possibility of ingesting debris from the runway and thrust compensation of the engines in the event of a failure. Laute concluded that there were as many disadvantages to engines on top of the wing as there were to engines below the wing and meaning "a distribution on the top and bottom side is therefore appropriate".

E 555-7 differed from those earlier in the sequence because it was not intended to investigate proportionality – it was a defensive armament demonstrator. Laute wrote: "The design E 555-7 contains a weapon system consisting of two rigid MK 103 firing forward and four movable MG 151 rearward. For this purpose, a special pressure-tight stern turret with a third crew member is provided. With the selected design, all four rear arms can shoot on both sides due to the tailless design, which significantly increases the fire force compared to the fuselage aircraft.

"The weight of the weapon system with ammunition is two tons. In order to free up space for the weapon system, the engines had to be pulled apart sideways. Two of the engines were placed on the wing over the landing gear shafts, one engine is in the middle on the underside."

Laute was clearly concerned about the handling characteristics of these huge flying wings and acknowledged that achieving satisfactory handling was likely to be "a big and time-consuming obstacle". He went on: "With the little present experience, it cannot be readily said whether a designed aircraft will later become satisfactory in its characteristics.

"It has to be expected that there will be a longer flight test period, especially since the characteristics are strongly coupled with each other and are not as easy to influence individually, as with a fuselage aircraft with tailplane. Thus, unpredictable delays can be caused.

"This uncertainty could be eliminated by attaching a tail unit to a sufficiently long boom. To compensate for the increase in drag, the wing surface could be somewhat reduced. From this idea, the designs E 555-8 to -10 were created."

Remarkably, Laute had effectively repeated Arado's experience of eight years earlier – by suggesting that the likely negative characteristics of a flying wing could be overcome by fitting it with tail booms. E 555-8a and -8b were to have a connecting plane between their tail booms, E 555-9 had just one tailplane each on the booms' outer sides and E 555-10 had two symmetrical full tailplanes. Laute explained: "The designs 8a and 8b differ only in the fuel load, which was first assumed to be 14.4 tons according to the quantities present in the previous designs, but later was increased to 20 tons.

"At the end of the investigations, a design with an ordinary fuselage was drawn. An even number of engines had to be used. There were four Jumo 012s, which gave almost the same total thrust as the previously used three BMW 018s."

Reducing the wing size for E 555-9 to -11 meant another sacrifice: "In the case of the last designs -9 to -11, the landing gear wheels partly protrude from the wing lower part to allow a thinner wing. This way, the largest wing thickness could be reduced from 17% to 10%.

"According to the previous designs, 40 to 50 tons flight weight was achieved with speeds of 800-950km/h and four-ton bomb load and 4000-5000km of flight distance. The fuel load ratio was between 30 and 45%. If the flight distance is to be increased further to 6000-7000 km, as was occasionally stated, an increase in the payload ratio to 50 to 55% would be necessary under similar conditions. This could be achieved with the given bombs at a flying weight of 60-70 tons."

Finally, Laute summarised his findings by showing that aircraft with jet engines could have a similar range to those powered by piston engines but carrying a larger bomb load and flying at almost twice the speed "so that their tactical value far exceeds that of the piston-engine aircraft, although it must be taken into account that fuel consumption is greater."

A new jet bomber development competition was launched around a month after the publication of 'A high-speed long-range bomber'. It was entitled Langstreckenbomber but there was no formal entry from Arado – the E 555 designs had been formulated primarily for the purposes of scientific investigation, rather than as blueprints that could readily be turned into real life aircraft. Instead, tail and fuselage designs from Messerschmitt and Junkers – to describe them as 'conventional' does not seem entirely accurate – would compete against one last flying wing from the Horten brothers.

By the end of 1944, work on E 555 had ceased, but the programme would be swiftly resurrected in January 1945 when it provided the basis for alternative wing layouts for Arado's entry in the night and bad-weather jet fighter competition – the last such design contest of the war. ●

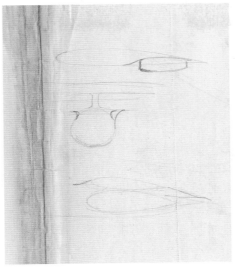
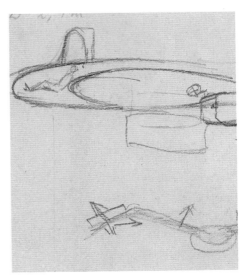

Arado sketches showing ways in which engines could be installed in a flying wing.

Side view detail from an E 555 sketch dated November 5, 1943.

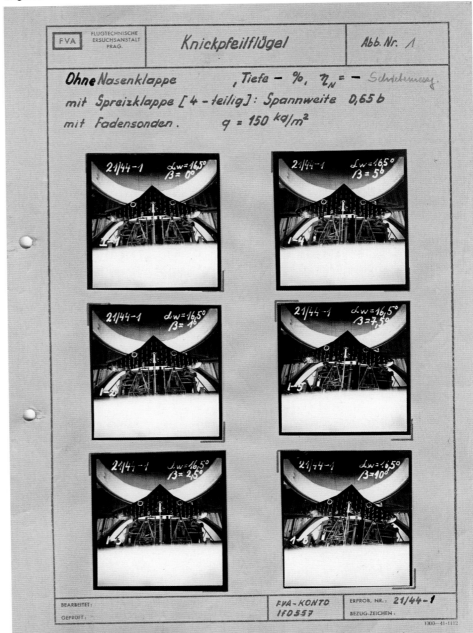

Wind tunnel tests were conducted on a model of the Arado 'knickpfeilflügel' shape. These photographs of the model were featured in a report dated October 12, 1944.

Big wing bomber

The final German aircraft design competition of the war was known as Langstreckenbomber. Messerschmitt had started it by putting forward a conventional four-jet design and the forward-swept Junkers Ju 287 was resurrected to compete against it. But at the last moment, another design was entered – the Horten brothers' H XVIII.

During November 1944, Willy Messerschmitt had suggested that an effort should be made to produce a four-jet bomber which could bypass Allied air defences and attack targets with relative impunity.

He was given until the end of January to work up a firm proposal for his P 1107 design while Junkers put forward its Ju 287 as an alternative that would be quicker to build, given that a 'flying mock-up' had already been tested during 1944. Towards the end of January a third design was added – an enormous flying wing design known as the Horten XVIII.

Dates were set for a four-day conference to discuss the designs at Junkers' Dessau headquarters, February 20-23, with a panel of interested parties and independent experts being assembled to go over the designs, establish their relative merits and identify their flaws.

Panel members included Ludwig Bölkow, representing Messerschmitt; Hans Gropler, head of Junkers' project office; Reimar and Walter Horten, representing themselves; Rüdiger Kosin of Arado; production management specialist Senior Staff Engineer Kohl; and Professor August Quick of the Deutsche Versuchsanstalt für Luftfahrt (DVL).

When the first day of the conference arrived, the delegates were clearly fascinated by the H XVIII. Worked up by the Hortens very quickly, the submitted design had outer wings made of wood with a metal centre section housing a large pressure cabin close to the forward tip of the aircraft's wing. Also attached to the central area were two large fixed sets of undercarriage wheels with the engines attached to them.

A report summarising the conference, published by the DVL at Berlin-Adlershof on February 25, 1945, states that each of the three designs – the Horten XVIII, the Messerschmitt P 1107 and the Junkers Ju 287 – was to be assessed with a fuel load of 15 tons and a payload of four tons of bombs. The Horten XVIII was also assessed with a fuel load of 19 tons because unlike the other two projects it had the capacity to carry that much. After briefly outlining the Messerschmitt and Junkers projects, the report states: "The Horten XVIII preliminary project differs from the other two types above all in its 'flying wing' type of construction and its by far greater wing surface area (156sq m instead of 60sq m). It is therefore as regards disposable load not fully exploited with the present power units."

It was found using the competition's approved mathematical formulas that the Horten XVIII would actually be 1000kg lighter than the brothers had worked out themselves, and making its outer wings from aluminium rather than wood could save another 300kg to 1360kg.

The P 1107 had the highest calculated top speed at 935km/h at 7000m, compared to 885km/h for the Ju 287 and 860km/h for the Horten XVIII. However, while the others were likely to suffer the effects of compressibility as they approached the subsonic range, no such problem was foreseen for the Horten design: "A study shows that at that speed the P 1107 enters a range in which the drag slopes up sharply as the speed of sound is approached. As a result possible disturbance in the flying characteristics appears which render it impossible to exploit this speed."

"The Horten XVIII is slightly slower than the 8-287, a fact attributable in the main to its larger wing surface. On the other hand its speed is within a range probably free from disturbances caused by approaching the speed of sound."

In terms of range, the Ju 287 was said to have a range of 4430km cruising at 785km/h, the P 1107 could do 4850km at 882km/h and the Horten XVIII had the potential for 5350km at 782km/h. The report does note however: "The range in the case of the Horten XVIII in spite of its higher drag, is the highest, because owing to its lower surface load, it possesses a higher ceiling, especially at the commencement of flight, and also owing to the performance characteristic of the jet power unit flight at high altitude is especially economical.

"As the Horten was originally designed for a larger fuel load than that indicated for the other types (15 tons) its load for the purpose of this comparison was taken at 19 tons and the airframe weight taken at 500kg higher in order to take into consideration the necessary reinforcement etc. The optimum range then obtained rose from 5350km to 6500km."

All three of the designs would have required a lengthy take-off run assisted by rockets, although the Horten XVIII "owing to its smaller surface load is materially superior to the other aircraft". And concerns were raised about the pronounced sweepback of the P 1107 and Horten XVIII's wings: "Up to now, apart from single small experimental aircraft, no experiences as to the practicability of sweepbacks of this size are available. Surprises are therefore to be expected, the overcoming of which will present new problems.

"The question of the probable flying characteristics of the Horten XVIII and the open questions arising therefrom are discussed later in this report. As a special point of some importance it may be here mentioned that the 'flying wing' aircraft of this size and shape have not hitherto been built for high speeds and that therefore difficulties of the most diverse character may be expected during development until personnel are fully trained.

"While we today have ample experience to draw upon when it is a question of eliminating unpleasant flying characteristics in aircraft of normal design and faults, for example, regarding stability, can usually be corrected by small alterations in design, this fund of experience is not yet available to us in the case of the 'flying wing' aircraft.

"Moreover, undesirable points in the flying characteristics of flying wing aircraft can often only be removed after alterations to the wing itself which in the majority of cases would involve considerable constructional outlay. For these reasons the time required for development and testing of a flying wing aircraft is even today greater than that in the case of an aircraft of normal type."

The Hortens were given an opportunity to make the case for their aircraft via a written statement, and Reimar used this opportunity to complain that his design was not being

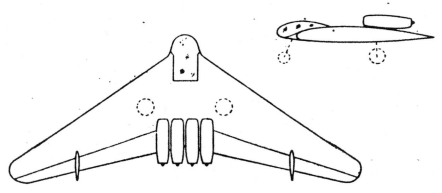

A postwar sketch of the Junkers EF 130 – a design intended to embody the work carried out on large flying wing bombers by the Hortens, Messerschmitt and Junkers itself.

allowed to show its true potential. He wrote: "For the purposes of comparison with the 8-287 and the P 1107 the Horten XVIII project was put back to four tons of bombs and 15 tons of fuel. By so doing the weight reserves of seven tons were left out of considerations."

Furthermore, he had understood that the competition required that the turbojets had to be placed in nacelles, yet now he found that Messerschmitt had submitted a design with the engines partially buried in the wings – which is what he had wanted to do in the first place.

At the end of the conference, the panel of experts concluded that, should the Horten XVIII be chosen for development, a lengthy programme of flight testing would be necessary yet they expected "that no insurmountable difficulties" would arise in this regard with the Horten XVIII.

They agreed that the positioning of the engines in nacelles under the wing, rather than installing them inside it, was less than ideal. There would be particular problems arising from boundary layer air at the engine intakes which would require "careful and exhaustive preliminary experiments either in the wind tunnel or during actual flight as on the basic experiences gained up to now they cannot be estimated and involve great uncertainties".

Following the meeting, on March 1, 1945, the Entwicklungshauptkommission 'Flugzeuge' met and it was reported that "the Junkers company was entrusted with development work for long-distance bombers with four jet engines each, i.e. the work on the 8-287 started again. Following this work, project work for a long-distance bomber in all-wing construction is planned for the same company".

The Ju 287 won the competition simply because it would be easiest to build – but Junkers was required to work with the Hortens on a flying-wing bomber design.

The situation was clarified a little further at another meeting of the Entwicklungshauptkommission on March 26, 1945. An appendix to the report, under the heading 'Bomberprojekte Horten', discusses plans for wind tunnel trials and construction of a flying mock-up before stating: "These whole works can only be done by an experienced sound company. The Horten brothers will only be involved as advisors, because they do not have any experience or knowledge about industrial aircraft manufacturing of that dimension and capacity.

"General Junck's opinion, to keep the Hortens' limited business to let them finish the Horten IX development and fulfil their own promises, is agreed. They will be involved as advisors in discussions about flying wing issues."

Still more evidence can be found in CIOS report XXXI-3 German High Speed Airplanes and Design Development written by Robert W Kluge and Charles L Fay on behalf of the US Technical Industrial Intelligence Committee and published in August 1945.

Under a heading of 'The Messerschmitt Tailless Jet Bomber', the report states: "Early in 1945 the Government decided that Messerschmitt did not have sufficient engineering manpower to handle the bomber design and turned it over to Junkers and the Horten Bros."

This would appear to refer to the P 1108. On the following page, under 'The Junkers

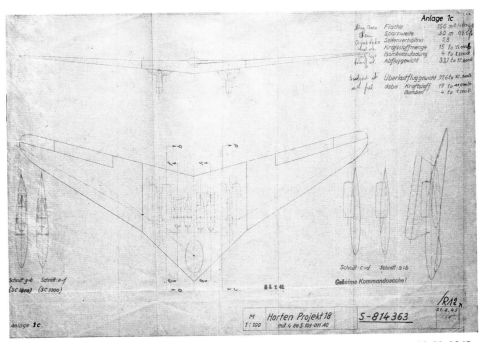

The Horten XVIII as presented to the Langstreckenbomber conference on February 20-23, 1945.

Tailless Jet Bomber', the report continues: "The Junkers Design Group had just begun work on a jet bomber to fulfil the specifications already mentioned for the Messerschmitt bomber. Although no drawings or data were available, the following information was obtained from Mr Gropler, chief designer of Junkers.

"The ship was to be tailless with the vertical stabilisers located at the trailing edge of the wing at approximately the middle of the semi-span. This is similar to the Junkers EF 128 arrangement. The wings have approximately 40-degree sweepback, aspect ratio of 4.8, area of 1290sq ft, span of 78.7ft. The gross weight is approximately 77,000lb and the maximum level flight speed approximately 620mph. The range is 3720 miles. All fuel is kept in the wings in tanks which are insulated because of the low melting point of the fuel. The tanks are not bulletproof.

"The fuselage consists only of a nacelle jutting forward of the wing at its centreline. This nacelle holds the crew, nosewheel and most of the equipment. The bomb bay is aft of the cabin and the bombs fit into the root airfoil contour. One layer of eight bombs (two rows of four) is provided for.

"The four HeS 011 jet units are mounted abreast above the trailing edge of the wing (about half of the power plant extends forward of the actual trailing edge of the wing and half aft of the trailing edge). All four motors are enclosed in one nacelle and a boundary layer duct runs between the nacelle and the wing surface.

"The centre section of the wing is the same span as the width of this nacelle and the bomb bay runs the full span of the centre panel. The main landing gear retracts forward and inboard to a location just outboard of the bomb bay. The nose wheel retracts aft. The plane carries no armament."

This would appear to suggest that the Messerschmitt P 1108 and Horten XVIII projects were both effectively handed to Junkers for further development as a single project – the Junkers EF 130 – with the Horten brothers retained as consultants.

Then again, when Myhra asked Reimar: "When was the H XVIII to have been built?" He replied: "I wanted to finish the H VIII and it was scheduled to be finished in the summer of 1945. I was then going to start on the H XVIII and make a scale model of the H XVIII for use in the H VIII flying wind tunnel. But I was only preparing for work on the H XVIII and anyway design work would not have started on the H XVIII until about July 1945.

"It was ordered at April 1 that I had to change locations to Kahla, near REIMAHG, and begin work on the H XVIII. It could not be because I was told to begin construction of the H XVIII in the workshop there but I needed at least six months more. Mr Saur, from the Ministry of Defence, did not understand that. He told me that I was to receive 2000 men and begin working on the H XVIII. I told him that I did not need 2000 men and at the present time I was only employing about 20 men. At most, all I'd need to build the H XVIII would be between 100 and 150 men. He told me that he had two hangars with 5.6m thick roofs which were bomb proof. Plus it was built into the side of a hill and had ventilation shafts for fresh air.

"Mr Saur wanted me to assemble the H XVIII and I told him that the span of the H XVIII would be able 40m. He said that a 40m span would be no problem at the Mühldorf hangers. I was still reluctant because I did not have a prototype of the H XVIII yet. To build the prototype I would have to build it with my men and could not possibly employ more than between 100 to 150 men.

"So the H XVIII was ordered without thinking. For my idea of thinking I required the entire second half of 1945 to begin production of the first H XVIII. I thought that I would be able to fly the first prototype in February 1946. Then after flying the prototype and making modifications, I could start production during the second half of 1946. This is what was possible. Mr Saur wanted all this at least one year earlier. This could not be."

It could not, since this was nearly the end of the war for the Horten brothers. But in the meantime work had continued on the 8-229. ●

One last Delta

Lacking the resources of the finely-tuned manufacturing machine that was Messerschmitt AG, Alexander Lippisch made slow progress on his P 11/Delta VI and was already losing interest in it when tragedy struck...

At the beginning of 1944, Alexander Lippisch confidently expected that his tailless P 11 multirole aircraft, now renamed Delta VI, would be built as a manned glider prototype and all being well would then enter full production.

His small workforce at the LFW in Vienna diligently laboured over his designs, even as these changed and evolved through an ever-increasing number of different versions, concepts and ideas. While the exterior appearance of the Delta VI remained loosely the same, Lippisch completely revised its internal structure as time went on.

Numerous drawings showing the Delta VI V1 glider's components, variously labelled P 11 or Delta VI depending on how long ago they had first been drafted, were compiled and work on a full scale mock-up was begun.

Work on building the glider itself had begun by June 1944 when disaster befell the project. According to Technical Intelligence report no. A.424: "The construction of this aeroplane was started in a factory in Vienna which was bombed out in June 1944 by the American Air Force.

"By this event Dr Lippisch lost 43 of his collaborators. The factory was then rebuilt in the Wiener Wald but the first experimental aircraft of this all-wing type, Li P 11, was never finished as the Russians invaded the region of Vienna."

Vienna was bombed twice in June 1944 by the USAAF – on the 16th and 24th. The former seems more likely to have hit the LFW.

Writing about the attack in his book Erinnerungen some 30 years later, Lippisch put the number of dead slightly higher: "At the time of the highest activity an air attack on aeronautics research in Vienna (LFW) occurred in June 1944, during which severe damage and, above all, 45 deaths were to be lamented; including some of my most valuable employees."

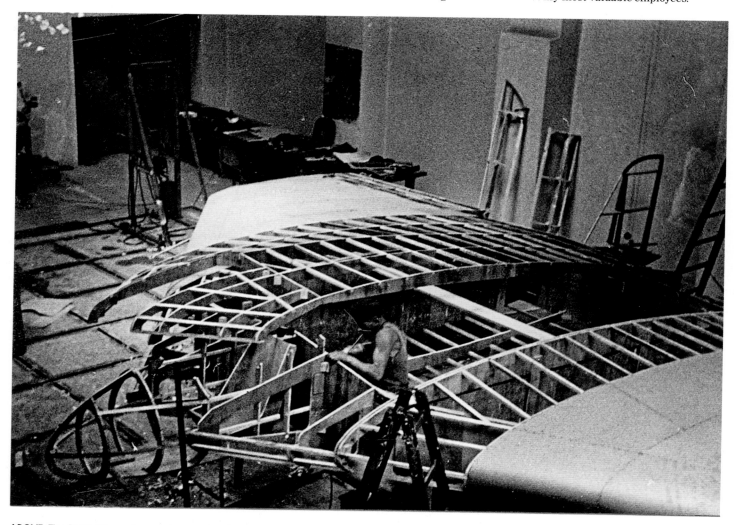

ABOVE: The Delta VI mockup under construction at the LFW in Vienna during 1944. Iowa State University Library Special Collections and University Archive

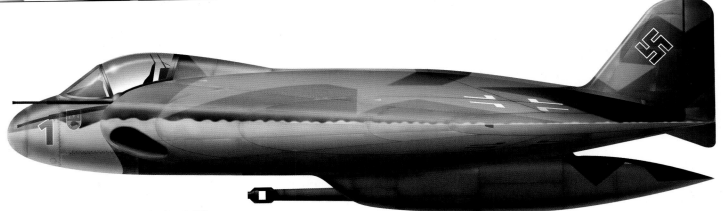

ABOVE: Lippisch Delta VI. Art by Daniel Uhr

Now work on the Delta VI slowed to a crawl as Lippisch became increasingly focused on a new project – the ramjet-powered P 12, P 13a and P 13b designs. Yet work did not stop completely. At one point Henschel appears to have become involved, perhaps as a construction partner to help with the construction of the Delta VI. The minutes from a meeting of the EHK on November 21-22 state "the Lippisch P 11, a parallel development with the Ho 229, was to be developed in collaboration with Henschel" but this does not seem to have come about.

Even as late as December 2, 1944, Junkers' special engines division OMW-Kobü Sondertriebwerke, was struggling to get a pair of Jumo 004s to fit inside the Delta VI V2 – the powered version that was to follow the unpowered glider V1.

The report begins: "The following difficulties have arisen during installation of the 004 device in the airframe VI 2:
1) Installation of the 004 inlet hood in the wing profile. According to the proposal put forward by the LF-Wien, inserting the inlet by cutting off the outer sheet metal jacket does not appear to be sufficient.

"We propose to investigate again whether it is not possible to modify the inlet hood somewhat in its present form, and to provide for the throughput of the cooling air the rear end of the hood jacket and the rear end wall with corresponding cutouts. With regard to cooling, we consider the measure to be appropriate for serial production, since the 004 device is already delivered in large quantities.

"2) Suspension of the engine in the tubing of the airframe. Since the engine is installed inside the wing and is suspended in a gantry, the joints had to be dispensed with because of the narrow installation."

It goes on to discuss the bolts needed to secure the engines, the need for tolerances to be used which take account of thermal expansion and the load-bearing capacity of the engine supports.

When the Russians reached Vienna at the beginning of April 1945, Lippisch found it necessary to abandon all the part-completed work already carried out on the Delta VI.

According to Erinnerungen: "The wind tunnel measurements were left in the cellar of a building where one of my aerodynamicists lived, or fell into the hands of the Russians, because this good aerodynamicist, who had carried out the measurements in Göttingen, took the train back to Vienna, and when he got out, he realised that the city was ▶

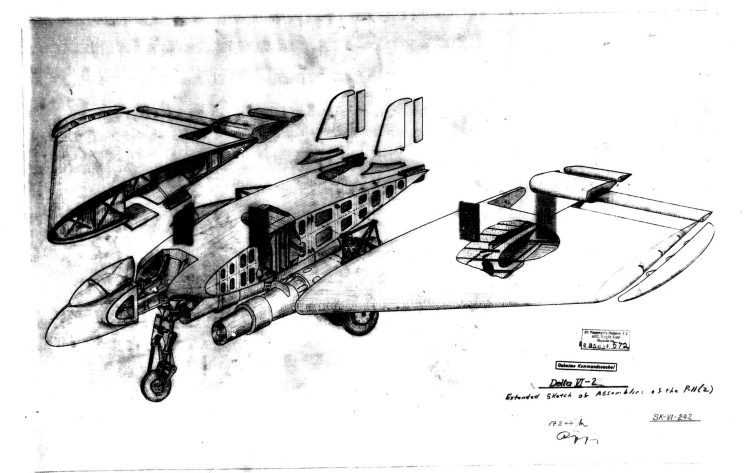

ABOVE: The second Delta VI prototype was to be powered by a pair of turbojets – following the same development trajectory as the Horten 8-229. This drawing from February 1944 shows its structure.

meanwhile occupied by the Russians.

"This material, which is nevertheless quite valuable, has been lost. A V-pattern begun in wood construction, which was to be used as a sailplane (with starting aid pack) to determine the flight characteristics, had been taken on a trailer during our escape from Vienna, but had to be left behind by the pressure of events on the edge of the motorway."

What became of the Delta VI V1 glider on its trailer and the Delta VI V2 airframe with which Junkers' engineers had been struggling is unknown. Presumably the Russians either captured or destroyed them both, along with much of the paperwork relating to the project.

But what happened to the 500,000 marks Lippisch was given by Reichsmarschall Hermann Göring with which to build the first powered prototype of the P 11, back in 1943? Evidently, Reimar Horten discussed the money with Lippisch either shortly before or shortly after the end of the war.

He gave David Myhra a possibly apocryphal account: "When Göring gave me 500,000 marks to work on an all-wing fighter I had a basis for starting my work in an official and highly organised manner. Lippisch told me also that Göring had given him 500,000 marks too for his research on delta wing aircraft.

"I asked Lippisch what he had done with his 500,000 marks and he said that he had purchased a stone quarry and after the war he'd provide stones needed to rebuild homes throughout Germany. However, he lost it all because these days it is now in Poland." ●

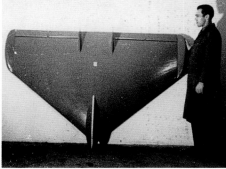

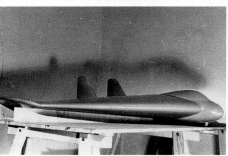

ABOVE: A huge display model of the Delta VI. The model would later be painted up and photographed against a 'sky' backdrop to help showcase the project. **Iowa State University Library Special Collections and University Archive**

ABOVE: Two views looking down on the Delta VI mockup from above. **Iowa State University Library Special Collections and University Archive**

ABOVE: The first page of a Junkers report dated December 2, 1944, discussing the difficulties of installing a pair of Jumo 004 turbojets in the Delta VI V2. A similar report on the Go 229 would be written three months later.

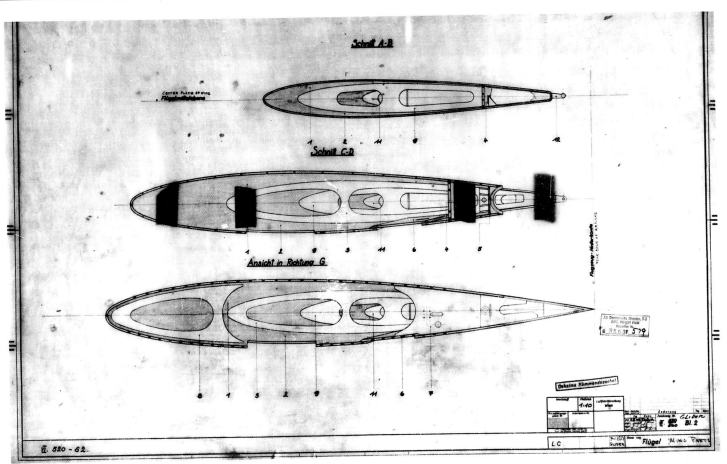

ABOVE: Wing structure of the Delta VI V1 glider – still very much a work in progress during the first half of 1944.

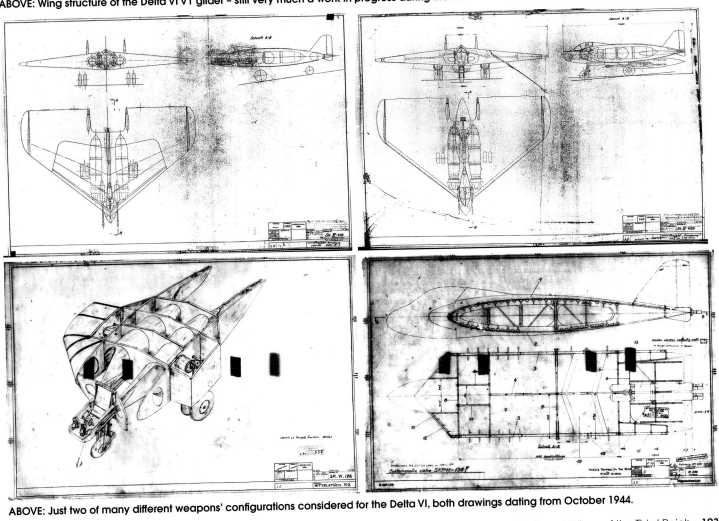

ABOVE: Just two of many different weapons' configurations considered for the Delta VI, both drawings dating from October 1944.

Last man standing

Horten H IXb/8-229/Go 229/Ho 267

As the end of the war approached, numerous projects fell by the wayside – but not the 8-229. Gotha continued attempting to build its prototypes right up to the end of the war, although the eventual production model might have been quite different from what was envisioned in 1943/44.

The first and only turbojet powered example of the 8-229, the V2, was completed on December 17, 1944, and transported by rail from Göttingen to Oranienburg, just north of Berlin, for flight testing.

The designated pilot, Erwin Ziller, received twin-engine jet flight training in a two-seat Me 262 B-1 on December 29-31 but apparently was not shown the proper procedure for starting the Jumo 004 engines.

Testing was halted while the brothers travelled back to Bonn to spend Christmas with their parents and during January Gotha appears to have slowed or even halted its programme of work on the V3, V4, V5 and V6. The firm's chief aerodynamicist, Rudolf Göthert, was certainly working on his P-60 designs and it is possible that the rest of the company was fully occupied with gearing up for and then commencing mass production of wings for the Heinkel He 162.

Ziller finally took the 8-229 V2 up for its first powered flight on February 2, 1945, having had the aircraft's engines started for him by another member of the Horten team – the only one who had received the appropriate training from Junkers – lying on the wing of the aircraft with his arm in the cockpit flicking the relevant switches.

Keeping the undercarriage locked in the 'down' position, he reached 300km/h before throttling back and landing again. A second flight is believed to have taken place on February 3 but this time a hard landing due to a too-early deployment of the aircraft's brake parachute resulted in undercarriage damage.

Following repairs, a third flight took place on February 18, 1945. Ziller made three passes over the airfield so that a team from the Rechlin test centre could make speed and altitude measurements – apparently clocking up 795km/h (494mph) below 2000m. The right engine failed after 45 minutes in the air and Ziller was unable to restart it. He tried to bring the aircraft in to land but put the gear down too soon – 400m from the landing strip. The landing gear hydraulic system, powered by the right engine, was inoperative so Ziller had to use the contents of a compressed air bottle, his emergency backup, to lower the gear. This meant that once it was down, it could not be retracted.

The increased drag slowed the aircraft and Ziller realised he wasn't going to make the strip. He powered up the remaining engine but the drag produced by the gear was too great and its airspeed could not be increased. The aircraft then entered a broad turn to the right which it maintained until it hit the ground. The impact was so great both engines and

Ziller himself were thrown from the aircraft. He hit a tree and was killed instantly.

It has been suggested that Ziller was rendered unconscious by engine fumes entering the cockpit during these final moments, which would explain why he made no further efforts to recover the aircraft after it entered its wide turn. It was found that his harness, though torn open by the force of the impact, had not been unfastened, and he had made no attempt to activate the ejection seat either.

Following Ziller's death, the Hortens were distracted by the inclusion of their H XVIII bomber in the Langstreckenbomber competition – the main conference for which took place from February 20-23. Once this was over, Reimar's thoughts returned to the 8-229 and he prepared a new report evidently intended to help Gotha acquire more resources for the production of the remaining prototypes.

The cover of the report folder was marked 'Horten (underlined) Flugzeugmuster 8-229 Zerstörer' and the first page read: "Preface. The airplane described in the following is a flying wing aircraft, which has neither fuselage nor special control surfaces. It was designed in 1943 on the basis of systematic preliminary work on more than 30 aircraft of the most varied tasks.

"The construction of the aircraft was carried out in two work-pieces by the Luftwaffen-Sonderkommando IX, Göttingen. Both aircraft have expanded our experience with numerous flights with various pilots in such a way that series construction can be realised on this basis. However, a further testing of pilot aircraft is required for the large series."

The page is signed by Reimar Horten, Göttingen, March 1, 1945. The next page is headed 'Description of the flying wing aircraft 8-229 (underlined) according to project "Horten IX"'. The 8-229 is described as a two-engine jet multipurpose two-seater aircraft for use as a) day-fighter and bad-weather fighter, b) destroyer, c) light bomber, d) reconnaissance, e) night fighter.

It is clear that, going forward, the 8-229 is to be a two-seater whatever its intended role. A construction description produced just over three months earlier by Gotha, on November 22, 1944, reiterated all other descriptions which had been given up to that point which it stated that "the aircraft is a single-seat fighter design. It can also be a bomber with a two-ton bomb load or a reconnaissance type".

The single-seater 8-229 appears, as of March 1, 1945, to have been abandoned.

The report description from that date continues: "The flying wing has 53.6sqm wings and a wingspan of 16.8m. It is three-part, the outer wings are made in wood construction, the wing middle part as steel tubular framework. The outer wings are supported by the rudder flaps acting as height and ailerons, as well as the side rudders configured as an air brake at the wing ends.

"On the wing root, drag flaps are sunk as take-off and landing aids. Inside the wings are four fuel tanks for 1200 litres of fuel. It is

ABOVE: Artwork showing the 8-229 in its final series production form – a two-seater – from Reimar Horten's March 1, 1945, Horten Flugzeugmuster 8-229 Zerstörer' report.

intended to glue and conserve the wing later, if necessary, so that approximately 2000-2200 litres of fuel tank space are produced per wing.

"The wing is lined with an auxiliary hull and with a 17mm thick solid wood shell. The dimension of the wing shell is selected to be this large for stiffness reasons, whereby it is at the same time possible to use locking wood of a poor quality without incurring disadvantages. The wing centrepiece with a width of 3.20m carries the landing gear, the two-seated pilot cabin, the engines 109 004 or 109 003 in the interior, as well as the weapons, armouring, bomb hanging devices and navigation equipment.

"The static assembly consists of untreated steel pipes; the claddings of plywood shells. These can be dismantled, so that the accessibility to the engines, weapons, picture frames and FT installations is ensured at all times.

"The landing gear is designed as a nose wheel gear and gives the aircraft an angle of 9°. By approximately 50% of the total load lying on the nose wheel, it necessarily forced this angle of attack when rolling, which significantly reduces the starting distance, especially in the case of lawns and soft ground. All wheels are retractable. The rear undercarriage, consisting of standard bogies from the Me 109 in the case of V-models, can be replaced later by the chassis of the Me 262 without major changes, which makes it possible to increase the weight of the aircraft up to 11.5 tons."

The engines, either Jumo 004s or BMW 003s, were to be installed inside the wing and would be as close as possible to the very centre of the aircraft. They could be installed or removed from the front via their intakes.

At the front of the aircraft "the cabin for the pilot and the observer is provided between the inlets of the engines. This cabin is designed as an armoured pressure cabin. It contains catapult seats for the successive, seated pilot and observer". Armour would be provided to protect the crew and ammunition boxes from

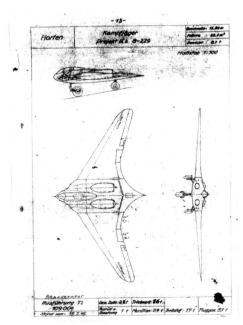

ABOVE: A three-view drawing of the two-seater production model 8-229. Whether it would have been the Ho 229, the Go 229 or even the Ho 267 is debatable.

ABOVE: Gotha Go 229 production version. Art by Daniel Uhr

bullets up to 12.7mm from the front and back. Weaponry would be four fixed forward-firing MK 108 cannon with 120 rounds each. The gunsight was to be an EZ 42 but also "the possibility to install an additional 24 to 36 R4M rockets is available. Between the engines, a 503 rack is installed for 1000kg bombs".

No detail is given on exactly how the unguided R4M rockets would be fitted but presumably they would be fitted to underwing racks as they were on the Me 262. Equipment in terms of radar units or other electronic devices would be "later determined by OKL", the Luftwaffe high command.

Weighing 7000kg, the 8-229 would require a take-off run of 520m. Landing speed with the same load was 144km/h but with a reduced fuel load (weight down to 5450kg) it was just 127km/h. The 'performance' section of the report also mentions a range of 4040km when fitted out for reconnaissance duties with a pair of 1000kg drop tanks. The drag from these would result in top speed being lowered from around 950km/h to 830km/h. Ceiling was 15-16km although the report notes that the available engine specifications were "not sufficient for more accurate height determination".

Next the report provides a summary of 22 advantages "of the 8-229 in front of today's jet fighters". These are given as "higher speed (950km/h near the ground), higher climbing speed, greater flight time and range, higher payload (2 tons bombs) higher ceiling (15-16km), shorter start run, narrow turn radius (smaller surface load), lower landing speed, jet inlets are higher (lower risk of contamination), airfield suitability, better visibility, better shooting position (side control), better accessibility (without tailplane), fuel is far from the pilot in the outer wing, lighter roll handling (nose wheel and intercepting force), two-seater, construction has less work required (4000 hours), building material wood and steel (65% wood), better single-engine flight due to closer engines, tactical brake in three stages, all three wheels can be braked, very short run-out due to: small landing speed, screen brake, 3 x wheel brake".

The final written section of Reimar's report is headed 'production' and gives the position as of March 1, 1945: "The company Gothaer Waggonfabrik 20 V samples have been ordered with DE-urgency starting from November 1944. The output begins with V3. From V3-incl. V5 is the single-seater. As of V6, the aircraft will be built as a double-seater. The standard processing can be carried out by the company GWF.

"In order to achieve the lowest possible risk during a series run, it is necessary that the test aircraft are manufactured as quickly as possible. The current deadline, which provides for the production of 1 piece per month, is sufficient to ensure a satisfactory trial during the course of the year 1945.

"The prerequisite for this is that the specified dates are kept. For example, the first aircraft to be deployed by the company

ABOVE: The Horten H IX V2 undergoing ground tests in late January or early February 1945. The aircraft would be destroyed in a fatal crash on February 18.

GWF has a deadline of three months, a larger support of the company is necessary."

On the same day, March 1, 1945, a meeting of the Entwicklungshauptkommission, discussing night- and bad-weather fighters, had confirmed that work on "another project, fighter variant Horten IX" was still ongoing at Gotha.

As previously mentioned, Junkers produced a brief report six days later, on March 7, 1945, entitled Triebwerkeinbau in Go 229 (Horten) (V3 + V5) which outlined the difficulties that the company was experiencing in fitting the engines into the airframe, primarily due to the lack of available space.

Under a heading of 'Horten IX' the war diary of the Chef-TLR for March 16 to April 4 states that "apart from the three V-patterns V3 to V5 in the V2 version, a further 10 aircraft V6 to V15 will be built at GWF".

This suggests that Gotha had been authorised to construct a series of 10 two-seater 8-229 aircraft, presumably some time between March 1 and April 4. There appears to be some evidence that the Go 229 received another redesignation before the war finally came to an end – the American T-2 Technical Intelligence Glossary of German Aeronautical Codes, Models, Project Numbers, Abbreviations, Etc. Final Edition, published in November 1947, has entries for both the Ho 229 and Go 229. Under 'Ho 229', it states: "Aircraft type number for an experimental flying-wing reconnaissance airplane powered by two Ju 004 turbojet engines redesignated as Ho 267." The entry for 'Ho 267' just below it reads: "Aircraft type number for a Horten flying wing powered by two Ju 004 turbojet engines."

The 'Go 229' entry states: "Aircraft type number for an experimental twin-jet flying-wing reconnaissance airplane developed from the Horten IX of which the Go 229 – V6 modification is known." Under 'Go 267' it simply states: "Aircraft type number for a Gotha airplane."

Evidently work on the V3 to V5 8-229 prototypes had been taking place on Gotha's behalf at the Ortlepp Möbel Fabrik at Friedrichroda – which is where the incomplete airframes were captured by elements of the American 3rd Army's VII Corps on April 14, 1945. Both the V3 and V4 had their engines fitted, the V3 being near completion. The V5 existed only as a steel frame.

By now both Horten brothers had also been captured and taken into custody as prisoners of war. ●

Collision course

As efforts to develop his P 11/Delta VI dragged on, Alexander Lippisch's attention switched to a new concept: ramjet propulsion. At first he envisioned it as the ideal powerplant for an aircraft designed to collide with and bring down Allied bombers. As the war approached its end however, he designed what amounted to a ramjet-powered Delta VI…

During the late summer of 1943, Alexander Lippisch conceived of a revenge weapon – a rocket-propelled manned aircraft shaped so that it could slice through Allied bombers. It would be a simple ramp-launched machine made in large quantities to create "a whole swarm" of "darts of death" according to a paper he wrote on the subject.

The ram-rocket itself would consist of a steel tube fuselage with a solid ram at one end, a central cockpit and three short swept wings to the rear. Once it had launched, cut through its target and burned through all its fuel and the pilot would bail out of the battered craft and take to his parachute.

Lippisch decided, however, that multiple or very large rocket engines on their own would not be ideal for this use due to the volatility of their fuel and the short duration of their thrust. However, towards the end of the year he became aware of promising research being carried out both at the DFS and in Vienna on a relatively new form of propulsion – the ramjet.

In order for a ramjet to work, it needs to already be travelling at speed before being lit up. The speed causes air to rush into the engine where it is mixed with fuel and combusted. The resulting blast is then directed through the engines exhaust to the rear, creating thrust. Lippisch realised that a rocket would be the ideal way of building up sufficient speed for a ramjet to begin working.

In Erinnerungen, he wrote: "Together with some competent thermodynamicists at the Vienna Institute, I succeeded in starting some basic work on the ramjet engine and also to carry out some fundamental and promising experiments. The engine, already invented by Lorin in 1912, but which can only operate economically at very high velocities, was moved into the interior of a thicker delta wing of small span, the jet emerging along the trailing edge being simultaneously used by appropriate deflection to control it.

"Such a combination is called a 'power wing'. The tests for the corresponding burners, which were originally to be operated with liquid fuel, later with solid fuel (carbon dust or paraffin-impregnated brown coal), were carried out by Dr Schwabl in Vienna and by Dr Sänger at the DFS.

"In March 1944, a corresponding design was created for a piloted aircraft, P 12, which would be brought to the required initial speed using a Mistel combination (on the back of another aircraft) or with the aid of a launching sled with rocket propulsion. After finding a more favourable form of the air intake, we had successfully let fly a corresponding model of the engine in May 1944 at the Spitzerberg in Vienna.

"This led to an improved draft, P 13, which was very much promoted by the Ministry of Defence."

Lippisch and his team worked on the P12/P 13 in parallel to the Delta VI for much of 1944. By October, Lippisch's interest in the Delta VI appears to have diminished and his work on ramjets correspondingly increased.

The P 12 and P 13 shared a near-identical delta wing planform with a nose intake for the internal ramjet at the forward tip and the exhaust venting from its trailing edge. They generally differed, however, in two key respects: the P 12's pilot sat within the wing, with the air for the liquid-fuelled ramjet passing on either side of him. He was covered over by a low canopy and at the rear of the aircraft was a vertical fin and rudder. The P 13's pilot sat on top of the wing in a large combined cockpit-fin, leaving the airflow to the solid-fuelled ramjet unobstructed.

However, Lippisch seems to have been unable to decide which layout was best – cockpit-in-fuselage or cockpit-in-fin. Although the former is usually associated with the P 12 and the latter with the P 13, period drawings exist of the P 12 with the

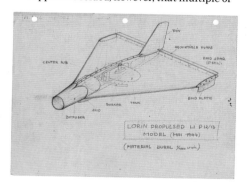

ABOVE: A sketch of the model used by Lippisch to test the flight characteristics of the P 12 and P 13 during May 1944. Iowa State University Library Special Collections and University Archive

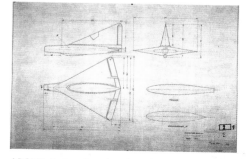

ABOVE: A drawing showing a model of the P 13a dated December 15, 1944. The external appearance of the design has changed little in two months.

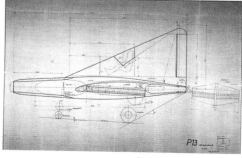

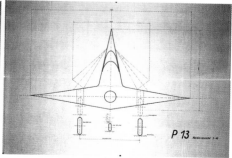

ABOVE: Side and front views of the wheeled undercarriage P 13, dated November 8, 1944 – over a month after the plan view. Iowa State University Library Special Collections and University Archive

ABOVE: Lippisch P 13 with wheeled undercarriage. Art by Daniel Uhr

cockpit-in-fin configuration and the P 13 with the cockpit-in-fuselage configuration.

Wind tunnel tests of a simplified P 12/13 model with different fin and cockpit arrangements were carried out during the early part of 1944 and a scale model was flight tested at Spitzerberg airfield near Vienna in May 1944.

Lippisch decided against the liquid fuelled version, abandoning the P 12 in the process, and concentrated on the coal-burning P 13. According to American Technical Intelligence report no. I-82 of July 28, 1945, a report of an interrogation of Lippisch: "He felt that at high velocities, solid fuels were more desirable than liquid fuels, the reason being that the solid fuel did not flow out into the velocity stream and, therefore, its burning took place at a predetermined place.

"For a solid fuel to be acceptable it must have good 'gas producing qualities', such

as has bituminous coal. The most intense heating among the solid fuels was provided by German normal pine wood 'cooked' in oil or paraffin in pieces 1 x 1 x 1cm."

Neither of Lippisch's 1976 books makes any mention of how the P 13 was to be used on active operations. When the British asked him whether the P 13a had been designed as a rammer, it was stated that: "The possibilities of using the P 13 as a ramming aircraft had been considered but Dr Lippisch did not think that athodyd propulsion was very suitable for this purpose owing to the risk of pieces of the rammed aircraft entering the intake. This would be avoided with a rocket-propelled rammer."

However, the LFW's undated P 13 Baubeschreibung or construction description of 1944, probably produced in October or early November, states: "The aircraft presented here is a jet with the task of fighter. The propulsion is by a Lorin engine, not using liquid fuel (gasoline, gas oil, J2 etc.) but with solid fuels (coal). Studies have been carried out on two forms – bulky pieces in a real grate or secondly with pressed coal in plates and hollow cylindrical shapes. Either can be used.

"The engine used allows, for the time being, no self-launch. The launch itself must be carried out with (powder) rockets,

a Madelung catapult or similar. Due to tactical considerations, among other things, the speed difference of fighters and bombers, preferably when attacking from behind, though thought was given to the installation of brakes (brake parachute, retractable screens similar to dive brakes etc.), and although ample room for weaponry is present, the task of ram fighter has been taken into account – so that the ramming attack will not lead to the loss of the aircraft, thanks to its shape and static structure."

The small rammer aircraft would be easily transported: "When the outer wings are folded, transport of the entire aircraft on a small open car is possible on the Deutsche Reichsbahn."

The fuselage section of the description gives the length of the fuselage as 6m, saying: "The wing attachment fittings (outer wing to wing centre section) are formed so that the outer wings can be folded upwards. This is necessary for two reasons. The 'up' position allows access to the engine through the wing centre section, and secondly for loading and offloading onto vehicles during transport." ▶

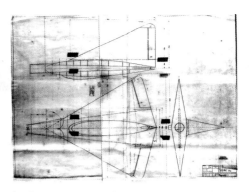
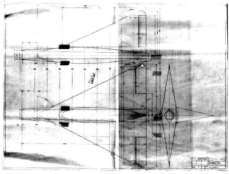

ABOVE: Drawings of diamond and simple delta planform P 13 models dated October 12 and October 25, 1944, respectively.

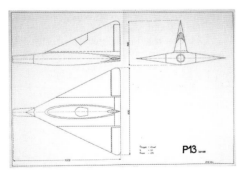
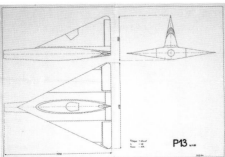

ABOVE: Two drawings of the P 13 simple delta, dated October 27 and October 30, 1944, showing minor detail refinements to trailing edge flaps and combustion chamber. Iowa State University Library Special Collections and University Archive

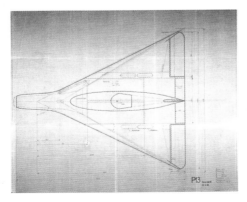

ABOVE: Plan view of the P 13 with wheeled undercarriage and straight trailing edge, dated October 4, 1944. The main wheels fit into the spaces between the main body section and the outer wings. Iowa State University Library Special Collections and University Archive

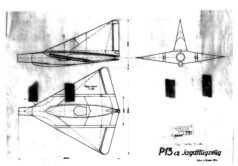

ABOVE: Lippisch seems to have worked on both simple delta and diamond wing configurations, and wheeled and landing skid arrangements, for the P 13 simultaneously.

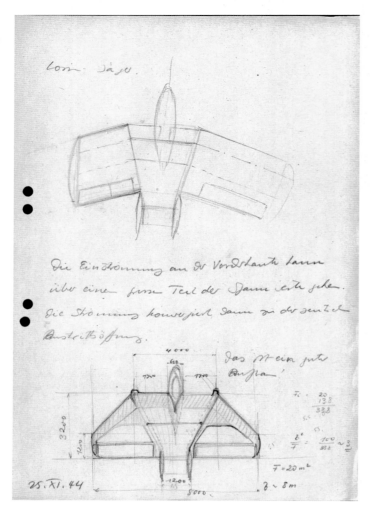
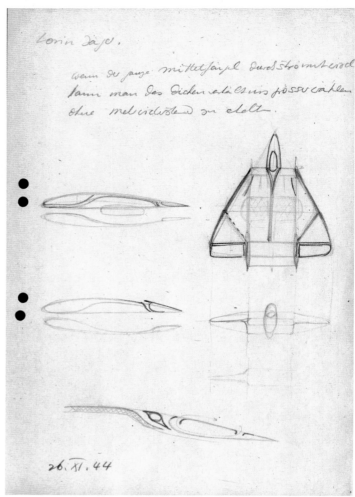

ABOVE: Lippisch's initial sketches for what would become the P 13b, dated November 25-26, 1944. Iowa State University Library Special Collections and University Archive

But how would the P 13a cut through Allied aircraft? "The edge cap is constructed as a deflector to avoid rudder damage if possible during ramming. The entire wing leading edge is reinforced with a knife (similar to the Kutonase)."

The Kutonase was originally developed to cut the steel cables anchoring barrage balloons. It was a hard steel blade that was fitted right the way along the leading edge of an aircraft's wing beneath an aerodynamic fairing of thin flexible metal. This concealed the Kutonase and made the wing fitted with it appear normal.

The fin was "designed just like the wing and built along similar lines" – presumably meaning that it too housed an aircraft-slicing Kutonase along its length. It was 2.28m high, with this being determined by the need to provide the pilot with good visibility, and was attached to the wing by four fittings, two of them on rockers to allow for expansion of the wing's surface due to intense heating by the ramjet.

The point of connection between the centre section of the aircraft and the outer wings served "as a cooling passage" and when the inner side changed in length due to heating, this was offset by a rocker.

The cockpit itself was "equipped with front and rear walls and is planned to be extremely spacious" and the glazing was designed to be simple to manufacture and distortion-free. The seat and joystick were to be "mounted on the detachable cabin floor" for "production reasons" and the portion of

the fin to the front of the cabin was designed to be easily removable for ease of access to the equipment housed beneath it.

Landing the P 13a would have been tricky given the nose-up attitude required. To this end, "a design was chosen where a blade flips open that is rotatable around its front end". This blade-skid with multiple torsion springs was only attached to the fuselage at one end, the other was intended to contact the ground and allow the aircraft to settle using the springs to cushion the impact.

Equipment fitted was to be "in accordance with its task" – horizon, artificial horizon, trip and altimeter, variometer and AFN2, compass, clock, FuG 16 ZY and FuG 25a. There was also an oxygen system installed but no pressure cabin.

Under the heading 'research aircraft' the minutes of the EHK's meeting on November 21-22, 1944, state: "Emphasis was placed on the athodyd propulsion system of the Lippisch P 13" and Lippisch says in Ein Dreieck Fliegt that "for a short time, series production of this type was planned".

Technical Intelligence report no. I-82 shows the Americans' surprise that the P 13a had been considered for construction: "It appears that Dr Lippisch's work was rather rushed, and that using simplified mathematical relations, he went directly into free flight tests made with scale models. His P 13 design incorporated design features, data on which were obtained from Dr Lippisch's model tests. It would therefore appear that some part of the German development

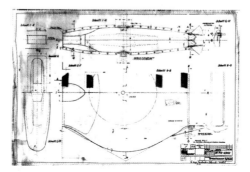
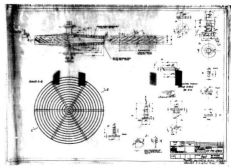

ABOVE: Drawings showing a model designed to demonstrate the workings of the P 13b's rotating coal grate and of the coal grate itself.

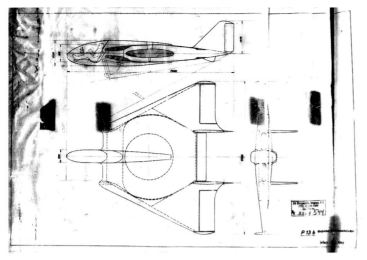 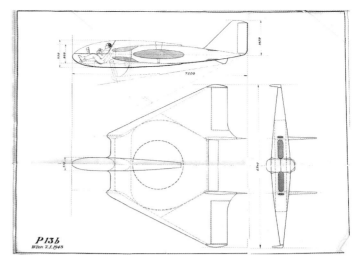

ABOVE: Two different versions of the P 13b three-view drawing, both dated January 7, 1945. The latter, from Lippisch's personal papers, appears to show a younger version of Lippisch himself at the controls! Iowa State University Library Special Collections and University Archive

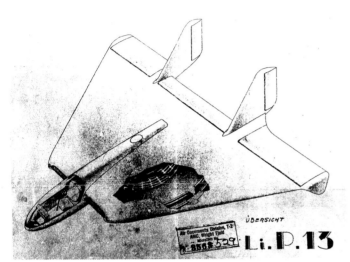

ABOVE: Contemporary artwork showing how the P 13b was intended to look, with cutaway showing its ramjet's combustion chamber.

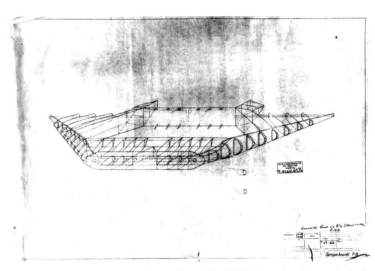

ABOVE: The proposed internal structure of the P 13b, showing the vents that would allow fast-flowing air to reach its ramjet's rotating circular coal grate.

work was actually going ahead on a high-performance fighter based on what appears to be elementary athodyd design information."

The British assessment of the P 12 and P 13a in German Aircraft: New and Projected Types revealed odd details about both types not mentioned elsewhere. The P 12 is described as "an unusual flying-wing design with built-in athodyd using liquid fuel. There is a large intake in the projecting nose and the pilot is seated above the combustion chamber, the cockpit canopy blending with the high single fin.

"The undercarriage comprises a single central wheel with a skid projecting downwards from each wing tip. The wing area is approximately 130sq ft and the aspect ratio 1.33."

The P 13 "was originally designed as a two-seater but it later assumed the form shown in the general-arrangement drawing (P 13a)". Sweep-back has been increased until the included angle of the leading-edges is only 60 degrees. The span is 19ft 8in the wing area 215sq ft and the aspect ratio 1.8. A very large fin accommodates the pilot."

In terms of performance: "It is estimated that 1760lb of coal will give an endurance of about 45 minutes. The all-up weight of the P 13 is 5060lb. Initial acceleration to the speed at which the athodyd will function effectively is provided by auxiliary rocket propulsion."

The report also mentions a 'Lippisch supersonic flying wing': "Another Lippisch project intended for supersonic speeds is an athodyd-propelled flying wing bearing a general resemblance to the P 13 but without the large vertical fin. Instead there is a small fin at the trailing edge and the cockpit canopy projects slightly from the wing surface. Sweep-back is even more pronounced than on the P 13."

Given the similarity between this design and the P.12/13, and since they were also intended to be supersonic, and had interchangeable cockpit/fin arrangements similar to this, it seems reasonable to assume that this design belongs to the same overall project.

LIPPISCH P 13B

Further experimentation with the P 13's coal grate arrangement seems to have resulted in the original P 13, the P 13a, being dropped and replaced by a new design which combined the latest coal grate design with an airframe derived from that of the P 11/Delta VI. German Aircraft: New and Projected Types' P 13 entry continues: "It was originally proposed that the solid fuel in the form of small pieces of brown coal should be carried in a wire mesh container set in the duct at a small angle to the air stream.

"The free flow of air through the lower portion of the duct was thus obstructed and it was hoped to obtain a progressive reaction with the oxygen passing through the fuel burning to CO which in turn would combine with oxygen in the air passing through the upper, unobstructed, portion of the duct to form CO_2. This arrangement proved inefficient and was abandoned.

"A later design called for a circular basket of oval axial section supported within the duct and positively rotated about its vertical axis at some 60rpm. Combustion is initiated by a gas flame and liquid fuel may be employed to facilitate starting up. Alternatively a more easily combustible material in the form of granules made from coal dust and an oxygen carrier may be distributed around the outside of the charge.

This was the P 13b. The first sketches for this seem to have been made on November 25-26, 1944. Although these show the form of the fighter emerging their do not show a circular basket for the ramjet's fuel. This does not appear, even in outline, until January 7, 1945. Then the fine detail of the basket and its construction is shown in drawings dating from early February.

No more work on the P 13b is evident after February 1945. But this was not quite the end of the story as the previously mentioned DM-1 at Prien-am-Chiemsee airfield was still under construction. ●

Tailless versus tailed: one last chance

Jäger mit Lorinantrieb

The RLM placed orders with both Skoda and Heinkel for ramjet-powered single-seat fighter designs just as the war was drawing to a close. While Skoda chose a relatively conventional layout, Heinkel opted for a tailless design one last time.

Austrian rocket scientist Eugen Sänger began work on ramjet or 'Lorin' powerplants at the DFS during 1942. After much experimentation with early ramjet designs, including carrying out practical tests of working ramjets fixed to the backs of lorries and later to the back of Dornier Do 17Z and Do 217E-2 aircraft, in 1943 he produced DFS report no. 3509 entitled Über einen Lorinantrieb für Strahljäger or 'On a Lorin Engine for Fighters'.

This proposed the creation of a flying "special structure" for the testing of ramjets which could be towed to an appropriate altitude before the engine was ignited and the "structure" put into a dive so that it could build up sufficient speed for the ramjet to produce maximum thrust. The report noted that work on this project was "under way".

Elsewhere in the report, he discusses the potential uses of a ramjet-powered fighter or fighter-bomber particularly for low-level operations – the ramjet would burn too much fuel if it was required to climb steeply for any length of time and would be increasingly ineffective running on thin high-altitude air.

The long tube of the ramjet itself is suggested as forming the fuselage of the fighter, with cockpit, fuel tank and tail all attached to the top of it. Landing gear would be attached to the lower surface of the tube and the wings could be either low or mid-set.

He wrote that "the whole aeroplane has no moving parts, but represents a pure shell design, when discounting the few auxiliaries for landing gear operation, cabin air system, fuel injection, nozzle and flap setting and so forth".

Take-off would be made with the help of two conventional rockets and once airborne the ramjet fighter would have a range of more than 100km at speeds ranging between 110km/h and 720km/h carrying 1000kg of bombs or other weaponry.

It had been thought that this report then formed the basis of an arrangement between Sänger and Otto Kauba or Skoda-Kauba. In 1942, Kauba convinced Hermann Göring to fund the development of a highly novel flying bomb – the stubby SK V-1 in Prague – and to require industrial giant Avia, a Skoda-owned company, to build it.

This project had resulted in a handful of prototypes and other work which had been largely unsuccessful but it had enabled Kauba to hire a workforce of 80 Czech and 40 German designers, engineers and craftsmen.

However, new evidence suggests that Sänger's report was actually left on the shelf for nearly two years until, in January 1945, the RLM commissioned both Skoda-Kauba and Heinkel to each design a new fighter based on Sänger's design. And while the former stuck reasonably closely to the original fighter envisioned in 1943, Heinkel had different ideas entirely.

CIOS Evaluation Report 118 of June 21, 1945, on the DFS at Ainring, says: "Dr Sänger, not listed in prior assessment report, was head of Triebwerkes Abteilung T-2, and was directly responsible to Professor Georgii. Triebwerkes Abteilung T-2 was concerned with development of athodyd propulsion units known in Germany as the Lorin Triebwerk. His department consisted of a total of 20 scientists, technicians and mechanics."

Evaluation Report 118 outlines the type and size of ramjets Sänger and his team were working on then states: "At the direction of RLM, Dr Sänger's group was in the process

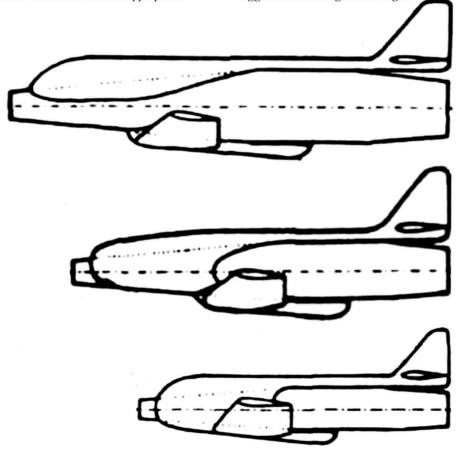

ABOVE: Three differently sized ramjet fighters were outlined by Sänger: the uppermost one was to be 15.59m long (by way of comparison, a Messerschmitt Bf 109 G-6 was 8.95m long), the one in the middle was 13.27m long and the one at the bottom was 10.95m long.

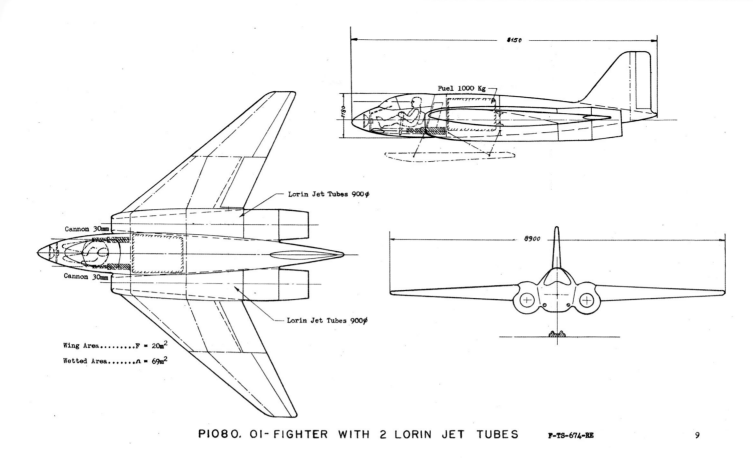

Lorin Jet Tubes 900∅

Cannon 30mm

Cannon 30mm

Lorin Jet Tubes 900∅

Wing Area........F = 20m²

Wetted Area.......Ω = 69m²

Fuel 1000 Kg

8150

8900

PIO8O. OI- FIGHTER WITH 2 LORIN JET TUBES   F-TS-674-RE   9

ABOVE: Heinkel's final project of the war – the tailless P 1080. It was a compact design based on two small ramjets rather than one large one.

of designing a new large athodyd, previously referred to, to be utilised in conjunction with a high performance fighter aircraft.

"The performance requirements demanded the transporting of 1000kg of armaments equipment from sea level to 12,000m in two minutes. It was further desired that the level flight endurance at altitude be of appreciable duration.

"Based on Dr Sänger's calculations, two airplanes were laid out, both of 5000 to 6000kg gross weight, carrying the aforementioned armament loads plus 2400kg of fuel. Of this fuel weight 600kg was required for climb to 12,000m and the balance would give the airplane one hour endurance at 12,000m when flying at a Mach no. between 0.7 and 0.8. Of the two airplanes laid out, the one airplane was designed by Skoda in Prague, and the other by the Heinkel organisation.

"The Skoda design was in a more advanced stage than Heinkel, although both designs were originated in 1945 and could hardly have progressed beyond the preliminary design stage. Discussions on the Heinkel airplane took place in Jenbach, Tyrol works with Dr Günter, but no evidence has been found to indicate that the actual design work was under way there."

Sänger evidently told his interrogators that both aircraft would have to overcome some problems specific to ramjet-powered aircraft: "For starting and take-off of the airplane, the use of solid fuel-assisted take-off rockets of conventional design was projected. An interesting point brought out by Dr Sänger was that an athodyd is no longer capable of providing sufficient

thrust to accelerate or maintain constant forward velocity of the airplane at low forward speeds, as for example 170km/h on the proposed aircraft under design.

"The designed landing speed for these aircraft was 120km/h. The landing characteristics of the airplane would accordingly have been very poor. The institute was ordered to develop a coal-burning version of the athodyd, and the Skoda airplane was being designed on this premise.

"While work was going ahead on this basis, Dr Sänger's group considered the arrangement very inferior to liquid fuel, and such developments in this direction as were carried on were apparently quite half-hearted in nature."

It is believed that most of Skoda-Kauba's paperwork concerning its ramjet design, the Skoda P 14, was destroyed shortly before the end of the war but enough seems to have survived to allow its inclusion in the German Aircraft: New and Projected Types report, which states: "This fighter, in which the pilot lies prone in the nose, is characterised by a very large fuselage in relation to the wing size. This is necessitated by the dimensions of the Sänger athodyd which has an overall length of no less than 31ft 2in and a maximum diameter, fairly far back, of 4ft 11in. The intake is carried forward slightly beyond the nose and there is a long, gradually tapering diffuser portion leading to the parallel combustion chamber.

"This wing is not swept back and there is a conventional fin and tailplane. A three-wheel bogie is used for take-off and there is a retractable skid for landing. The armament comprises a single MK 103 mounted above

the pilot and in the upper portion of the fuselage behind the cockpit there is a single large fuel tank containing 297 gal."

Exactly how far Heinkel got with its ramjet fighter design, designated P 1080, before the war ended is uncertain. What is known about it comes from a report written in German by Siegfried Günter then translated by American Technical Intelligence (T-2) and issued on July 15, 1946, as F-TS-674-RE.

According to the report: "Shortly before the end of the war the project design office of the Heinkel firm received data concerning the Lorin jet developed by Dr Sänger from the RLM. The RLM ordered the design of a single-seat fighter with this powerplant."

He then outlines the same take-off and landing problems mentioned by Sänger during his interrogation, stating that the P 1080 would use four 500kg solid fuel rockets providing 1000kg thrust each for 12 seconds attached to a take-off trolley to get airborne, then the same number of rockets attached to the aircraft itself would enable it to climb up to the ramjet's operating altitude and speed.

The next section of the report is headed 'comparison of Lorin-jet with turbojet' and begins: "In order to obtain a judgement of the possibilities of the new propulsion power plant, a comparison with the turbojet engine is computed. Basis for the computation: as an example for a turbojet airplane the tailless P 1079 B [although this appears to be an error – the aircraft referred to throughout is in fact the P 1078 B] with HeS 011 (static thrust = 1300kg) is used. The weight of structure, military load, mean flight weight, wing area and drags were ▶

likewise taken from the tailless airplane P 1078 B. The computation was accomplished for several very different modifications of the Lorin and the turbojet power plants.

"As a base for these power plants, the Lorin tube suggested by Dr Sänger and the HeS 011 were chosen. The weight per thrust unit of these power plants was retained for the modifications with changed thrust. By these reasons the different thrusts of power plants result in different fuel weights."

A full comparison of performance is then made between the tailless P 1078 B and the tailless P 1080 – presumably to eliminate any question of performance being affected by the type's layout and avoiding any discussion concerning the merits of a tailless design.

He concludes: "The airplanes with turbojet engines attain essentially smaller climb performances. By enlarging the turbojet engine, the climb performances are only a little improved while endurance is considerably decreased.

"By reducing the turbojet engine there is a great gain of endurance with a great decrease of speed. The latter airplane also needs rockets for take-off, but essentially smaller ones. The loss of endurance because of the fuel consumed for take-off is unimportant for turbojet airplanes.

"The comparison shows that airplanes with Lorin-jet propulsion are eminently suited for flying in the stratosphere. However, it must be kept in mind that the data of the Lorin-jet are not yet sufficiently tested."

In the following section, headed 'remarks regarding the design', he says: "There are two important advantages of the design fitted with two Lorin-tubes as compared to the design with one tube. First, the favourable installation of the cockpit and the better vision. Secondly, two small tubes result in smaller unstable moments about the normal axis.

"The tubes are placed at the most aft possible position in order to keep the hot part of the tube free of structure details and cowling, and to get effective cooling. A Lorin-jet powered aeroplane is not able to accelerate again in the case that the landing cannot be completed (because of landing errors or emergency). Thus, decreased landing speed is urgently necessary.

"Power required for pumps, compressor, armament and radio is furnished by two generators installed inside the Lorin-tubes. The considerable decrease of air speed in the diffuser of the Lorin-jet improves the efficiency of this device.

"When starting, the skid is retracted. The springs of the retracted skid legs are compressed. It is then possible to extend the skid without additional power."

This is where the very brief text of the report ends. No mention is made of armament, but the drawings provided show the P 1080 fitted with a pair of 30mm cannon.

For the Skoda-Kauba single ramjet design, wingspan was given as 25.9ft (7.9m), no value is given for length but based on the drawing it appears to have been 9.85m, wing area is given as 134sq ft (12.45sq m), aspect ratio 5, fuel 297 gallons or 154 gallons "plus 1870lb of coal". All-up weight was 6270-6820lb. Maximum speed was, at sea level, 620mph or 545mph at 33,000ft and 535mph at 49,000ft with a ceiling

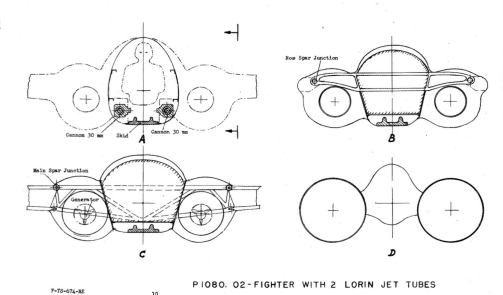

P 1080. 02 - FIGHTER WITH 2 LORIN JET TUBES

F-TS-674-RE   10

ABOVE: The diminutive size of the P 1080 is illustrated by this sectional view – showing the pilot, cannon and ramjets all positioned within a short distance of one another.

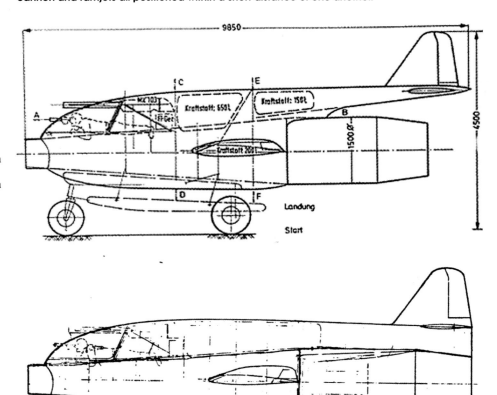

ABOVE: Two slightly different versions of the Skoda-Kauba ramjet fighter of early 1945. While their dimensions are broadly similar, their undercarriage arrangements and tails are slightly different.

of 60,000ft. Climb to 20,000ft would take 1.7 minutes. Its ramjet was 150cm in diameter.

For the Heinkel twin ramjet design, wingspan is shown as 8.9m, length is 8.15m and wing area is 20sq m. Its ramjets were each 90cm in diameter.

It is tempting to suggest that the Heinkel design was superior to that of Skoda if only due to the deceptive simplicity of its tailless layout – particularly the clever way

in which it enables the inclusion of a seated rather than prone cockpit by using two smaller ramjets rather than one large one.

It was also capable of carrying heavier armament while remaining relatively compact in size thanks to its departure from the strictures of Sänger's 1943 design. But in the end, neither design got anywhere due to Germany's final defeat and the end of the war in Europe on May 8, 1945. ●

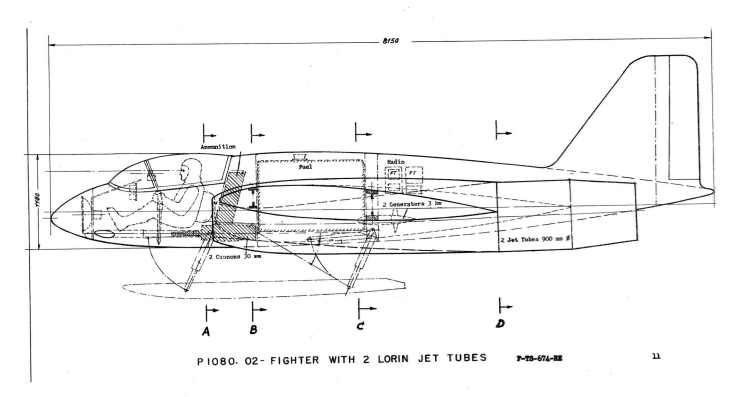

P 1080. 02 - FIGHTER WITH 2 LORIN JET TUBES   F-TS-674-RE   11

ABOVE: The P 1080 would have been a relatively simple aircraft, utilising what appears to be a He 162 canopy and cockpit but with a different nose.

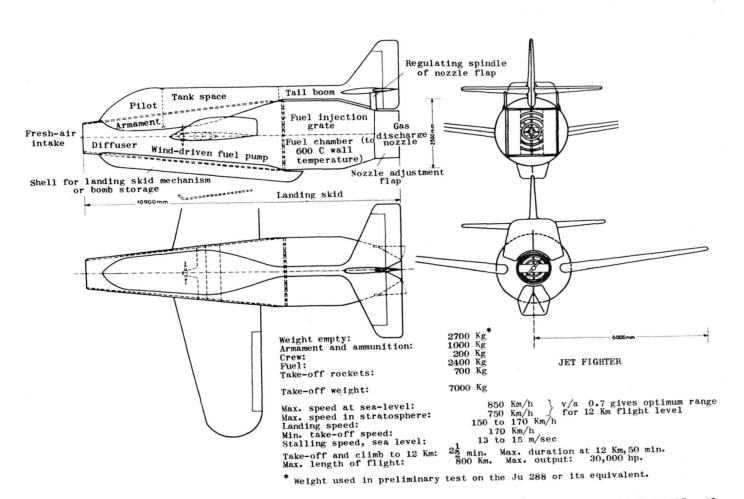

Weight empty:	2700 Kg *
Armament and ammunition:	1000 Kg
Crew:	200 Kg
Fuel:	2400 Kg
Take-off rockets:	700 Kg
Take-off weight:	7000 Kg

JET FIGHTER

Max. speed at sea-level:	850 Km/h } v/a 0.7 gives optimum range
Max. speed in stratosphere:	750 Km/h } for 12 Km flight level
Landing speed:	150 to 170 Km/h
Min. take-off speed:	170 Km/h
Stalling speed, sea level:	13 to 15 m/sec
Take-off and climb to 12 Km:	2½ min. Max. duration at 12 Km, 50 min.
Max. length of flight:	800 Km. Max. output: 30,000 hp.

* Weight used in preliminary test on the Ju 288 or its equivalent.

ABOVE: Eugen Sänger's ramjet-powered fighter design from an Allied translation of his 1943 DFS report Über einen Lorinantrieb für Strahljäger 'On a Lorin Engine for Fighters'. Work on designing it in more detail would not take place until around two years after its publication.

The Hortens and the Chimney Sweep

Stealth during WW2

Reimar Horten claimed in 1983 that he had planned to make the H IX invisible to radar by putting sawdust and charcoal into the glue used to make it. But was this a wartime plan or did he only think of it later?

Writing about the outer shell of the H IX in his book Nurflügel, Reimar claimed that it had been his intention to sandwich a 12mm thick layer of sawdust, charcoal and glue mix between two 1.5mm thick outer plywood layers. As a result, he wrote: "The entire aircraft would have been protected against detection by radar devices, since the charcoal should absorb the electrical waves. Under this protective shield the steel tube framework and the engines were 'invisible'."

This innovative sawdust, charcoal and glue layer had not been used on the V1, however, because the engineer who pressed the wing shells at a Silesian workshop, Oberingenieur Hans Herrmann, was unequipped to make them like this, the shells were made out of 10 layers of 1.5mm plywood instead.

The English translation of Nurflügel states that the radar-absorbing sandwich shell was only intended for the production version of the H IX, which in 2014 resulted in the Americans, who currently hold the captured remains of the H IX V3,

assessing its structure to see if it had the 'stealth' sandwich shell – which it apparently did not. But then Reimar never claimed that the V3 was built that way.

Interviewed by David Myhra several years after Nurflügel was published, Reimar said: "We wished to have the plane which would not reflect the beams from radar. I had heard in 1933 that the length of the radar wave had been 9cm, therefore I looked for all the boards and things and on the outside of the plywood had been a minimum dimension of 8cm.

"Therefore, in order to build the all-wing so that it would not give results to radar we had to construct this way. If we would have used metal we would not have had these problems. These were problems which come in designing with wood."

Myhra asked: "What, did you not use metal?" Reimar said: "We had the idea that the wood we needed we would first glue. For the glue when used makes the wing like a tank for fuel. Second, metal must be covered with wood to make it unresponsive to radar waves. Wood does not reflect the wave of radar.

"We wanted to make sure that the aircraft would not be seen by the radar. That was the idea. Therefore, the centre section which was made of steel tubes, had to be covered also with wood. This wood had glue with coal to absorb the radar waves. All this was for the H IX."

The idea that a wooden aircraft would be 'invisible' appears to disregard the fact that largely wooden aircraft such as the De Havilland Mosquito were certainly visible to German radar during the war. Myhra asks: "Could you have built the wings out of aluminum if you wanted to?"

"Yes, in fact it would have been very much more easier."

"Why not build it out of metal then?"

"If we would have built it out of metal then it would not have been undetectable by radar. In addition, our workmen did not have the skills needed in metalwork. Metalwork requires a great deal more time and skill manpower to achieve.

"Also, we could not use the aluminium as fuel tanks. We would then have to use tanks and they would have about half the volume of sealed wing tanks."

Later, talking about the H XVIII bomber, Myhra asks: "Would the H XVIII have been built out of wood?"

Reimar: "Yes. The H XVIII was to have been built out of wood because I thought that the most important part of the H XVIII would be that it would not be observed by radar. Wood absorbs radar so the use of wood was another important reason for using it. I had been told by radio-radar specialists that radar was not able to pick up materials made out of carbon or coal.

"Therefore we began to mix our glue with carbon to have non-readable by radar. The same thinking applied to the H IX. All the plywood on the centre section and on the wings had been glued together with carbon-mixed glue."

While no contemporary document has ever been found which even mentions in passing the idea of making a German aircraft invisible or even simply less visible to radar – including the March 1 brochure on the H IX b personally signed by Reimar – the Germans did develop and actively use 'stealth' technology during the war.

It is worth looking at the radar-absorbing projects that were worked on, for which hard evidence exists, how they were deployed, and why, before assessing Reimar's 1983 claim.

During 1940, the British began fitting ASV (Airborne Surface Vehicle)

ABOVE: When the Americans took possession of Type XXI U-boat U-3008 at Wilhelmshaven following the surrender of Germany on May 8, 1945, they examined its Wesch absorber-covered schnorkel in detail.

ABOVE: The positioning of the U-3008's schnorkel relative to its periscopes.

ABOVE: A close-up view of the U-3008's schnorkel, showing its dense, rubbery, waffle-form Wesch mat covering. The absorber's use by the Kriegsmarine appears to have been the only example of 'stealth' technology in use during the Second World War.

radar sets to Coastal Command Hudson and Sunderland aircraft. This was initially unreliable but an improved version, the ASV Mk.II, was more successful. A Whitley Mk.VI was able to detect and attack a U-boat, U-71, using it on November 30, 1940.

By late 1942, the Germans had developed a radio receiver, Metox, that could detect the ASV Mk.II, enabling the U-boat to dive out of sight to avoid an attack before it happened.

However, in March 1943 Coastal Command began to use ASV Mk.III – a centimetric radar that was extremely effective at detecting U-boats. Most of the U-boats in the Bay of Biscay had been detected and attacked within two months, 56 being sunk, and Allied shipping losses fell from 400,000 tonnes a month to just 100,000.

So, according to CIOS Report XXVI-24 The Schornsteinfeger Project: "In June of 1943, a conference was apparently called in Berlin by the OKM (Ober Kommando der Marine) at the instigation of Admiral Dönitz for the purpose of presenting the problem of protecting U-boats against Allied radar. It was realised at this time that the U-boat war would be lost unless a successful countermeasure could be found.

"At this conference, which was attended by about 400 technical representatives from various organisations in Germany, the problem was discussed by Konter Admiral Stummel, who was designated as the senior naval officer for the project, which was named Schornsteinfeger (Chimney Sweep). It appears that the military requirements of the problem were not clearly defined at this time, particularly with respect to wave length coverage, allowed weight and thickness of the coating, durability standards etc.

"Plans for operational use of the schnorkel were not presented, as the discussion concerned the need for providing radar camouflage for the conning tower and possibly for part of the hull. Top priority was assigned, and

the representatives were asked to submit proposals immediately, with the aim of solving the problem within three months!"

Research efforts slackened off during early 1944 when it was decided that the schnorkel should be fitted to U-boats. This device, originally invented by the Dutch and found on captured Dutch submarines, allowed U-boats to remain submerged for much longer by enabling them to drawn down fresh air.

However, in the autumn of 1944 it was decided that the schnorkels themselves needed to be shielded from radar. According to the report: "Plans were made and put into effect at this time to provide microwave protection for all U-boats."

From the large number of radar-absorbing proposals put forward, four were chosen for further development – the Netzhemd or 'mesh hat', the Becker-Hellwege absorber, the Jaumann absorber and the Wesch absorber.

The first two were abandoned as failures but the latter two worked. The Jaumann absorber, invented by Professor Johannes Jaumann of Brünn, was produced by IG Farben. It consisted of a hollow cylinder around 76mm thick, which could be fitted over the schnorkel. The cylinder was made up of seven layers of thin, semi-conducting paper separated by layers of PVC 9mm thick.

The CIOS team could find no documentary evidence of effectiveness tests but "according to verbal reports the range of detection was reduced to 15% of uncoated schnorkel range against airborne Rotterdam radar on 9.3cm, under calm sea conditions". Due to the difficulty of bending the PVC to fit different shapes, the Jaumann absorber was only really suitable for covering certain types of schnorkel, rather than conning towers or hulls.

The Wesch absorber or 'Wesch mat' was developed by Professor Ludwig Wesch of the Institut für Weltpost in

Heidelberg. Wesch, whose research on radar camouflage coatings was apparently underwritten by Austrian company Deutsche Magnesit AG, carried out tests at IG Farben's Oppau facilities between November 1943 and January 1944 and after many failed experiments by September 1944 he had come up with something that worked.

The Wesch absorber went into production in December 1944. It was effectively a waffle-form rubber-like mat 4mm thick with the 'waffle' ridges standing about 4mm up from the surface. It contained a high percentage of iron powder and was made in flexible pieces measuring about 50sq cm. In operational use, these were glued to sheets of rubber about 1mm thick before being glued directly onto the metal surface of the submarine.

About 100 U-boats were fitted with either Wesch mats or Jaumann absorbers or a combination of both between January and March 1945.

It took Jaumann and Wesch, both professors with a solid understanding of chemistry and physics, not to mention radar, months of theoretical work followed by months of practical chemistry in Germany's best-equipped laboratories with full teams of chemists working for them to develop bulky, heavy, rather inflexible hard coverings for submarines – for which weight was not much of an issue.

It is possible that the Hortens, with their uncanny ability to catch wind of the latest scientific developments in aviation, might somehow have heard about naval radar camouflage materials. However, it is highly doubtful that they would have been able to produce an effective lightweight stealth coating for aircraft without everything mentioned above.

The documents they produced at the time attempt to make strong arguments for the full-scale production and introduction into service of their aircraft – particularly the H IX. They are trying to persuade the sceptics that their designs possess qualities superior to those of their rivals.

This being the case, why not mention the incredible opportunities apparently represented by the radar-absorbing properties of wood and carbon-infused glue? An aircraft that was provably 'invisible' to radar would surely attract a production contract immediately. None of the other aircraft companies seem to mention radar camouflage in any of their reports, and neither do any of the experimental institutions.

Similarly, Reimar makes no mention of the idea that the very shape of the H IX might make it less visible to radar – only that its wooden construction would help it.

The only possible conclusion must be that if Reimar Horten did have plans to make the H IX a 'stealth fighter', and the know how to do it successfully, he strangely kept it all to himself at a time when such an innovation could have brought him boundless praise and might have given his flagging country a genuine wartime advantage. ●

Working for the British

Horten VIII revived

Both Horten brothers were captured by the Allies on or around April 7, 1945, and within a few months they were given an opportunity to revisit a project of which the partially completed remains were found in a garage near Göttingen when the war ended – the H VIII.

The Horten brothers were caught not far from one another and were sent together as POWs to Brunswick in northern central Germany on April 11, 1945. From here, they were transferred to Wiebaden. By mid-May they had been transferred to London and they were interrogated from May 19-21.

In the meantime, Allied intelligence officers had discovered evidence of their work at several locations across Germany.

A fragmentary USAAF memo kept at the National Archives in London, headed "interview with Horten bros May 21, 1945", states: "The steel framework in the garage

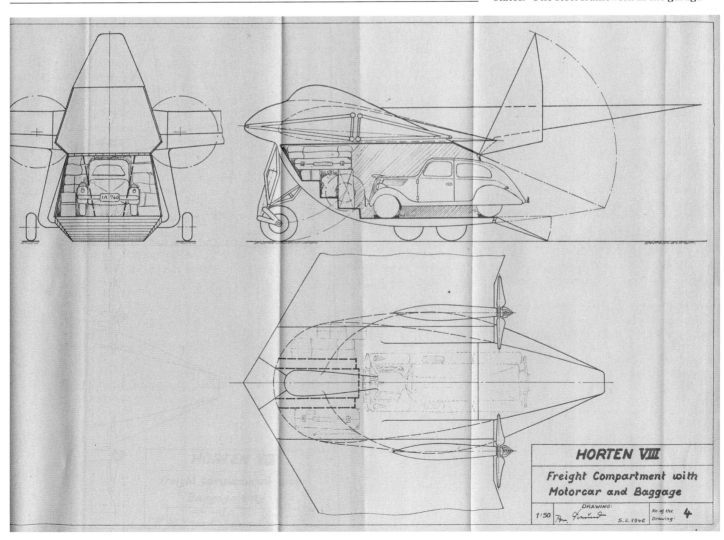

ABOVE: The Horten VIII was capacious enough to swallow a car with room to spare.

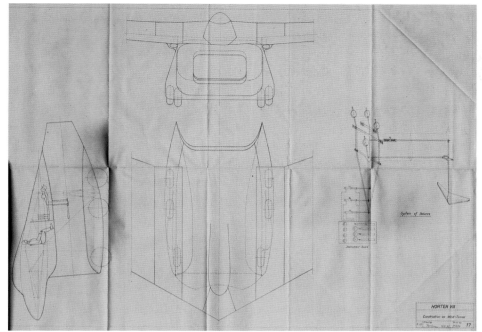

ABOVE: The Horten brothers regarded the H VIII primarily as a research aircraft with which to gather data for larger flying wings. To this end, they hoped to build a number of H VIIIs as flying wind tunnels.

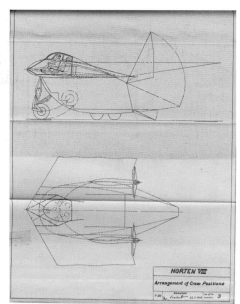

ABOVE: The cockpit of the H VIII would have been relatively cramped for the three crewmen – though communication between them would have been easy.

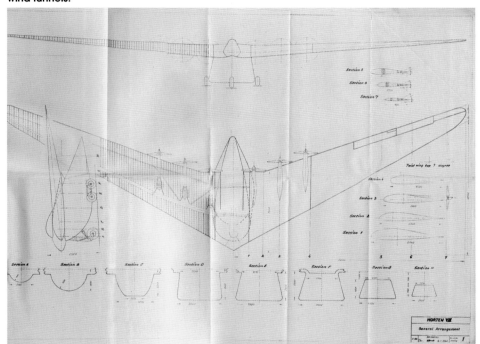

ABOVE: General arrangement of the H VIII design prepared for the British.

was extremely interesting. The Horten brothers finally received support from the Air Ministry in February 1945. The time estimate for the construction of a metal wind-tunnel model of the high-speed twin turbo-jet design which would be satisfactory for the tests was so great that the Horten brothers conceived a new method of experiment.

"They proposed to build a flying wind tunnel. The carrier was a six-motored tailless airplane with conventional motors and the comparatively slow speed of 350kph. Within the large central fuselage, they proposed to build a wind tunnel, i.e. entrance cone, working section and diffuser. A speed of 500-550kph was expected in the working section.

"This wind tunnel would be turbulence-free. Hence it would be suitable for tests of laminar flow airfoils and other high-speed tests. This project was kept quite secret and was not discussed with the professors at LFA or AVA. They thought this proposal would be a surprise to German aeronautical scientists. The welded steel frame in the garage outside Göttingen was the fuselage section of this flying laboratory."

Further on, the memo states: "A 6-engine prototype (the Ho VIII) was undergoing

ABOVE: Horten H VIII. Art by Daniel Uhr

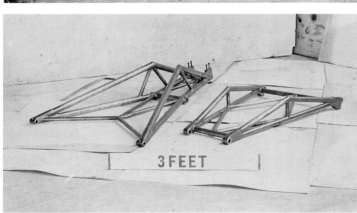

FACING PAGE & ABOVE: Manufactured components of the prototype Horten H VIII photographed by the British in 1945.

flight trials for larger projects. It was planned to make a 40-ton flying wing with 4 x 011 units and a 100-ton flying wing with eight 011 units. The prototype had 6 x As 10 reciprocating engines and was also to be used as a flying wind tunnel for research on Reynolds and Mach numbers.

"It was found by this method that wooden models could be used, although the speed of air-flow inside a tunnel approached 900kph because the air was free from dust and consequently there was no pitting of the aerofoils."

Evidently the six-engined H VIII had piqued the interrogators' interest. The H VIII, although it had originally been conceived before the war in 1939 as an up-scaled H III, had lain dormant for more than five years. Reimar told David Myhra: "At the end of 1944, when the H IX V2 was in Oranienburg ready to fly, we worked on a little plane we called the H VIII."

He said he had thought it would not take much effort to build this six-engined aircraft, based on a design that was twice the span and twice the wing dimensions of the H III, "and we would have experience in great planes. This was in preparation along with the long-range H XVIII bomber with six turbines. They had the same shape of the wings only less high."

He said that work on the H VIII "had begun in Göttingen with about 100 men in March and April 1945. The English took many photographs of the work in progress when they overran our Göttingen facilities in April 1945. It had not been destroyed or so I

was told but most of our sailplanes had been once the army of occupation had moved in".

Following their interrogation in England, the brothers were moved back to Germany – specifically back to Göttingen where a selection of parts for the first H VIII had been found. They were then asked to complete new drawings for the project and also to design a gigantic 120-ton flying wing passenger aircraft for which it would serve as a half-scale prototype. Reimar said: "When I was working for the RAE in Göttingen designing an all-wing passenger aircraft with an airscrew for passenger transport, one of the RAE officials there said that the British air ministry was really interested in all-wing passenger transport planes. I thought that if I did a really good job for the RAE, they would want me to go to England and help them build the passenger transport I was then designing. This would not be.

"However, in designing the all-wing passenger transport, great concern was given that every passenger have a window for a view of the outside. Also, they wanted a design with a high wing so that the passengers could have an excellent view all around and not have anything hidden by the wing. I think that my plans called for about a 40-passenger aircraft. I think that the plans called for Rolls-Royce Merlin engines in this proposed all-wing passenger plane for production of these engines was being continued after the war."

The report on the H VIII, published in February 1946, was entitled simply "Aeroplane Type Horten VIII" with the authors' names

"W. & R. Horten" printed below.

The introduction began: "Description of the design of an all-wing-wind-tunnel-plane. The present design was projected in 1944, and the work in the shops was started in the beginning of the year 1945. Its purpose is to be on the one hand a first study of an all-wing-'giant' aeroplane of about 120 tons total weight for transcontinental transport; on the other hand it is to serve as an aeroplane carrying the funnel of a wind tunnel to give a possibility of measuring model-aerofoils with a span of more than 6ft 6in (2m).

"In the first application, the design corresponds to a 'model' of a scale of length of 1:2. By this special problem, the aspect ratio was first defined to be 1:10. The cargo space within the wing itself given by the volume scale of 1:2 cubed = 1:8 naturally is insufficient in the 'model' without fuselage-like additional structure. Therefore it is provided to employ the wind-tunnel funnel arranged under the centre portion of the wing also as freight compartment.

"Due to this it is possible to carry out all performance flights with this 'model-aeroplane'. These flights are made for determining the take-off lengths, performance of climb and velocity with different load conditions. Beside the variation of the total weight, that of the centre of gravity, too, is important. For these flight-performance investigations the effect of the fuselage must be subtracted in the performance calculation, as it is eliminated in the realisation in full scale.

"Apart from these investigations,

also problems of flight mechanics and construction must be solved. Some of them are enumerated here: investigations of flight characteristics and stability: determination of control areas for giant aeroplanes of this type: combination of high lift devices and control flaps, fitting of control devices, course instruments or automatic piloting apparatuses in the aileron and elevator systems which are combined in this aeroplane type; fitting of the power plants in the wing with pusher airscrews operated by remote driving shafts; fuel distributing systems for avoiding disadvantageous trims; power-controlled anti-oscillating hydraulic devices for the control flaps etc. These tasks alone justify the realisation of the project."

In short, the British H VIII design would serve not only as a scaled down prototype but also as a flying wind tunnel to test models of the new intercontinental giant flying wing in the appropriate flight conditions without substantial additional expense.

A trio of prototypes was initially projected, one without the wind tunnel and the next two with it installed. Fitting this ungainly structure would mean a revision to the undercarriage however: "It was provided to construct the first aeroplane with a fuselage and to fit the following two with the wind-tunnel. The retractability of the front wheel is renounced with the latter form, i.e. two front wheels are provided in front, one at the right and the other at

the left side of the wind-tunnel funnel.

"Owing to the six engines, embedded in soft rubber, which are arranged in the wings outside the centre portion, only slight oscillations are expected to occur, and the slipstream of the pusher airscrews are expected not to influence the conditions of measurement and flow in the funnel. Thus a wind tunnel will be formed which, according to the ratio of flight velocity to jet velocity in the working plane, will have a turbulence less considerable than that prevailing in the open atmosphere.

"We can expect that hereby boundary layer measurements will be rendered possible, which imitate the conditions of free flight in the best possible manner. An investigation will be made in order to state, how far laminar state of the boundary layer at suitable aerofoil sections can be maintained with certainty at high Mach numbers (in the working plane a maximum Mach number of 0.8 will be reached).

"Moreover the manner of the drag rise at the swept-back aerofoil is of interest in this range of the Mach number and higher ones, and so forth. These problems can influence the future production of aircraft considerably. They are likely to be solved satisfactorily by means of the 'flying wind-tunnel' by extending the tests at the same time to the flying object itself.

"Summarizing, we want to mention again that this aeroplane project does not represent an optimum solution of some problem, but, beside the employment as wind-tunnel carrier, is to furnish practical data, so that it may become possible to realise optimum designs in 'all-wing construction'."

The Horten VIII would have a wingspan of 131ft (40m) and a maximum total weight of 17 tons. The six engines would be De Havilland Gipsy Queen 51s, driving pusher propellers via long drive shafts. Unusually for a Horten design, it would also have a fuselage of sorts: "A spacious, fuselage-like thickening under the centre part of the aerofoil permits the accommodation of testing devices, cargo and persons for test or transport flights, beside a rigid main undercarriage arranged at the rear near the centre of gravity, it has a nose wheel retractable into the fuselage.

"If the aeroplane is employed as a 'wind-tunnel carrier', however, this nose wheel is substituted by two wheels arranged in the track of the main undercarriage. The main undercarriage will comprise four wheels, arranged in pairs according to the tandem-principle."

The aircraft would be built in five sections – the centre, two middle wing parts and two outer wing parts. The centre portion would be made of welded steel tubes covered with plywood and with side walls covered with fabric. The middle parts of the wings carrying the engines would be made from a mixture of wood and steel while the outer wings would be made entirely from wood.

As for the crew compartment: "The cockpit will contain three seats, for pilot, wireless operator (navigator), and air-mechanic; it is arranged in the foremost part of the wing. The pilot is seated in the centre with forward direction of view, whereas the two other members of the crew

HORTEN VIII
Freight Compartment with Baggage only

ABOVE: The H VIII was envisioned as a cargo aircraft in civil service.

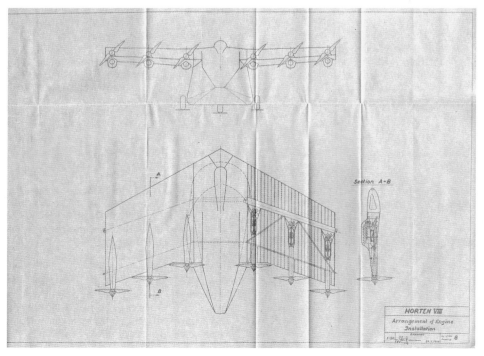

Section A-B

HORTEN VIII
Arrangement of Engine Installation

ABOVE: Arrangement of the H VIII's six De Havilland Gipsy Queen 51 engines.

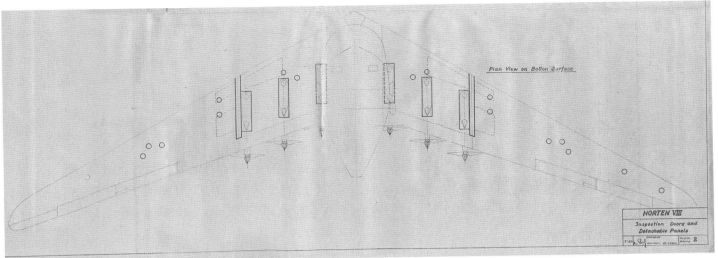

ABOVE: Positioning the engines within the wing meant they needed to be access from below. This view shows the locations of maintenance hatches on the H VIII's underside.

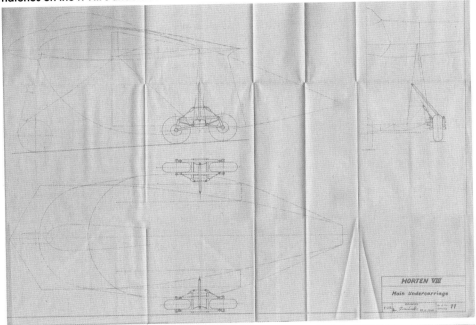

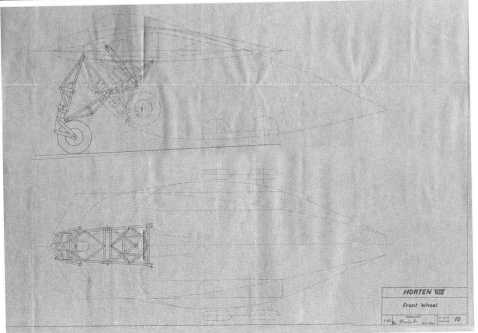

ABOVE: Main gear and nosewheel arrangement. The nosewheel structure is particularly large due to the high proportion of the aircraft's weight it would be expected to bear.

have their seats behind him at the right side and the left with directions of view deflected laterally forwards by 45 . Thus a convenient accommodation of the crew is secured, whereby a too wide ceiling of the cockpit is avoided. The sight conditions are very good, especially those for the pilot.

"The control system of the aeroplane is operated by a hand-control stick for elevator and lateral control; the rudders are moved by the foot pedals. The control flaps at the wing tips are employed in combination as elevator and lateral controls. The rudders ("resistance rudder") in form of a brake to be extended from each wing tip, produce the moments about the vertical axis with the semi-span as lever arm. Easy handling and good stiffness in the transmission of the whole control system has been paid special attention to. Ball bearings are employed for the bearings of all double-armed levers."

In an emergency, the Plexiglass cockpit canopy was detachable. There were no ejection seats though – the pilot was to have a seat-type parachute while the radio operator and mechanic each got a chest parachute. A further emergency escape feature was provision for jettisoning the propellers of the inner engines so that the crew would not risk hitting them on the way out. But "the normal way for getting in and out is through the fuselage".

Reimar told Myhra: "I had hoped that in 1946 the English would be interested in finishing the H VIII but they expressed no interest in it. We had produced all the drawings for the H VIII but even these they apparently were not interested in either.

"At this time they did not want any work performed in aerodynamics and I saw that the whole time we had spent with the English at Göttingen after the war making drawings of proposed projects was really just a make-work type of exercise. So I went along with this 'make work'."

The Hortens' brief association with the British failed to bear fruit, particularly when Reimar discovered that no British aircraft company was interested in employing him. He would eventually go on to work with former Focke-Wulf chief executive Kurt Tank and other former German aero engineers on projects in Argentina. ●

Science fiction

Leopold Harbich's Arctur

Almost a year after Germany's defeat a former associate of Lippisch's emerged from the rubble of Vienna to offer the Americans a tailless 'secret project' the like of which neither they nor anyone else had seen before.

Soviet forces rolled into Austria at the end of March 1945 and laid siege to the capital Vienna, in the east of the country, from April 2-13. Austria had technically ceased to exist in 1938, being annexed by Germany and absorbed into the Third Reich, but the Allies disregarded the annexation and had agreed in 1943 that it should be treated as a separate country again when the war ended.

In the days leading up to the arrival of the Red Army on Vienna's outskirts, chaos reigned in the numerous aviation industry offices and research bureaus which had relocated to Vienna during the war in an attempt, futile as it turned out, to escape bombing raids carried out by the British and Americans from bases in Britain. The Heinkel design office was in Vienna, Lippisch was based there at the LFW and Daimler-Benz had built its enormous Flugmotorenwerk Ostmark facility there. Many who were able fled the city in an attempt to go west towards the advancing Americans but many more were left to face the Russians.

Among those who remained behind were pre-war glider designer and engineer Leopold Harbich, who had worked for Lippisch, and his colleague Gustav Staatz. When the war finally ended, the Soviets controlled much of Austria

and all of Vienna but reluctantly agreed to abide by the 1943 agreement and the country was divided up into zones of occupation. Vienna, like Berlin, became a microcosm of the wider situation – it ended up deep within the Soviet zone but with its centre divided up into British, American, French and Soviet sectors.

The first Americans did not arrive in Vienna until the end of July 1945, by which time the Soviets had already found and taken away all equipment, machinery, documents and other materials of value that had remained in the city during the siege. Even so, it took until mid-September for the different sectors to be established.

Harbich and Staatz were fortunate to find themselves within the American zone when the dust began to settle. The pair had evidently worked together on a highly ambitious private project of their own devising during the war and now had the opportunity, having learned what had become of some of their fellow engineers, to present it to the Americans in the hope of winning employment, financial backing or both.

Precisely how much work was done on the tailless aircraft project Harbich dubbed 'Arctur' during the war remains to be seen, although his report mentions models tests

taking place – which are unlikely to have been carried out during the months of lockdown following the Soviet invasion and occupation without attracting unwanted and unwelcome attention. In addition, although Harbich told the Americans that he "was formerly employed by Dr Alexander Lippisch, a German scientist carrying on current research in the United States", the nature of his employment is unclear. There was a 'Harbich' on the list of Abteilung L workers redeployed at Messerschmitt following the department's dissolution but this may simply be a coincidence.

While Harbich was responsible for the design of the Arctur aircraft, with jet engines, Staatz had designed an alternative powerplant – an axial or 'barrel' engine where the cylinders are formed into a ring, resulting in a barrel-shaped powerplant. In operation, each cylinder would press down on a 'wobble plate' in turn, generating a rotary motion.

Harbich wrote an outline description of his ideas as Beschreibung des Projektes Arctur during the winter of 1945/46 and published it in February 1946. The Americans received their copy during April and it was translated as F-TS-789-RE, being eventually republished in English in February 1948.

The Arctur was to be a high-speed tailless touring jet for civilian passengers, although military applications were not ruled out.

Harbich wrote: "The creation of a high-speed touring plane, with as wide a cruising range as possible, of the tailless type and of narrow wing span, has been set up as the aim of the design. The practice of long-range flying reveals that the safety factor increases with speed. In terms of the weather, the smaller the time interval between the weather report of the pilot and the stop at the airfield of destination, the less trouble will be encountered.

"High-speed flying necessary for mail, express, and commercial airplanes offers an ideal field of activity for this aircraft. A military version, if desired, is always feasible with the aid of appropriate installations. This plane presents numerous novel ideas for the construction of tailless aircraft as well as for general aircraft construction. The innovations are described in the various structural groups.

"The mid-wing monoplane arrangement was chosen in order to fulfil the requirements of low air resistance and symmetrical drag in high-speed flight. Here, the thrust

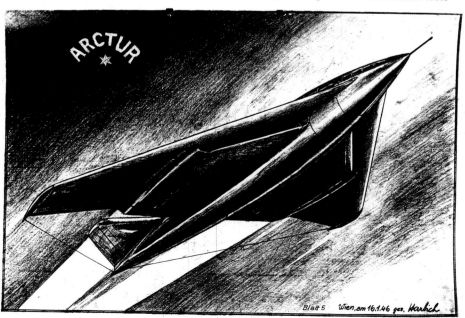

ABOVE: Artwork from the cover of Leopold Harbich's brochure for his jet-propelled flying wing – Arctur.

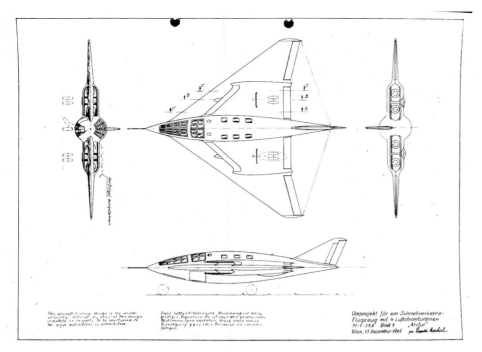

ABOVE: The four-jet Arctur flying wing. The diamond shape is created only by two cables running from the wingtips to the end of the fuselage.

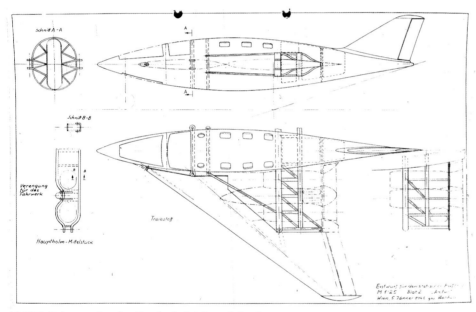

ABOVE: Cutaway showing the Arctur's internal structure.

of the power plant passes through the centre of gravity. The power plant, built completely within the wing and studied in the preliminary work, has very long air inlet ducts for the inner turbines, and the outer wing thickness becomes unnecessarily great.

"The installation of the power plant according to this design, brings about a decrease in the wetted area, in contrast with free suspension under the wing, as for instance in the Me 262 or the Gloster Comet. The wing arrangement was tested on a model in a free flight and showed good stability. In this case, the turbines were replaced by open air ducts. In collaboration with Gustav Staatz, his new type engines 'TM 32' were provided for installation in this project. The low fuel consumption and small size of the engine make it especially suitable for high-speed aircraft."

Harbich then gave a detailed breakdown of Arctur's features. It was to have a monocoque fuselage, nose-mounted pitot tube and a steerable nosewheel actuated either electrically or hydraulically. Visibility for the co-pilot on landing was to be improved by "arranging the sidewalls of the fuselage in front of the cockpit so that they can fold inward. This break in the outer form of the fuselage produces a desirable, additional air resistance for landing. A closure pane, vertical or inclined slightly forward between the cockpit and the hinged window, offers the pilot a good, undistorted field of vision. The cockpit is enclosed by windows that open upward".

Passengers and crew would climb aboard through a fuselage hatch complete with folding footboard and the radio operator's seat was to be folded up for better access. And while up to six passengers enjoyed a pressurised cabin, the crew had to put up with an unpressurised cockpit. However, there was to be an air-tight section between the two fitted with a toilet. This section could be accessed by either the passengers or the crew but not both at the same time to avoid depressurisation.

Having been familiar with the use of jet engines during wartime, Harbich saw that for civil aviation measures would need to be taken to compensate for their shortcomings during manoeuvring on the ground. He wrote: "The slight static

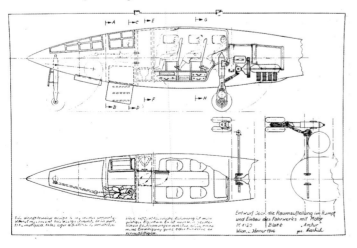

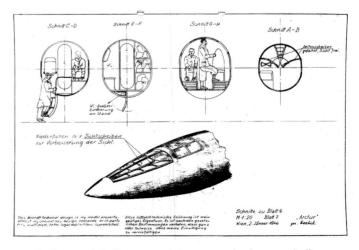

ABOVE: Arctur interior – the passenger compartment was pressurised but the cockpit was not. Both crew and passengers had access to the toilet but not at the same time. The curved sections of glazing on either side of the nose could be hinged downwards for improved visibility when landing.

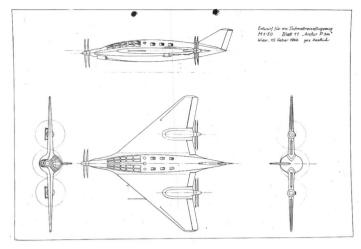

ABOVE: The three-prop Arctur P 3m, fitted with a trio of TM 32 barrel motors.

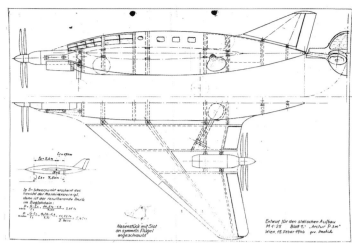

ABOVE: The relatively compact dimensions of the TM 32 engines are evident in this detailed view of the Arctur P 3m.

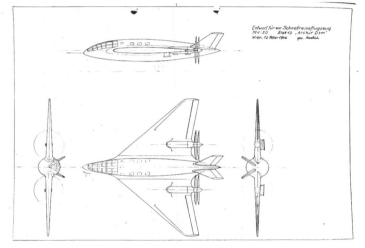

ABOVE: Pusher prop-only Arctur D 2m. This design featured a V-tail and blunt nose but was otherwise similar to the jet-propelled Arctur.

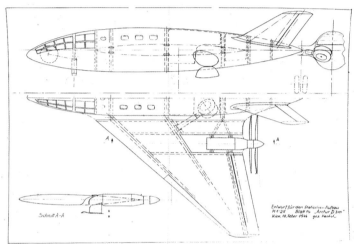

ABOVE: Arctur D 2m detailed view.

thrust of jet engines, and particularly that of air-flow turbines caused a complication in flying routine by necessitating droppable starting assists, starting rockets, catapults, and similar devices.

"Furthermore, the awkwardness of the device on the ground, the necessity of towing it by tractor before a take-off and recovering it after landing, proved to be serious defects. All these faults were tolerable from a military viewpoint, but are inconceivable for civil aviation, especially, when after an intermediate landing, a resumption of flight is intended.

"All these faults are eliminated by the drive provided for the landing gear unit, in the form of a light type motor or 'barrel-type motor of the Staatz system' which at the same time can be used as an electric motordrive."

Harbich acknowledged that reducing a tailless aircraft's landing speed was a significant difficulty and proposed a novel solution. The upper lips of the Arctur's engine air intakes were to function as leading edge slats, which could be closed during high-speed flight. The lower intake lips were to form split flaps. As he explained it: "The lower lips of the inlet ducts carry a spit flap, which, when deflected, increases this nose-up moment further. Therefore, no moment has to be produced by the elevator for setting the control planes or at any rate

not so great a moment as heretofore. This gives rise to gentler elevator deflections, and with it, to higher total lift by the wing."

Arctur's jet engines were to be "air stream turbines (BMW, Jumo 4 or those in the American type P-59 and P-80 Shooting Star)" and they would be "spread out in the rear between the trim tabs into a rectangular form".

Structural weight was 3800kg (8379lb) while engines, fuel tanks and pipes accounted for another 3330kg (7341lb). Equipment added 550kg (1212.2lb) and along with pilot, radio operator, six passengers, and 400kg (881.8lb) of baggage and airmail the total empty weight came to 7680kg (16,931.3lb). Fuel load was to be 5700kg (12,566.2lb) for a total loaded weight of 14,500kg (31,966.7lb).

Arctur was 13.3m long without the pitot, with a span of 12.3m and height on the ground of 3.9m. Wing area was 52m sq.

Again, the nature of Harbich's association with Lippisch comes into question when he writes: "Due to lack of authentic data concerning the power plant, performance calculations for the Arctur have not been made." Lippisch and his designers certainly had access to a wealth of data concerning German jet engines.

But if this were to prove a problem, Harbich had another solution. Jet engines had their advantages, he wrote, but these advantages

"disappear when longer flying time and greater range are required. Here the fuel consumption of jet engines, which is still high, becomes a burden. For this very reason the 'Arctur propeller' has been constructed with a triple-engined drive and the 'Arctur pusher propeller' with a two-engined drive".

The Arctur with jets was simply the Arctur, but the design with one tractor and two pusher propellers was known as the Arctur P 3m. The design with two pusher props was the Arctur D 2m.

Concerning the Arctur P 3m, Harbich wrote: "This project shows a variation of the Arctur consisting in the installation of the new barrel-type engines 'TM 32' of the Staatz system. Long-range flights were used to determine the fuel consumption of the power plants.

"The barrel-type engines excel in their unusually low fuel consumption. In collaboration with engineer Staatz, this new power plant is being developed as a large unit with counter-rotating propellers."

Most of the P 3m's features were the same as those of the jet Arctur except the piston engines required a radiator. Harbich wrote: "The cooler is located under the engine. The flow of air from the cooler can be regulated. The bulge on the fuselage underside needed for this purpose is used for housing the landing gear." Also, "the exhaust of the front engine is utilised for heating the cabin". There would be no need for landing gear drive either if a propeller configuration was used.

Concerning Staatz's 'Trommelmotor' design: "The barrel type engines developed by engineer Staatz after many years of work have, according to the dynamometer test stand reports, an unusually low fuel consumption, which is the result of the type of engine construction, since damaging piston side pressure on the cylinder walls is eliminated.

"In addition, the compact type of construction of the engines is so low in drag that these engines are especially suitable for airplanes at high horsepower. The engines are liquid-cooled. The engine cowling is round and smooth and can be retained as outer skin. This will cause the relative wind to conduct heat from the cooling jacket which results in smaller cooling surface.

"A standard power plant of 3300PS (3253.8hp) is being prepared for the P 3m and D 2m designs, in collaboration with engineer Staatz. The supercharger is located in the front on the engine shaft; behind it is the starter which can be switched in as an electric motor. The slight starting moment of the engine makes the push-button type of starter possible.

"The 32 cylinders are arranged around the crankshaft like the cylinders of a revolver. The reduction gear for the two counter-rotating propellers is attached to the crankcase. Efficiency is increased further by conducting the exhaust into two thrust nozzles which, especially in high-altitude flight, utilise in the familiar way the difference between cylinder and atmospheric pressure."

Performance data had been calculated for the P 3m – at 5000m it would reach a speed of 800km/h (497mph) using just 52% of its engine power and achieve a range of 3880km in four and three quarter hours. Ceiling was 10,000m and landing speed 176km/h. It was 15m long, 4.33m tall and had a span of 14m.

The pusher prop D 2m was structurally similar to the P 3m and aside from the engine change-around the biggest difference was the adoption of a V-tail. According to the report: "The trim tab is omitted owing to the compactness of the engines. For this reason the rudder unit has a V-shape, the control surfaces are manoeuvrable in the same and in the opposite direction. When the latter adjustment is chosen, the rudder unit takes the place of the trim tab."

Length excluding the pitot tube was 15m, span 14m and height 4.15m. At 5000m and 800km/h, a range of 5040km was to be achievable in six hours 20 minutes. Landing speed was just 132km/h.

It undoubtedly surprised no one who was aware of it that the Arctur was never taken any further than Harbich's optimistic brochure. While there is no doubting his ambition, Arctur amounted to little more than fantasy amid the ruins of bombed-out, looted, burned and occupied Vienna.

The seemingly miraculously small, light, efficient and powerful barrel motor being developed by Staatz was actually not a new idea. Similar, albeit much smaller, designs had been around since the early 1910s in the US, Switzerland, Australia, Spain and England – none of them proving to be particularly successful, although a design by John O Almen of Seattle, USA, during the 1920s, had actually passed US Army Air Corps acceptance tests.

Today, barrel motors are produced for industrial applications and a similar design is used to power torpedoes. None of these is derived from the proposals of Gustav Staatz, however. Arctur represents a last dying gasp of work on tailless designs during the final days of the Third Reich and its ultimate fate was the same. ●

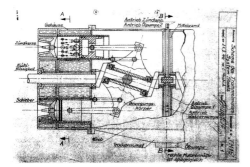
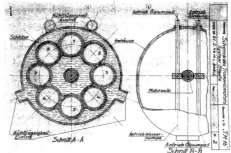
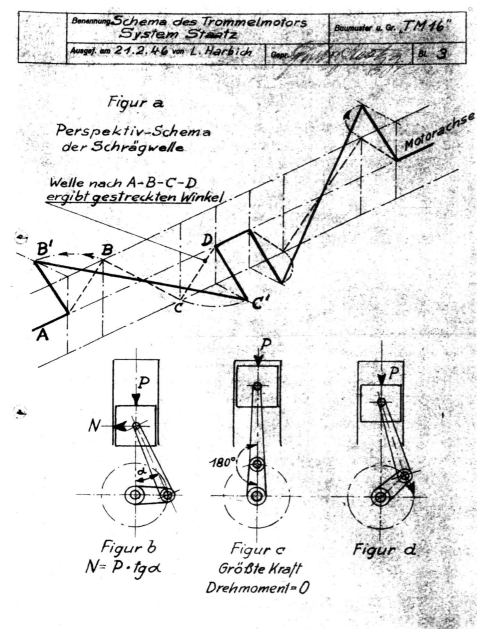

ABOVE: Diagrams showing the operation of Gustav Staatz's experimental barrel motor, the TM 16, designed in conjunction with Harbich's Arctur. The circular 'barrel' arrangement of the eight pistons is evident. A larger type, designated TM 32, was proposed for the production version of Arctur.

A prototype rammer by any other name…

When American forces captured Prien-am-Chiemsee airfield, they took possession of a very odd looking glider evidently designed and built by aeronautical technology students. It was returned to the US for testing but what was it?

Lippisch had always been a firm believer in testing prototypes of new designs rather than simply relying on a combination of wind-tunnel testing and mathematical formulas to determine what their flight characteristics might be.

When the German armaments ministry showed an interest in his P 13a, he decided that practical flight tests were needed to work out how it was likely to handle in the air. However, since every aircraft company was already operating at maximum capacity, he needed an alternative if his P 13a V1 was to be constructed. So he enlisted the aid of some students.

In his book, Ein Dreieck Fliegt, Lippisch writes of the P 13: "Admittedly this project of a Delta wing of very low aspect ratio and with the location of the cockpit on top of a wing that had been converted into a combustion chamber was rather unusual and there loomed the possibility of flight attitudes which might have to be mastered by special procedures.

"However, wind-tunnel and free-flight model tests did not reveal any especially problematical characteristics. We therefore deemed it practical to start construction of an experimental, manned powered craft of this design (scale 1:1).

"The difficult military situation demanded the drafting of many of the remaining civilian employees for service in the Volkssturm, which was regarded by the powers-that-be as the last line of defence. This meant that the aeronautical engineering students also had to join.

"Only work of highest priority rating could protect these students from being drafted. Aeronautical students of the Institutes of Technology of Darmstadt and Munich approached me in the hope of obtaining work in connection with the P 13. Since the end of the war obviously was imminent anyway, I created the project of a wooden flying-glider of the P 13, which the students were to build under the direction of my assistant, Heinemann, in a hangar of the small airfield in Prien on the Chiemsee.

"The students designated this project D 33 (Darmstadt 33) which was later changed to DM-1. We succeeded in obtaining deferment for the students. The DM-1 was almost completed when the war ended and the Prien airfield was occupied by American forces.

"In response to the suggestion of Professor Theodor von Karman the project was completed under US direction."

So the DM-1 was only built to help some students dodge the draft and they had simply omitted to mention its connection to Lippisch when questioned by the Americans.

But in his memoir Erinnerungen, Lippisch's account is slightly different: "After finding a more favourable form of the air intake [than that of the P 12], we had successfully let fly a corresponding model of the engine in May 1944 at the Spitzerberg in Vienna. This led to an improved draft 'P 13', which was very much supported by the Rüstungsministerium.

"Since the design of a thick delta wing with a low aspect ratio and a cockpit on top was novel and the Academic Aviation Groups Darmstadt and Munich had approached me with a high degree of urgency, I handed over the construction of a flyable wooden model in a 1:1 scale. They built this P 13a V1 in Prien-am-Chiemsee under the designation 'DM-1'.

"In Prien the students there, under the direction of my assistant Heinemann, handed over the almost completed DM-1 to the Americans as their own development, without mentioning that it was actually my P 13a V1. At the instigation of Theodor von Karman, it was completed and brought to the USA for survey."

While the two versions are not

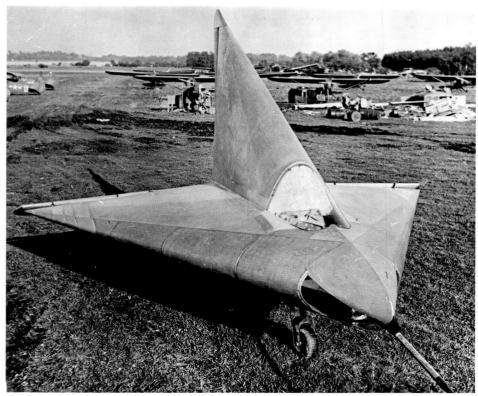

The P 13a V1 aka Akaflieg Darmstadt/Akaflieg München DM-1 as it appeared from the front when American forces occupied Prien am Chiemsee on May 3, 1945. NASA

incompatible, there are two facts presented in Erinnerungen which are omitted from Ein Dreieck Fliegt – firstly the reference to strong support for the P 13 from Albert Speer's Rüstungsministerium, which was now able to exert some influence on which aviation projects were to be built during the closing stages of the war, and secondly the fact that Lippisch very much regarded what was being constructed at Prien as the P 13a V1, whatever the students chose to call it.

The Rüstungsministerium's support was based on the model tests Lippisch mentions plus wind tunnel tests of the P 13 in model form carried out by the AVA up to August 1944. Wolfgang Heinemann, who Lippisch mentions as his assistant,

had been studying at Darmstadt but a bombing raid on September 11-12 had resulted in him and his fellow students moving to Prien-am-Chiemsee in Bavaria.

Evidently, as part of his studies, Heinemann had been given a work placement at the LFW in Vienna, where he met Lippisch, and in November 1944 Heinemann persuaded Lippisch to let him build the P 13a V1 with the help of his fellow students back at Prien. It was initially called 'D 33' as the 33rd Darmstadt project, then 'DM-1' for 'Darmstadt and Munich' because the Darmstadt students were using the Munich students' workshop and enlisted their help during the build.

In fact, Lippisch was wrong about

Heinemann – he did tell the Americans exactly what the DM-1 really was. CIOS Evaluation Report 68 Flugtechnisches Fachgruppe, dated June 1945 and compiled by H C Ashley and Major C F White is largely based on their interrogation of Heinemann and it states: "Target: Flugtechnisches Fachgruppe. Location: Prien Chien See. 1. Interviewed Heinemann. This firm evacuated to Prien from Darmstadt and Munich last September. Previously, they had only made gliders, but were now working on a prototype glider of the P 13 (DM-1) type (see report on Dr Lippisch).

"One interesting fact quoted by him was that on the P 13, the speed was too great to use a gun in attacks on bombers, and it was hoped to use a kind of sword suspended below the plane by a pendulum suspension which would cut through the fuselage of the bomber as the P 13 flew over.

"The Flugtechnische Fachgruppe Prien – before 1933 known as Academische Fliegergruppen (Akafliegs) – were independent associations of students of aircraft construction and similar faculties, who in addition to their studies voluntarily and without any payment designed, built and flew aeroplanes in order to complete their knowledge and instruction.

"Present aim of the Akaflieg Prien. During the war, the rooms of the Akaflieg Darmstadt and Munich were destroyed by air bombardment, and they therefore moved to Prien. In November 1944, they began in cooperation with Dr Lippisch, Vienna, the development of a completely new aeroplane type in order to conquer the stratosphere and attain supersonic speed, both necessary for aeroplane traffic over long ranges and 'to other stars'. In consequence of low air density at high altitudes, load capacity of the aeroplane could only be utilised if necessary lift was attained by high flying speed.

"In order to increase the speed of an aeroplane of standard construction, a long and difficult development would be necessary. Velocity of sound could not be surmounted because of resistance, rigidity and flying qualities. It was, therefore, very uneconomical to continue working in this direction.

"Though not difficult to develop an aeroplane for supersonic speed only, it was very difficult to design a plane which could fly as well in subsonic as in supersonic. The present state of flight research and flight testing in the sphere of high speed promised that the form chosen would correspond to both demands. Relation of rigidity to weight and of surface to useful inner room as well as the change of the flying qualities in passing the velocity of sound would be much better than in planes of standard construction. Only one tenth of performance would be needed.

"In order to be able to fly slowly as well a compromise was necessary, which made aeroplanes of standard construction superior to the DM-1. The main point however was to design a plane which could fly in both cases. At present, the principal problem was to find out the necessary shape of aeroplane. Afterwards, the development of an appropriate power plant might be started." ▶

ABOVE: A rear view of the P 13a V1/DM-1. The shape of the glider suggests that Lippisch favoured the diamond planform over the simple delta for his P 13. NASA

ABOVE: Viewed from the side, the P 13a V1/DM-1's true nature is readily apparent. Even though the glider's pilot was to sit at the base of the fin, in the nose, it is easy to imagine the P 13's pilot seated entirely within the fin above the wing, looking out through a canopy about halfway up the slope. NASA

ABOVE: The P 13a V1/DM-1 was taken apart piece by piece at the Langley Memorial Aeronautical Laboratory at Langley Field, Virginia, during 1946 and reassembled in this radically altered form. Its wings received sharp leading edges, the fin was removed, a new smaller fin was fitted and a canopy borrowed from a P-80 was installed. The goal was to test the likely effect of these innovations on lift and handling performance of a sharply swept delta form. NASA

ABOVE: Tests on the P 13a V1/DM-1 in its original form began at NACA Langley in April 1946. NASA

Heinemann told his interrogators that it would be impossible for a propeller-driven aircraft to reach supersonic speeds and that it "was uncertain whether it would be possible by a turbine though at least higher speed could be attained. But it could positively be stated that the supersonic speed would be attained by means of rocket propulsion of the same kind as in the Messerschmitt 163. This rocket propulsion however began to be economical only in flying speeds of more than 2000km/h".

Evidently Lippisch had mapped out a three-stage testing process for the P 13: "The first model would have no power plant and would only show whether the chosen shape would be corresponding to the demands of slow-speed flight though assimilated to the demands of high-speed flight, especially whether it could start and land. This aeroplane would be towed in 'Huckepack' by a normal plane to 8000-10,000 yards, when released and in glide would test the qualities of slow-speed flight, in diving those of high-speed flight (perhaps a rocket would be built in) until about 800km/h (500mph).

"The second model would have a jet power similar to that of the Messerschmitt

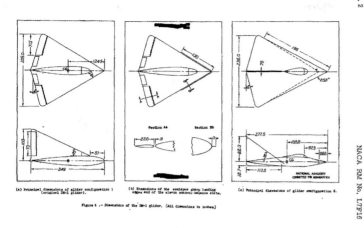

Fig. 2

ABOVE: Dimensions of the glider in unaltered and altered forms as shown in a NACA report. NASA

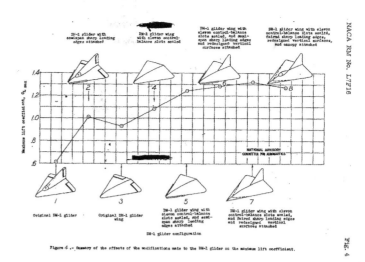

Fig. 4

ABOVE: Diagram showing the eight different stages of modification carried out on the glider. NASA

262 or P 38 [presumably Heinemann meant either P 59 or P 80 here]. With it the critical range of speed of 800-1200km/h (500-750mph) would be tested.

"The third model would have a rocket propulsion (as for the Me 163) and with it the plane would attain a maximum speed of 2000km/h (1250mph). The newly developed shape of aeroplane could also be used for testing other possible drives for high speed."

Some technical details of the DM-1 followed, primarily relating to its wing form. Concerning its structure, the report states: "The plane is built in wood construction. Wings and tail are developable surfaces and cantilever shells without spar. As the DM has no power plant, the pilot's seat is not completely put into the tail, but a little in front on account of the centre of gravity. On account of the low aspect ratio unusual angles of attack can be obtained, in theory up to 35°. Therefore, there are two hoods for the pilot, a normal one at height for his head for high-speed flight, the second is set at the bottom of the fuselage for landing.

"Also the undercarriage is a new construction. It is a tricycle undercarriage with a stroke of 60cm and permits a sinking speed of 6m/sec in landing. Stressed steel tubes will be the material for it. Therewith a good method of retracting will be obtained. The holes for accommodating the retractable undercarriage have the size of the lowest wheel section."

The glider also had two water tanks on board – one in the nose and one in the tail – connected via a hand pump so the pilot could move 35 litres of water back and forth to alter the centre of gravity as required. It would seem that the solid shock absorber-less undercarriage was of the students' own invention and may have only been intended for moving the glider around the airfield, since landing on it would probably have damaged the DM-1's delicate wooden structure.

Take-off would have been on the back of a powered aircraft, such as a Siebel Si 204 or Focke-Wulf Fw 58, with the glider's pilot detaching once a suitable speed was achieved. A test pilot had been recruited to fly the DM-1, Hans Zacher

from the DFS, but by the time American troops arrived at the airfield on May 3, 1945, the glider was still incomplete.

While he clearly outlined every other aspect of the P 13's design process and its purpose, Heinemann does seem to have entirely omitted the P 13's intended ramjet powerplant from his account. Why he should have left this out is unclear, unless Lippisch had kept it from him. The Americans, however, seem to have had no real interest in the DM-1's origin as an experimental prototype for a ramjet-powered rammer intended to destroy USAAF bombers over Germany. What caught their attention was the idea that its form had been designed specifically for supersonic flight.

Apparently General George S Patton saw the DM-1 during a visit to Prien on May 9 and authorised the students to complete it, which they did several months later. On November 9, 1945, it was crated up and taken to Mannheim, Germany, on the back of a truck. It was then loaded onto a ship and taken to Rotterdam, then on to Boston where it arrived on January 19, 1946. On January 21, the Army Air Forces Material Command asked the National Advisory Committee for Aeronautics (NACA) to evaluate it. Loaded onto another ship, it was taken down the American east coast to Norfolk, loaded onto another truck, and carried to the Langley Memorial Aeronautical Laboratory at Langley Field, Virginia.

Wind-tunnel testing took place in three phases – in April, June and November 1946; the off periods during this process resulting from delays while radical changes were made to the glider's form. On August 5, 1947, J Calvin Lovell and Herbert A Wilson Jr published the results of the programme in a research memorandum.

The introduction states: "Research directed toward the attainment of supersonic flight has led to interest in the characteristics of wings of high sweep and of low aspect ratio. Since there are only limited full-scale data on such wings, an investigation of the German DM-1 glider has been conducted in the Langley full-scale tunnel. The DM-1 glider, which was designed for the investigation

of the low-speed characteristics of an airplane configuration believed suitable for supersonic flight, has approximately triangular plan form, airfoil sections similar to the NACA 0015-64, an aspect ratio of 1.8, and a 60° sweptback leading edge.

"Preliminary tests of the DM-1 glider in the Langley full-scale tunnel disclosed that the maximum lift coefficient was considerably lower than had been indicated by low-scale tests of similar configurations. In an effort to increase the maximum lift coefficient, the effects of sharp leading edges, redesigned vertical surfaces, and other modifications to the DM-1 glider were investigated. In addition to the maximum-lift tests, an investigation was made of the stability and control characteristics of those glider configurations believed most suitable."

In other words, rather than simply test the DM-1 as it was, the NACA team took the glider apart and rebuilt it in a variety of different arrangements, even to the extent of adding new parts. Six major revisions were attempted: installation of sharp leading edges for its wings, removal of the vertical fin, sealing the elevon control-balance slots, installing a new smaller thinner fin, installing faired sharp leading edges and finally installing a conventional cockpit canopy borrowed from a P-80 Shooting Star jet fighter.

When the thin fin and sharp leading edges were fitted in combination with the cockpitcanopy: "The results indicate that airplanes having approximately triangular plan form with 60° sweepback and sharp leading edges can be designed to have acceptable stability characteristics in the subcritical speed range."

American historians have recently re-evaluated the significance of the DM-1 glider and credited it as the inspiration for Convair's successful series of delta-winged Cold War interceptors beginning in 1948 with the XF-92 and progressing on to types such as the F-102 Delta Dagger in 1953 and Delta Dart in 1959, which themselves went on to inspire further delta-wing designs – a lasting legacy for Alexander Lippisch's years of work on tailless deltas. ●

Unknown!

Other tailless types

There remain several German wartime tailless and flying designs about which very little is known – either because they were only fleeting concepts or because the documentation describing them was destroyed or otherwise unavailable. Here are a handful of the more elusive designs.

HENSCHEL

When it comes to companies with designs about which very little is known, Henschel must top the list of any German 'secret projects' researcher.

Certainly the Berlin-based design office of Henschel under Friedrich Nicolaus, according to his 1946 report Bericht über die Entwickling der Henschel Flugzeugwerke, came up with a whole host of interesting tailless designs such as the P 130 and P 135 – two designs worked on in parallel. The former was powered by a Jumo 213 piston engine and the latter by a BMW 003 turbojet, which was later swapped for an HeS 011.

The P 135 design later formed the basis for the P 136, a rocket-propelled interceptor which had a landing skid instead of a wheeled undercarriage and was armed with a pair of rocket launchers instead of cannon. The P 136 itself was then reworked to include an annular ramjet around the rear fuselage, which would operate independently of the rocket engine.

Henschel went even further with the P 135, the company's apparently final project of the war involving the marrying up of the P 135's wings with a new fuselage and the pressure cabin of the DFS 228 high-altitude reconnaissance aircraft, which Henschel had designed.

Less well-known is Henschel's involvement with the Horten brothers. During 1944, the company designed a flying wing based on the Horten IX but powered by a pair of linked Jumo 213s and with a central fin for directional stability.

Perhaps the most mysterious Henschel design of all is the P 122. Nicolaus makes no mention of it in his report but it does appear in German Aircraft: New and Projected Types. It states: "This Henschel bomber project has a low wing without dihedral but only moderate sweepback. There is no tailplane but the normal fin and rudder has been retained. In plan the fuselage has a sharply pointed nose. The span is approximately 70ft and the overall length 38ft. Two BMW 018 turbojet units, each developing 7500lb static thrust are slung below the wing.

With a crew of two the aircraft has a normal all-up weight of 33,100lb (bomb load not stated). The maximum speed is 627mph at sea level and 580mph at 33,000ft. The rate of climb at sea level is 11,200ft/min. The maximum range is 690 miles at 33,000ft and 1240 miles at 55,700ft."

The words are accompanied by a rather blurry drawing of the aircraft which makes the design of the cockpit unclear, seemingly leaves little room for landing gear and begs the question as to where the bomb load, whatever it was, would actually be kept.

LIPPISCH/MESSERSCHMITT

Alexander Lippisch's Abteilung L used a clear numerical sequence for its designs, most of which are relatively well known, but there are some gaps. The first of these is the P 02 – no information about which has ever surfaced. The second is the P 07, which author Stephen Ransom has said is what, elsewhere, has been referred to as the Me 334. This is a small single-seater similar to the P 06 but with a pusher prop rather than tractor, and designed as a fighter rather than a trainer. Also somewhat unknown is the precise appearance of the P 15 Diana – a single-jet interceptor to be made from bits of other aircraft already in production.

In his outline document Flugtechnische Grundlagen für Projekt P 15 Diana, dated March 4, 1945, Lippisch wrote that this aircraft would be made "from the components of the design Me 163 B and C, He 162 and Ju 248 or 263". The engine would be "He S 11 (BMW)", presumably whichever was available, and the nosewheel gear would be "same as He 162".

Oddly, the wings would come unaltered from the Me 163 C, which was not in fact in production, the cockpit from the He 162 the main gear from the He 162 or Me 109 G, the instruments and controls from the Me 163 B and the weapons installation from the He 162 or Me 163 B.

There is actually no mention of which specific parts would come from the Ju 248/Me 263. Writing in the 1970s, shortly before his death, Lippisch wrote: "Projekt Diana – P 15 was to be built using the wing of the Me 163 C, the cockpit of the He 162, and the modified fuselage (with nosewheel and turbojet) of the Ju 248".

The reference to the Ju 248 having a turbojet is strange, since it was actually powered by two rocket engines, yet no original drawing of the P 15 has yet been unearthed so exactly how this unlikely marriage of components would have worked remains unclear.

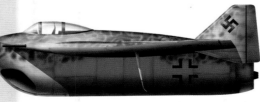

ABOVE: Arado E 581-4. Art by Daniel Uhr

ARADO

Aside from its night-fighter projects and E 555 bomber designs, Arado worked on a number of flying-wing projects. As early as September 1943, the company designed an aircraft that was perfectly triangular in plan view, powered by a pair of HeS 011 turbojets buried entirely within the wing and, most bizarrely, a small central tail fin similar to that of the Ar 96.

Information about another tailless project, the E 581 single-jet fighter, is extremely sketchy but it is known that the E 581-2 was dated November 18, 1944, and was powered by a BMW 003, making it a potential Volksjäger alternative, whereas the E 581-4 and E 581-5, the latter dated January 8, 1945, were both powered by the HeS 011. Neither was a contender for the 1-TL-Jäger competition, despite being contemporaries of those designs.

BMW

Two tailless bomber designs were presented in BMW's six-page EZS – Bericht Nr. 47 EZV Nr. 537/44 of May 25, 1944, entitled Flugleistungen von TL-Bombern or 'Flight performance of jet bombers'. The first bomber design, powered by six BMW 003 As was labelled 'Strabo I' and the second, powered by a pair of BMW 018s, was labelled 'Strabo II'. The report, which was apparently produced in collaboration with Junkers, aims to compare the performance of both the engines themselves and the design of the aircraft.

It suggests that the idea of flying-wing aircraft, which had been thought particularly suitable for jet aircraft design, might need a rethink and that a return to aircraft with tails might be necessary. In addition, it unsurprisingly concludes that jet engines are better than piston engines for high-speed performance, that two 018s still provides a much better performance than six 003s and that due to its speed the Strabo II might make an effective fighter-bomber.

The drawings accompanying the report are dated slightly later, June 2 for the Strabo I and June 6 for the Strabo II, suggesting that these were perhaps supplied by Junkers' designers after the BMW engineers had already completed the written portion of the report.

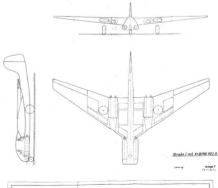

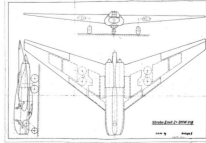

ABOVE: Bomber designs from BMW's report of June 1944. Evidence suggests that these designs were actually the work of project partner Junke